THE SERVANT OF THE LORD AND HIS SERVANT PEOPLE

NEW STUDIES IN BIBLICAL THEOLOGY 54

Series editor: D. A. Carson

THE SERVANT OF THE LORD AND HIS SERVANT PEOPLE

Tracing a biblical theme through the canon

Matthew S. Harmon

APOLLOS

An imprint of InterVarsity Press
Downers Grove, Illinois

APOLLOS (an imprint of Inter-Varsity Press)
36 Causton Street
London SW1P 4ST, England
ivpbooks.com
ivp@ivpbooks.com

InterVarsity Press, USA
P.O. Box 1400
Downers Grove, IL 60515, USA
ivpress.com
email@ivpress.com

InterVarsity Press® is the book-publishing division of InterVarsity Christian Fellowship/USA®, a movement of students and faculty active on campus at hundreds of universities, colleges, and schools of nursing in the United States of America, and a member movement of the International Fellowship of Evangelical Students. For information about local and regional activities, visit intervarsity.org.

Inter-Varsity Press, England, originated within the Inter-Varsity Fellowship, now the Universities and Colleges Christian Fellowship, a student movement connecting Christian Unions in universities and colleges throughout Great Britain, and a member movement of the International Fellowship of Evangelical Students. That historic association is maintained, and all senior IVP staff and committee members subscribe to the UCCF Basis of Faith. Website: www.uccf.org.uk.

Typeset in Great Britain by CRB Associates, Potterhanworth, Lincolnshire

USA ISBN 978-0-8308-1035-2 (print)
USA ISBN 978-0-8308-1306-3 (digital)
UK ISBN 978-1-78974-210-7 (print)
UK ISBN 978-1-789749-211-4 (digital)

Printed in the United States of America

InterVarsity Press is committed to ecological stewardship and to the conservation of natural resources in all our operations. This book was printed using sustainably sourced paper.

British Library Cataloguing-in-Publication Data
A catalogue record for this book is available from the British Library.

Library of Congress Cataloging-in-Publication Data
A catalog record for this book is available from the Library of Congress.

P 22 21 20 19 18 17 16 15 14 13 12 11 10 9 8 7 6 5 4 3 2 1

Y 38 37 36 35 34 33 32 31 30 29 28 27 26 25 24 23 22 21 20

For Kate
the most Christlike servant I know

Contents

Series preface

New Studies in Biblical Theology is a series of monographs that address key issues in the discipline of biblical theology. Contributions to the series focus on one or more of three areas: (1) the nature and status of biblical theology, including its relations with other disciplines (e.g. historical theology, exegesis, systematic theology, historical criticism, narrative theology); (2) the articulation and exposition of the structure of thought of a particular biblical writer or corpus; and (3) the delineation of a biblical theme across all or part of the biblical corpora.

Above all, these monographs are creative attempts to help thinking Christians understand their Bibles better. The series aims simultaneously to instruct and to edify, to interact with the current literature, and to point the way ahead. In God's universe, mind and heart should not be divorced: in this series we will try not to separate what God has joined together. While the notes interact with the best of scholarly literature, the text is uncluttered with untransliterated Greek and Hebrew, and tries to avoid too much technical jargon. The volumes are written within the framework of confessional evangelicalism, but there is always an attempt at thoughtful engagement with the sweep of the relevant literature.

When most Christians hear the expression 'the servant of the Lord', they think of the portrait of the suffering servant painted in Isaiah 52:13 – 53:12. This is not so much wrong as reductionistic. Displaying a variety of dominating characteristics, other servants of the Lord (whether that terminology is used or not) repeatedly surface in Scripture, including Adam, Moses, Joshua, David and the apostles. Jesus appears as the servant par excellence, the One who fulfils the patterns they establish. After Jesus, it soon transpires that his apostles are also servants, and collectively his redeemed followers are to be a servant people. In this distinctive volume of biblical theology Dr Harmon connects the dots that some of us have overlooked, and enriches not only our understanding but also our discipleship.

D. A. Carson
Trinity Evangelical Divinity School

Author's preface

For as long as I can remember, I have been fascinated with the servant of the Lord figure described in Isaiah 53. That fascination only grew as I worked on my dissertation, which explored Paul's extensive engagement with Isaiah in his letter to the Galatians. Recognizing that Paul applies servant of the Lord language to himself as well as Jesus piqued my curiosity about other biblical figures given this special designation. In the years that followed, my interest in this theme continued, and when I eventually approached Don Carson about a volume in this series pursuing this theme, he graciously accepted. Although completing this study took longer than I originally hoped, God has used this extended time pursuing this theme through Scripture to deepen my love for him, his Word and his people. Seeing afresh the beauty of Christ as the servant who loved me and gave himself for me is a priceless gift for which I am eternally grateful.

The process of moving from an idea to a published book involves numerous people, many whose contributions might otherwise be unknown without acknowledging them here. Philip Duce at Inter-Varsity Press has patiently guided this manuscript through the editorial process. As the project editor, Michelle Clark made sure the publication process stayed on track. The careful copy-editorial eye of Eldo Barkhuizen improved the readability of this book.

I am blessed to serve at Grace College and Theological Seminary, where I have the privilege of teaching and mentoring students. For many years they have heard me talk about the servant of the Lord in the classroom, and my interaction with them has frequently stimulated my own thinking. The administration has enthusiastically supported my research and writing, even granting me a reduced teaching load and a sabbatical that has enabled me to devote extended time to this project and others. Thank you, Bill Katip, John Lillis, Jeff Gill and Freddy Cardoza for affirming God's call on my life to serve others through writing.

Biblical theology has become an essential foundation and framework for how I interpret, apply and teach the Bible. I have been privileged to study under scholars such as Don Carson, Greg Beale and Doug Moo:

each of them have made their own unique contributions to my love for Scripture in all of its unity and diversity. Conversations with fellow scholars such as Ben Gladd and Jim Hamilton have also spurred me to see fresh truths in Scripture. I am grateful for their friendship.

But when it comes to those who, humanly speaking, have played the biggest role in making this book possible, it is without question my family. In the nearly six years I have been working on this book, my two sons have grown from boys to young men. What a joy it has been to watch God at work in their lives and I am eager to see how God uses them to advance his kingdom. When it comes to my wife, Kate, I am regularly at a loss to express how grateful I am to God for her. She is my greatest earthly treasure and I cannot imagine my life without her. As long as the Lord gives us life together, it will always be 'us against the world'. Her self-sacrificial love for me, our sons and others is a beautiful picture of Jesus to those around her. She is the most Christlike servant I know, so it is with gratitude and joy that I dedicate this book to her.

Matthew S. Harmon

Abbreviations

4Q265	*4QMiscellaneous Rules* (Dead Sea Scrolls)
4Q418 frag. 81	*4QInstruction*[d] (Dead Sea Scrolls)
4Q423	*4QInstruction* (Dead Sea Scrolls)
4Q423 frag. 2	*4QInstruction* (Dead Sea Scrolls)
4Q423 8+24	*4QInstruction*[d] (Dead Sea Scrolls)
4Q504	*4QWords of the Luminaries* (Dead Sea Scrolls)
4Q504 frag. 8	*4QWords of the Luminaries* (Dead Sea Scrolls)
4QIsa[a]	*4QIsaiah*[a] (Dead Sea Scrolls)
4QIsa[b]	*4QIsaiah*[b] (Dead Sea Scrolls)
4QIsa[d]	*4QIsaiah*[d] (Dead Sea Scrolls)
AB	Anchor Bible
ANTJ	Arbeiten zum Neuen Testament und Judentum
AT	author's translation
B	Codex Vaticanus
b. Meg.	Babylonian Talmud Tractate *Megillah*
b. Ned.	Babylonian Talmud Tractate *Nedarim*
b. Sabb.	Babylonian Talmud Tractate *Shabbat*
b. Sanh.	Babylonian Talmud Tractate *Sanhedrin*
BA	*The Biblical Archaeologist*
BBR	*Bulletin for Biblical Research*
BDAG	W. Bauer, F. W. Danker, W. F. Arndt and W. F. Gingrich, *A Greek-English Lexicon of the New Testament and Other Early Christian Literature*, 3rd edn, Chicago: University of Chicago Press, 2000
BDB	*The New Brown-Diver-Briggs-Gesenius Hebrew and English Lexicon*, ed. F. Brown, Peabody: Hendrickson, 1979
BECNT	Baker Exegetical Commentary on the New Testament
BETL	Bibliotheca ephemeridum theologicarum lovaniensium
BHT	Beiträge zur historischen Theologie
Bib	*Biblica*
BN	*Biblische Notizen*

BNTC	Black's New Testament Commentary
BT	*The Bible Translator*
BTCP	Biblical Theology for Christian Proclamation
BZAW	Beihefte zur Zeitschrift für die alttestamentliche Wissenschaft
BZNW	Beihefte zur Zeitschrift für die neutestamentliche Wissenschaft und die Kunde der älteren Kirche
c.	circa
CBET	Contributions to Biblical Exegesis and Theology
CBQ	*Catholic Biblical Quarterly*
CBQMS	Catholic Biblical Quarterly Monograph Series
COS	*The Context of Scripture*, ed. W. W. Hallo. 3 vols., Leiden: Brill, 1997–
CSB	Christian Standard Bible
D*	Codex Bezae
DCH	*Dictionary of Classical Hebrew*, D. J. A. Clines, Sheffield; Sheffield Academic Press, 1993–2011
DPL	*Dictionary of Paul and His Letters*, ed. G. F. Hawthorne and R. P. Martin, Downers Grove: InterVarsity Press, 1993
EBC	The Expositor's Bible Commentary, ed. F. E. Gaebelein, Grand Rapids: Zondervan
ESBT	Essential Studies in Biblical Theology
ESV	English Standard Version
EvQ	*Evangelical Quarterly*
FRLANT	Forschungen zur Religion und Literatur des Alten und Neuen Testaments
GHAT	Göttingen Handkommentar zum Alten Testament
HALOT	*The Hebrew and Aramaic Lexicon of the Old Testament*, L. Koehler and W. Baumgartner, Leiden; Brill, 1994–2000
HBM	Hebrew Biblical Monographs
ICC	International Critical Commentary
IEJ	*Israel Exploration Journal*
JANER	*Journal of Ancient Near Eastern Religions*
JBL	*Journal of Biblical Literature*
JETS	*Journal of the Evangelical Theological Society*
JSNT	*Journal for the Study of the New Testament*

JSNTSup	Journal for the Study of the New Testament, Supplement Series
JSOTSup	Journal for the Study of the Old Testament, Supplement Series
JSPL	*Journal for the Study of Paul and His Letters*
LNTS	Library of New Testament Studies
LXX	Septuagint
MT	Masoretic Text
NAC	New American Commentary
NASB	New American Standard Bible
NETS	New English Translation of the Septuagint
NICNT	New International Commentary on the New Testament
NICOT	New International Commentary on the Old Testament
NIDNTT	*The New International Dictionary of New Testament Theology*, C. Brown, 4 vols., Grand Rapids: Regency Reference Library, 1986
NIDNTTE	*New International Dictionary of New Testament Theology and Exegesis*, ed. M. S. Silva, 2nd edn, Grand Rapids: Zondervan, 2014
NIDOTTE	*New International Dictionary of Old Testament Theology and Exegesis*, ed. W. A. VanGemeren, Grand Rapids: Zondervan, 1997
NIGTC	New International Greek Testament Commentary
NIV	New International Version
NovTSup	Supplements to Novum Testamentum
NSBT	New Studies in Biblical Theology
NT	New Testament
NTS	*New Testament Studies*
OT	Old Testament
OTL	Old Testament Library
P^{75}	Papyrus 75
PNTC	Pillar New Testament Commentary
Q	Codex Guelferbytanus B
SBLMS	Society of Biblical Literature Monograph Series
SBTS	Sources for Biblical and Theological Study
SCHT	Studies in Christian History and Thought
SHM	Studies in the History of Missions
SNTMS	Society for New Testament Studies Monograph series

SubBi	Subsidia Biblica
s.v.	(sub verbo) under the heading or word given
Tg. Ps.-J.	*Targum Pseudo-Jonathan*
T. Jos.	*Testament of Joseph*
TDNT	*Theological Dictionary of the New Testament*, ed. G. Kittel and G. Friedrich, tr. G. W. Bromiley, 10 vols., Grand Rapids: Eerdmans, 1964–76.
TNTC	Tyndale New Testament Commentaries
TOTC	Tyndale Old Testament Commentaries
TWOT	*Theological Wordbook of the Old Testament*, ed. R. L. Harris, G. L. Archer Jr, 2 vols., Chicago: Moody, 1980
tr.	translation, translated by
TrinJ	*Trinity Journal*
TynB	*Tyndale Bulletin*
UF	*Ugarit-Forschungen*
VT	*Vetus Testamentum*
VTSup	Supplements to Vetus Testamentum
W	Codex Washington
WBC	Word Biblical Commentary
WMANT	Wissenschaftliche Monographien zum Alten und Neuen Testament
WTJ	*Westminster Theological Journal*
WUNT	Wissenschaftliche Untersuchungen zum Neuen Testament
ZECNT	Zondervan Exegetical Commentary on the New Testament
ZNW	*Zeitschrift für die neutestamentliche Wissenschaft und die Kunde der älteren Kirche*

1 Introduction

> Better to reign in Hell, than serve in Heav'n.
> (Milton, *Paradise Lost*, Book I, line 263)

Satan's words to his demonic forces in John Milton's *Paradise Lost* capture well the lie he has told to humanity throughout the ages – rather than joyfully serve the true and living God, it is better to reject his authority and determine one's own destiny even if that leads to an eternity in hell. Satan used a form of this lie in the Garden of Eden with Adam and Eve, persuading them to rebel against their sovereign Lord and determine for themselves good and evil. Rather than embrace their identity as servants of the Lord, our first parents chose instead to pursue the subtle but deadly slavery of perceived self-autonomy.

Identity is arguably the defining issue of our contemporary Western culture. At one level humanity has always sought to understand who we are, but developments within the past 500 years have brought the issue of identity to the forefront in fresh ways.[1] The question of identity affects us as individuals, as communities and as the people of God. Yet sadly, in the contemporary quest for identity, the Bible is often neglected or ignored, even among professing Christians. But only in Scripture do we find authoritative and infallible answers to the question of who we are as human beings. In order for the church to proclaim and live out a compelling picture of what it means to be human, we must first understand what Scripture says about our identity.

Yet therein lies part of the challenge. The Bible has so much to say about our identity as human beings that it is challenging to know where to begin. But rather than paralyse us, the presence of so much material

[1] See especially Taylor 1989 and 2007. For an accessible summary and engagement with Taylor's work from a Christian perspective, see Smith 2014.

allows us to explore the question of identity from a wide variety of entry points.

In one sense this book is a contribution to understanding our identity as human beings from a biblical perspective. The specific angle will be to trace the key biblical theme of the servant of the Lord from Genesis to Revelation. I am not arguing that this is the most significant biblical theme for understanding our identity as human beings; rather, I am proposing that it is an important and sometimes overlooked theme that helps us better understand the metanarrative of Scripture as well as our identity as human beings.

But before we begin to trace our theme through the canon, we must first address some preliminary issues.

Preliminary issues

The nature of servitude in the ancient world

A significant body of literature exists on slavery in the ancient world, the New Testament, and the early church.[2] The nature of these discussions is at times complex, even to the point of debates over how slavery itself should be defined![3] Further complications arise when studying slavery and servitude in the biblical world from a contemporary perspective that lives under the shadow of the history of race-based slavery in the New World and the present-day forms of slavery that continue. Such contemporary perspectives can blind the reader of Scripture to important differences in slavery in the ancient world. While such differences must not be overemphasized in an attempt to anaesthetize

[2] For helpful summaries of slavery in the ancient Near East, see Matthews and Benjamin 1993: 199–210; Averbeck 2018: 423–430. For helpful summaries of slavery in the Roman Empire during the NT period, see Martin 1990: 1–49; Combes 1998; Harris 2001: 25–45; and McKnight 2017: 6–29 (see p. 6, n. 18 for an extended list of recent studies). A sampling of primary source materials on slavery in the Roman period can be found in Shelton 1998: 163–185.

[3] See the helpful summary in Combes 1998: 21–29. McKnight (2017: 15–16) offers this expanded definition: 'Slavery describes *a perceived inferior human (the other) under the total authority of another perceived superior human, and that perceived (and false) reality is established by power and authority for the sake of profit (for the owner) and publication of the owner's wealth*. Slavery then is about *voluntary exploitation* of an *involuntary* human and in most cases slavery was for life. Slavery is about status, integrity, identity, and utility' (emphases original).

the evils of slavery, responsible interpretation of Scripture must take them into account.

Three differences in particular stand out. The first regards the entry point. While being taken against one's will (e.g. kidnapping, prisoner of war, etc.) was the most common way to become a slave in the ancient world, some people chose to sell themselves into slavery because of crippling debt. Second, slavery in the ancient world was not necessarily a permanent state of affairs. The Israelites were specifically instructed to release any Hebrew slave from service in the sabbatical year (Lev. 25:35–43).[4] In the Roman Empire, upon their death, masters would sometimes free their slaves; indeed, at one point the practice became so common that the emperor Augustus passed legislation establishing certain limits.[5] During the first century it was also possible for some slaves to purchase their freedom, though such a process was usually lengthy and tedious.[6] Finally, in the ancient world slaves served in virtually every area of society. While the experience of rural slaves was often similar to the predominantly agricultural nature of New World slavery, urban slaves served in a wide range that ran the gamut of education, government and business.[7]

In sharp contrast to our contemporary situation in many parts of the world, slavery and servitude were simply a given in the biblical world of both the Old and New Testaments. Regardless of how this reality strikes our contemporary sensibilities, we must allow the biblical text to speak on its own terms within its own context.

---

[4] For succinct summaries, see Harris 2001: 38–40 and Averbeck 2018: 424–428. These regulations were unique in the ancient Near East and are rooted theologically in the identity of Israel as a people brought out of slavery from Egypt (e.g. Lev. 25:42, 55; Deut. 5:15; 16:12).

[5] Referred to as the *lex Fufia Caninia* (2 BC), Harris (2001: 40–41) notes that Augustus created a sliding scale (based on the total number of slaves owned) that limited the number of slaves a master could manumit in his will.

[6] The Romans referred to this as the *peculium*. The master would allow the slave to save up money (usually gained through services performed on behalf of the master), and once those savings equalled the amount the slave was worth he or she could purchase his or her freedom. Such an incentive was thought to motivate the slave to work harder, though the process of saving a sufficient sum often took a minimum of seven to ten years (this summary was adapted from Aldrete [2004: 66–67]). For a description of the manumission ceremony based on the account in Epictetus, see McKnight 2017: 23–25.

[7] In a sense, the living conditions of slaves depended on the wealth and social status of their owner. Aldrete (2004: 66) notes that 'Some of these [urban] slaves, particularly family ones raised together with the master's children, were the confidantes and even friends of their masters and might receive educations, have their own families, and live nearly as well as the free members of the family.'

Servant, slave or none of the above?

One significant challenge in studying this theme is the vocabulary and overlapping conceptual realms of slavery and servanthood. Both the Old and New Testaments use a range of words to capture these ideas, and often do so in ways that defy precise distinctions.[8] As well as the fluidity of vocabulary used, there were significant differences in how slavery and servanthood were practised and perceived in different ancient cultures. In addition to these challenges, there is also the fact that the various LXX translators use a variety of Greek terms to render Hebrew terms that refer to slavery and servanthood, even using two different Greek words to render one Hebrew word within the span of a few verses with no discernable nuance in meaning between the two.[9]

This challenge is multiplied when one translates from Hebrew and/or Greek into a modern language such as English. The meaning of an individual word is determined by its use in context, and words have semantic ranges. For example, the Hebrew word *'ebed* occurs over 800 times in the Old Testament, but this same word can refer to someone who is a lowly and menial slave (Lev. 26:13) or a high-ranking official in the service of a king (Gen. 41:37–38). Even an English translation such as the English Standard Version (ESVUK), which strives for a 'word-for-word' translation that renders Hebrew words with the same English words where possible, rightly recognizes that the use of *'ebed* in 1 Kings 1:9 refers to Solomon's high-ranking attendants and translates it as 'officials'. Similar difficulties arise in the New Testament when attempting to translate *doulos*, as that term also allows for a range of meanings (e.g. slave, bondservant, servant) depending on the context and the nature of the relationship in view. According to the preface of the ESVUK, where *doulos* refers to 'absolute ownership by a master' they render it 'slave' (e.g. Rom. 6:16), but when a 'more limited form of servitude is in view' they translate it 'bondservant' (e.g. 1 Cor. 7:21–24) or 'servant' (e.g. John 4:51).[10] Although other English

---

[8] As but one example, in Mark 10:43–45, *diakonos/diakoneō* and *doulos* are used interchangeably of the kind of service that should characterize Christ's followers in the light of his work as the Isaianic suffering servant.

[9] For example, in Isa. 49:1–8 the Hebrew word *'ebed* is translated as *doulos* (49:3, 5, 7) and *pais* (49:6) with no discernable nuance of meaning between the choices.

[10] For the preface to the ESVUK, see <https://www.esv.org/preface>, accessed 21 August 2020.

versions do not raise this issue in their preface, they regularly practise similar approaches.[11]

As if those difficulties are not enough, there is the further challenge of accounting for how the original audiences of the Bible would have understood the language of servitude. As we have already noted, various forms of servitude were part of the fabric of both the ancient Near East and the Greco-Roman world. Based on the various ways that the Hebrew word *'ebed* (as well as other related terms) is used in the Old Testament, there is clear evidence that in certain contexts the term has an honorary sense. In other words, far from communicating a sense of bondage or oppression, it communicated a privileged position of authority and status.[12] The work of scholars such as Gerhard Sass, Walter Ollrog and Dale Martin has shown that the Greek word *doulos* could also refer to a person in a position of honour or leadership.[13] There should be little doubt that when the New Testament writers used expressions such as 'slave of Christ/God' or 'servant of Christ/God' that many of the original readers/hearers initially understood such references through the framework of their cultural experience of slavery in the Greco-Roman world. This would have been especially true of Gentile converts who had little or no exposure to the Old Testament. However, that does not mean that the New Testament authors *intended* such references to be *exclusively* or even *primarily* understood against this Greco-Roman cultural background.[14] Indeed, there are often strong contextual indicators that expressions such as 'slave of Christ/God' or 'servant of Christ/God' have as their *primary* referent the Old Testament background of key individuals raised up by God to further his creational and redemptive purposes in the world. Furthermore, the New Testament writers often take language and concepts that had

---

[11] Murray Harris notes that part of the impetus for his excellent book *Slave of Christ* was his work on the translation committee for the New International Version and the difficulties they encountered translating *doulos* in its various contexts (Harris 2001: 17).

[12] See the very helpful summary in Schultz 1997: 4.1184–1196.

[13] Sass 1941: 24–32; Ollrog 1979: 75–76. The work of Martin (1990: 30–49) is focused on slavery more broadly considered and is especially helpful in showing how slavery could even be a means of upward mobility within Greco-Roman society.

[14] This either/or approach is a flaw in the otherwise excellent work of Combes (1998). For example, he dismisses the 'servant of God' tradition as a backdrop for Paul's self-reference as a *doulos Christou* (slave of Christ) on the flimsy basis that Paul never calls himself a *doulos theou* (slave of God) and that Paul's theology would not allow him to simply substitute Christ for God in such formulations (77–79). Yet as we shall see, such a conclusion does not account for Paul's repeated use of language drawn from Isaianic servant texts to describe his apostolic commission.

certain meanings and connotations in the Greco-Roman world and reframe them in the light of the truth of the gospel such that they take on fresh significance.[15] As the chapters that follow will demonstrate, that is certainly the case with the use of servant language.

Approach of this study

It is important to note that this is not a word study, as Scripture uses a variety of terms and expressions to both identify and describe these key individuals. There are a variety of different terms and expressions that together express the servant of the Lord theme. Indeed, as we will see, in some instances the biblical text portrays an individual or group of people acting as a servant of the Lord without explicitly using such terminology. Thus, our interest is in the concept of the servant of the Lord, not merely the expression or terminology itself.[16]

Each chapter will address a specific individual who is identified as a servant of the Lord. Based on a careful reading of the biblical text (with insight from the broader historical, cultural and social contexts along the way), I will attempt to identify and summarize the nature of his role within God's purposes for both creation and redemption. Along the way we will see the consistent pattern that God uses each individual servant to produce a servant people. Therefore, tracing this servant thread throughout Scripture sheds fresh light on (1) the role of these key figures in redemptive history; (2) how these key figures point forward to Christ; (3) the identity of God's people; and (4) how we interact with fellow believers and the world around us.

---

15 As but one example of this, in Phil. 4:10–20 Paul uses language and concepts that were part of the Greco-Roman patron–client system. Yet he transforms this language and concept through the lens of the gospel to help the Philippians understand the true nature of their financial partnership in the advancement of the gospel.

16 On this important distinction, see Silva 1994: 22–32. In his revision (now titled *New International Dictionary of New Testament Theology and Exegesis*) of the *New International Dictionary of New Testament Theology*, Silva has attempted to address some of these challenges; see the summary in Silva 2014c: 1.5–14.

2
Adam: the first servant

> And God blessed them. And God said to them, 'Be fruitful and multiply and fill the earth and subdue it, and have dominion over the fish of the sea and over the birds of the heavens and over every living thing that moves on the earth.'
> (Gen. 1:28)

> The LORD God took the man and put him in the garden of Eden to work it and keep it.
> (Gen. 2:15)

Origin stories have become increasingly popular in recent years. This trend has been reflected in popular culture through literature, film and other forms of media. Related to this trend has been the growing popularity of services that analyse a person's DNA. Based on their analysis these services tell a person the various components of his or her ethnicity as well as the region of the world the person is likely from. People pursue such information about their origins because they believe it will help them understand who they are and why they are the way they are.

The opening chapters of Genesis provide us with the ultimate origins story.[1] They explain to us who God is, how the world came into existence and who we are as human beings. Genesis 1 – 3 also reveals what is wrong with the world and introduces the first hints of what God will do to fix what is broken. Thus, it is no exaggeration to say that a correct understanding of these chapters is essential for formulating a biblical world view.

---

[1] The reading of Gen. 1 – 3 that follows lies somewhere between a seminal and maximalist approach; on these categories and how they influence one's interpretation of Gen. 1 – 3, see Carson 2018: 143–163.

While Genesis 1 – 3 has much to say about our identity as human beings, the focus of this chapter will be to demonstrate that God created humanity to be his servants. But what exactly does it mean to be a servant of the Lord? How does God intend us to live out this identity? What effect has humanity's rebellion had on our ability and desire to live out our identity as servants? These are the questions we must answer if we are to live as God designed us to live.

God creates a servant

The starting point for understanding humanity's identity as servants of God is a close look at Genesis 1 – 2. Although nowhere in these chapters is Adam or humanity in general referred to with the title/label servant, the picture that emerges from these chapters is that human beings were created as divine image-bearers who serve God as kings and priests.

Commissioned as a king

Genesis 1 opens with a two-verse introduction that sets the stage for the rest of the creation story that stretches from 1:1 to 2:3. The emphasis in these two verses falls on God creating the universe *ex nihilo*, though in an initial state that is described as 'without form and void'.[2] The darkness that hangs over the deep is matched by the Spirit of God hovering over the face of the waters. What follows in 1:3–31 is a description of the six days of creation, each of which follows the same basic pattern: (1) God commands something to happen;[3] (2) what God commands happens; (3) the formula 'there was evening and there was morning, the . . . day'. In several of the days God gives specific names to the things he creates, and beginning with the third day the text notes that 'God saw that it was good'. The seventh day breaks the pattern, since, rather than creating anything, God rests (2:1–3).

As Bruce Waltke notes, the first six days can be broken down further into two triads, with the first triad (days 1–3) corresponding to the earth being 'without form' and the second triad (days 4–6) aligning with the earth being 'void' (see Table 1).[4]

---

[2] The phrase seems to stress the emptiness of creation, with particular emphasis on the lack of life (Tsumura 1989: 42–43).

[3] With the exception of the form in 1:26 (a first-person cohortative), each example (1:3, 6, 9, 11, 14, 20, 24) of the verb form is a third-person jussive. Both the jussive and the cohortative have the force of a command in this chapter.

[4] Waltke and Fredricks 2001: 57. I have made slight adaptations to their table.

Table 1 The pattern of creation in Genesis 1

Day	*Form/'the resource'*	*Day*	*Fill/'the utilizer'*
1	Light (1:3–5)	4	Lights: sun, moon and stars (1:14–19)
2	Firmament (1:6–8): Sky Seas	5	Inhabitants (1:20–23): Birds Fish
3	Dry land (1:9–10) Vegetation (1:11–13)	6	Land animals (1:24–25) Human beings (1:26–31)

Within this broader framework we will focus on the sixth day (1:26–31). Up to this point in the narrative, God has commanded some aspect of creation to come into existence or perform an action. But here in 1:26 God 'commands himself' to do something: 'Let us make man'.[5] The Hebrew noun *'ādām* can refer to humanity in general or can be the proper name of the first man (it is in fact used both ways here in Gen. 1 – 3). What is most significant for our purposes are the two prepositional phrases that further describe man.

First, man is made 'in our image'. We have already dealt with the use of the plural with reference to God, but this phrase contains two additional interpretive challenges: (1) the force of the preposition 'in' (*bĕ*); and (2) the meaning of the word 'image' (*ṣelem*). As used here, the force of the preposition seems to indicate the standard by which humanity is created.[6] With respect to the word *ṣelem*, in the Hebrew Bible it communicates some kind of resemblance between an original 'object' and some form of visible representation.[7] The nature of the connection is not necessarily physical, as any quick survey of idols recovered from the ancient Near East reveals.[8]

[5] According to Gesenius (2006: 318) the use of the cohortative stresses the determination and personal interest of the subject in performing the action (§108a). The plural 'us' has provoked no shortage of discussion and debate. See the helpful summary in Waltke and Fredricks 2001: 64–65. My discussion here does not depend on any specific conclusion.

[6] See both BDB s.v. *bĕ* III.8 and *HALOT* s.v. *bĕ* 8.

[7] In using the term 'object' I am not indicating that the original must be physical in nature; it could be something immaterial as well. There are three basic categories of usage for *ṣĕlĕm* in the OT: (1) references to humanity being made in the image of God (Gen. 1:26–27; 9:6); (2) references to a child being in the image of a father (Gen. 5:3); (3) references describing some form of idolatry (Num. 33:52; 1 Sam. 6:5, 11; 2 Kgs 11:18; 2 Chr. 23:17; Pss 39:7; 73:20; Ezek. 7:20; 16:17; 23:14; Amos 5:26).

[8] On whether the image of God in view here is physical or non-physical, see Clines 1968: 70–101.

Instead, an image was 'a more abstract, idealized representation of identity relating to the office/role and the value connected to the image'.[9] So as a starting point, humanity being made in the image of God means that in some sense we were created both to reflect who God is and represent his purposes here on earth.

Second, God makes man 'in our likeness'. Again, two interpretive issues confront the reader: (1) the force of the preposition 'according to' (*kĕ*); and the meaning of 'likeness' (*dĕmût*). Although a different preposition is used, the sense is essentially the same as the previous phrase: it communicates conformity to a standard.[10] The noun *dĕmût* communicates the idea of correspondence or similarity. It is especially common in Ezekiel, where it occurs in descriptions of supernatural beings, including God himself (e.g. 1:5, 10, 13).[11] As with the noun *ṣelem*, the point of comparison communicated by *dĕmût* is not necessarily physical.[12] For example, in Isaiah 13:4 the noun is used to compare a sound on a mountain to that of a great multitude of people. So to be in the likeness of God means that in some sense human beings are comparable to him.

Based on study of the words themselves as well as how they are used in Genesis (as well as the rest of the OT), no sharp distinction should be drawn between *ṣelem* and *dĕmût*.[13] This conclusion seems to be confirmed by Genesis 5:3, the only other passage where the two terms are used in close proximity to each other. Introducing the line of promise that begins from Adam, the text notes that 'When Adam had lived 130 years, he fathered a son in his own likeness [*dĕmût*], after his image [*ṣelem*], and named him Seth.' Here the order is reversed from Genesis 1:26 and the prepositions used are flipped, with no discernable significance. The point seems to be simply that Seth is every bit as much a human being made in the image of God as his father Adam was. Perhaps the most one can say is that *dĕmût* reinforces *ṣelem*, such that it amplifies and specifies its

---

9 Walton 2006: 212. Walton goes on to note an Aramaic inscription that uses cognates of the terms for image and likeness to describe a statue that physically represents both the essence and substance of an earthly king (*COS* 2.34).

10 Again, see both BDB s.v. *kĕ* 1.a and *HALOT* s.v. *kĕ* 3.

11 Sixteen of the twenty-five OT occurrences are in Ezekiel, and ten of those are in chapter 1 alone!

12 In her study of royal images of Assyrian kings, Winter (1997: 359–851) demonstrates that such images were not intended to reflect the physical features of the king but rather represent his values and role.

13 For a concise summary of the different ways scholars have construed the relationship between the two terms, see Hamilton 1980: 192.

meaning: 'Man is not just an image but a likeness-image. He is not simply representative but representational. Man is the visible, corporeal representative of the invisible, bodiless God.'[14]

An additional window into what it means that humanity was created in the image and likeness of God can be found in exploring the ancient Near Eastern parallels to image-of-God language.[15] Three elements of this background are particularly relevant for our purposes.[16] The first is the observation that the king is often described as representing the image of God. David Clines notes several examples from Assyria, such as the following, where Esarhaddon is addressed in a letter as follows: 'The father of the king, my lord, was the very image (*ṣalmu*) of Bel, and the king, my lord, is likewise the very image of Bel.'[17] Clines further notes several texts from Egyptian literature that describe the king as the image of a god, including the following example where Amosis I is addressed as 'A prince like Re, the child of Qeb, his heir, the image of Re, whom he created, the avenger (or the representative), for whom he has set himself on earth.'[18] Thus, when read in the light of the ancient Near Eastern background of Genesis, we should be alert to the possibility that when Genesis 1 describes humanity as made in the image of God, there are royal overtones to such language.[19]

A second observation from the ancient Near Eastern background is the common practice whereby kings would set up an image of themselves in a territory they had conquered.[20] Consider, for example, this inscription discovered on an Assyrian statue:

---

14 Clines 1968: 101.

15 See e.g. ibid. 80–85; Curtis 1987: 80–90; Middleton 2005: 93–231; Walton 2006: 78–80; Walton 2011: 74–86; Crouch 2016: 7–13.

16 It should be noted that in using such information from the ancient Near Eastern background, I am not arguing that Genesis simply 'borrows' from these texts or traditions. Rather, I am attempting to highlight the presence of similar concepts as part of the larger cultural milieu within which Genesis was written. As Beale (2004: 87) helpfully notes: 'The biblical writers were sometimes aware of the ideas reflected in this [i.e. ancient Near Eastern] literature and sometimes intentionally presented their versions as the true ones in contrast and even in contradiction to the others. The narrative of creation, especially the creation of humanity, would have been a prime place to point out the unique witness of the biblical revelation.' On this important subject, see further Oswalt 2009 and Currid 2013.

17 Clines 1968: 83–85.

18 Ibid. 85.

19 It is also worth noting in passing a portion of a Babylonian ritual exorcism that identifies the priest as an image of God: 'The exorcism (which is recited) is the exorcism of Marduk, the priest is the image (*ṣalmu*) of Marduk' (ibid. 84)

20 See Cogan 1974: 58–61; Curtis 1987: 119–120; Walton 2011: 80–81. For a succinct and helpful discussion of the various ways these statues were thought to function in the ancient Near East, see Middleton 2005: 104–108.

> The statue of Adad-it'i (Hadad-yis'ī) governor (king) of Guzan, (and of) Sikan, (and of) Azran, for perpetuating (exalting and continuing?) his throne, (and) for the length of his rule (life), (and) so that his word might be pleasing to gods and (to people), this statue (image) he made better than before. Before Adad (Hadad) who dwells in Sikan, lord of the Khabur, he has set up his statue.[21]

Such images served to remind the local inhabitants of the authority of a ruler who was not physically present, acting as a symbol of his presence, power and even protection. Such images were often placed in temples,[22] an observation that I will return to later in my discussion of Genesis 2:4–25. It would seem plausible, then, that God's placing image-bearing humanity on earth is at least in part intended as a representation of his own rule over creation, the true reality behind the distorted pagan practice reflected in the ancient Near East.

A third observation is that creation accounts from the ancient Near East often frame the creation of humanity as a way for the gods to find relief from their labour. Humanity will serve the gods by doing tasks that the gods find burdensome. This comes out especially clearly in the Babylonian creation epic commonly called *Enuma Elish*:

> From his [i.e. Tiamat's] blood he [i.e. Ea] made mankind,
> He imposed the burden of the gods and exempted the gods.
> (35) After Ea the wise had made mankind,
> They imposed the burden of the gods on them.
> (*COS* 1.111: 401)

A similar train of thought is present in the Akkadian text *Atra-Hasis*. The text begins as follows:

> (1) When gods were man,
> They did forced labor, they bore drudgery.
> Great indeed was the drudgery of the gods,
> The forced labor was heavy, the misery too much:

21 The text of the inscription is taken from Millard and Bordreuil 1982: 137–138. The Aramaic portion of this inscription uses the language of both image and likeness; see further Garr 2000: 227–234.

22 On this see especially Beale 2004: 87–93.

> The seven (?) great Anunna-gods were burdening
> The Igigi-gods with forced labor.
> (*COS* 1.111: 450)

After further describing the misery of the labours the gods performed, the god Ea steps forward and offers a solution:

> '[Belet-ili, the midwife], is present.
> Let her create, then, a hum[an, a man],
> (j) Let him bear the yoke [ ],
> Let him bear the yoke [ ]!
> [Let man assume the drud]gery of god . . .'
>
> '[Belet-ili, the midwife], is present,
> Let the midwife create a human being,
> Let man assume the drudgery of god.'
> They summoned and asked the goddess,
> The midwife of the gods, wise Mami:
> 'Will you be the birth goddess, creatress of mankind?
> Create a human being that he bear the yoke,
> Let him bear the yoke, the task of Enlil,
> Let man assume the drudgery of god.'
> (*COS* 1.111: 451)

Both of these texts stress that a driving motivation behind the creation of humanity was to provide the gods relief from their labours by having humanity serve them, with emphasis on the difficulty of the work.

Based on his careful study of ancient Near Eastern creation accounts, Walton proposes three main categories that summarize how human beings were created to function:

- Function *in place of* the gods (menial labor; Mesopotamia only)
- Function *in service to* the gods (performance of ritual, supply of temple; Mesopotamia, Egypt, and Gen 2:15)
- Function *on behalf of* the gods (rule, either over nonhuman creation or over other people; role of the image in Mesopotamia, Egypt, and Genesis 1)[23]

[23] Walton 2011: 85.

These categories help provide a larger context for what Genesis itself says about humanity.

So based on the Hebrew terms and the ancient Near Eastern background, we can summarize that being made in the image and likeness of God means at least two interrelated things. First, human beings in some sense *reflect* who God is and what he is like. Just as looking at the reflection of an object in the mirror reveals something about the object, so too observing human beings shows something about the very nature of God himself. Second, human beings *represent* God. They act in ways that advance the interests and purposes of the God who created them. Human beings are thus like envoys sent by an authority figure, authorized to act on behalf of the authority figure in ways that are consistent with the agenda of that authority figure.

While both studying the Hebrew terms used in Genesis 1:26 to describe humanity as created in the image and likeness of God and exploring the ancient Near Eastern background are helpful starting points, ultimately the larger context of Genesis 1 – 2 must determine what these expressions mean. The remainder of Genesis 1:26 sheds some immediate light when God says: 'And let them have dominion over the fish of the sea and over the birds of the heavens and over the livestock and over all the earth and over every creeping thing that creeps on the earth.' So the very first way the text expands what being made in the image of God entails is to stress humanity's authority over the various creatures God has already made. The Hebrew verb rendered 'have dominion' (*rādâ*) refers to exercising authority over someone or something.[24] In itself the term is neutral: only the context can determine whether such dominion is beneficial or oppressive. Thus, in Leviticus 25:43–53 the verb occurs three times to warn the Israelites not to oppress the poor among them, while in the very next chapter it describes Israel's enemies ruling over them as one of the curses that will befall them when they break the covenant (26:17). Nehemiah 9:38 uses the verb to describe the oppressive rule of foreign nations over Israel throughout their history. But there are a number of positive uses where the term has the sense of to exercise authority in a way that benefits those ruled over. Numbers 24:19 foresees a day when a descendant of Judah will rule over the nations currently troubling Israel. Solomon's rule is positively

[24] This verb is often (16 of the 23 OT occurrences) used with the preposition *bĕ* expressing the persons(s), object(s) or realm(s) over which authority is exercised.

described with this term (1 Kgs 4:24), and Solomon himself uses this verb in Psalm 72:8 to pray that God will extend the rule of Israel's king 'from sea to sea'. Psalm 110:2 records Yahweh using this verb to command his anointed king: 'Rule in the midst of your enemies!' The context of Genesis 1 clearly presents this exercise of authority in this positive sense, and such dominion is exercised over the totality of creation (sea, sky, land and the creatures that inhabit each of those spheres).

After this initial statement of God's purpose in creating humanity, the narrative pauses to describe God creating humanity in poetic terms:

> So God created man in his own image,
> in the image of God he created him;
> male and female he created them.
> (Gen. 1:27)

The development in this verse is the recognition that humanity, considered both as a whole as well as individuals, bears the image of God. Furthermore, humanity's identity as divine image-bearers extends to both male and female. Thus, each individual human being – male and female alike – bears the image of God, yet at the same time there seems to be a sense in which reflecting the fullness of God's image requires humanity working together.

The narrative resumes in 1:28, where God blesses humanity by issuing five imperatives that lay out how humanity is called to live out their identity as God's image-bearers: 'Be fruitful and multiply and fill the earth and subdue it, and have dominion over the fish of the sea and over the birds of the heavens and over every living thing that moves on the earth' (Gen. 1:28). These five imperatives sequentially build upon each other such that obeying the first enables the second, which in turn enables the third, which in turn enables the fourth, which in turn enables the fifth. Yet the fact that the first three imperatives are repeated from God's command to the creatures inhabiting the seas indicates that humanity's unique identity as divine imager-bearers rests in the final two imperatives. Nonetheless, it will be helpful briefly to treat each imperative to trace the logic.

The first command is to 'be fruitful'. Just as the animals that God created were to produce offspring according to their kind (cf. 1:24), so too human beings are commanded to procreate. The use of this verb (*pārâ*) suggests an abundance of offspring. It occurs regularly in Genesis in connection with human beings reproducing (e.g. 8:17; 9:1, 7; 17:6, 20; 28:3). Being fruitful will lead to the fulfilment of the second imperative: 'multiply'. God has in mind far more than human beings simply producing enough offspring to replace themselves, or perhaps slowly adding to their number. He intends for humanity to produce offspring to such a degree that they multiply – that is, grow exponentially in number. These two verbs appear frequently together in the Old Testament, usually in the context either of God's command to increase numerically or his promise to cause people to do so.[25]

Obedience to the first two commands eventually leads to the third imperative: 'fill the earth'. This command signals the scope of God's commission to humanity. Just as God commanded the creatures he created to fill their respective spheres (1:22), so too he commands human beings to increase in number to such a degree that they fill the earth he has created. Of course, as human beings are fruitful, multiply and fill the earth, they will inevitably come into potential conflict with the other creatures that God has made. So the fourth command addresses this situation: 'subdue it'. To 'subdue' (*kābaš*) means to bring under one's control to the extent that what was once hostile is no longer so. It frequently refers to the Promised Land being subdued before the Lord and/or Israel (Num. 32:22, 29; Josh. 18:1; 2 Sam. 8:11; 1 Chr. 22:18) as well as foreign powers subduing Israel (2 Chr. 28:10; Neh. 5:5).[26] The object that must be subdued is the earth, and by implication the creatures that inhabit it. As used here this verb 'implies that creation will not do man's bidding gladly or easily and that man must now bring creation into submission' through force.[27]

These four commands (be fruitful, multiply, fill the earth, subdue it) set the stage for the final imperative, which is a repetition of the original command connected to being created in the image of God: 'have dominion'. Whereas in 1:26 this verb is a third-person plural jussive ('let them have dominion') that God speaks with reference to humanity that he is about to create, here in 1:28 it is a plural imperative ('have dominion') spoken directly to the first human couple. The presence of the four preceding imperatives that unpack what it means to have dominion over

---

[25] See Gen. 1:22, 28; 8:17; 9:1, 7; 17:20; 28:3; 35:11; 47:27; 48:4; Exod. 1:7; Lev. 26:9; Jer. 3:16; 23:3; Ezek. 36:11.

[26] One of the more interesting occurrences is the promise in Mic. 7:19 that Yahweh 'will subdue our iniquities'.

[27] Oswalt 1980: 430.

creation provide humanity a roadmap of sorts in exercising their royal function as divine image-bearers exercising dominion over the earth.

God does not leave humanity on their own to accomplish this commission. He provides food for both them and the rest of the creatures he has made (Gen. 1:29–30). With that provision in place, God declares all that he has created 'very good' (1:31).

But this initial creation account is not over yet. After noting the completion of God's work (2:1–2a), the text notes that God 'rested on the seventh day from all his work that he had done' (2:2b). The rest in view is far more than simply cessation of activity. As Beale notes:

> God's rest both at the conclusion of Genesis 1–2 and later in Israel's temple indicates not mere inactivity but that he had demonstrated his sovereignty over the forces of chaos (e.g. the enemies of Israel) and now has assumed a position of kingly rest further revealing his sovereign power.[28]

With his image-bearing vicegerents in place to rule over creation under his ultimate authority, God enters into a state of rest from his creation labours.

Based, then, on the picture that emerges from Genesis 1:1 – 2:3, God created humanity in his image to be his servant. In this initial creation account, the focus is on humanity's royal function as vicegerents over creation. As an image-bearing servant, humanity is commissioned to reflect who God is and what he is like, represent his purposes, and rule over creation within the parameters established by God, who is the Great King. Humanity does this in the context of a relationship with God, which comes into greater focus in the second creation account. Through this initial pair of individual servants, God intends to produce a servant people who carry out this commission for humanity.

Consecrated as a priest

While the first creation account (Gen. 1:1 – 2:3) emphasizes humanity serving God as vicegerents ruling over creation, the second account (Gen. 2:4–25) highlights humanity's service to God as priests who mediate God's presence in creation. To demonstrate this, we will look first at how the

[28] Beale 2004: 62; see also Kline 2000: 33–40.

biblical text presents Eden as Yahweh's temple sanctuary here on earth. Then we will turn our attention to humanity's role as priests within this garden temple sanctuary.

That the Garden of Eden should be understood as the temple sanctuary of Yahweh here on earth has been argued by a number of scholars, so here I will simply summarize the evidence.[29] While some of the following evidence is more persuasive than other evidence, the cumulative effect establishes the point. We begin by noting that Eden is the place where Yahweh 'walks' (*hālak*) with Adam and Eve (Gen. 3:8); this same verb in the same (hithpael) stem describes how Yahweh 'walks in the midst of your camp' (Deut. 23:14) and walks to and fro through his presence in the tabernacle (cf. 2 Sam. 7:6–7). When Adam and Eve are exiled from Eden after their rebellion, God stations cherubim at the entrance to prevent them from re-entering the garden (Gen. 3:24). These angelic creatures are regularly associated with God's presence, and are present with Yahweh in his heavenly sanctuary (Isa. 37:16; Pss 18:10; 80:1; 99:1) as well as being visually depicted in Israel's tabernacle (e.g. Exod. 25:18–22; 37:8–9) and temple (1 Kgs 6:23–35). The presence of 'botanical and arboreal imagery'[30] in both the tabernacle and temple suggests they were intentionally modelled on Eden: gourds, flowers, pomegranates and trees proliferate in the description of Solomon's temple (1 Kgs 6 – 7). Also worth noting is that later Scripture makes the connection between Eden and the temple. Ezekiel 28:13–18 refers to Eden as the garden of God and associates it with the holy mountain and sanctuaries, both of which allude to the temple. These lines in themselves are sufficient to establish Eden as a temple sanctuary where God's presence dwelled.[31]

This portrayal is also consistent with evidence from ancient Near Eastern literature, which often associated the cosmos with a temple.[32] Gardens are regularly associated with such temples; note for example, the following text:

> In Eridu the black tragacanth tree grew in a pure place it was created. Its appearance is lapis lazuli stretched out on the Apsu

[29] On this point I am largely following Beale 2004: 66–80, who in turn notes the following predecessors: Kline 1980: 35–42; Barker 1991: 68–103; Parry 1994: 126–251; Wenham 1994: 399–404; Kline 2000: 31–32, 54–56.

[30] The phrase is borrowed from Beale (2004: 71).

[31] Additional, albeit perhaps less persuasive, parallels are provided in ibid. (66–80).

[32] See especially Walton 2011: 100–121.

> [fresh water or sea] of [the god] Ea – his promenade in Eridu filled with abundance . . . its shrine is the bed of Nammu. In the holy temple in which like a forest it casts its shadow, into which no one has entered, in its midst are the [the gods] Shamash and Tammuz, in between the mouths of the two rivers.[33]

The presence of gardens in conjunction with temples appear to have symbolized the fertility of the deity, an idea that was sometimes reinforced by the presence of rivers or streams that flowed from the temple into the gardens and outwards from there.[34] Given the parallels with Eden in Genesis 2, the biblical text may contain an implicit polemic against similar descriptions in ancient Near Eastern thought, showing that those traditions are faint distortions of the real garden temple sanctuary of Eden.[35]

Perhaps even more to the point is evidence from late Jewish texts that portray Eden as a temple.[36] The most explicit example is from Jubilees 8.19, which asserts that Noah 'knew that the garden of Eden was the holy of holies and the dwelling of the LORD'.[37] In *Testament of Levi* 18.1–14 the author looks forward to a day when God would raise up a new priest, who 'shall open the gates of paradise [i.e. Eden]; he shall remove the sword that has threatened since Adam [Gen. 3:24], and he will grant to the saints to eat of the tree of life' (18:10–11a).[38] Several texts in the Dead Sea Scrolls also seem to connect temple imagery with the Garden of Eden, describing it as an 'eternal plantation' where Adam's descendants consecrate themselves and are placed as a 'Holy of Holies' over all of creation (4Q418 frag. 81= 4Q423 8 +24?).

In the light of these various lines of evidence there should be little doubt that Eden is presented as a temple sanctuary for Yahweh. As a result, we should expect to find evidence that Adam is described in priestly terms, and that is in fact the case. The place to begin is with the text of Genesis itself, before moving on to supporting evidence from ancient Near Eastern and Second Temple Jewish texts.

---

33 Cited from Beale (2004: 76).
34 Walton 2006: 122–123.
35 Similarly, Beale 2004: 77.
36 Here we are again largely following ibid. (77–79).
37 Charlesworth 2010: 2.73.
38 Ibid. 1.795

The key verse is Genesis 2:15, which says: 'The LORD God took the man and put him in the garden of Eden to work it and keep it.' The first thing to note is the unusual verb used to describe God placing Adam in the garden. Genesis 2:8 uses the common verb *śîm* when it states that Yahweh 'put the man whom he formed' in the garden. Yet Genesis 2:15 uses the verb *nûaḥ*, which comes from a root that has the sense of 'coming to rest upon some place, or of being caused to rest, or being placed, in a certain spot'.[39] The hiphil stem of this verb is frequently used to describe the placement of objects in the tabernacle or temple, such as priestly garments (Lev. 16:23; Ezek. 42:14; 44:19), various instruments (Ezek. 40:42), holy things (Ezek. 42:13), staffs (Num. 17:22 [Eng. 17:7]), baskets of firstfruits (Deut. 26:4, 10), tables (2 Chr. 4:8) and even a book of regulations for the king (1 Sam. 10:25). It also describes placing an idol in a shrine (2 Kgs 17:29; Zech. 5:11). Based on this data Beale is likely right to conclude that 'the implication may be that God places Adam into a royal temple to begin to reign as his priestly vice-regent'.[40]

The second thing to note from Genesis 2:15 is the combination of verbs used to describe the purpose of placing Adam in the garden: 'to work it and keep it'. The verb rendered 'work' (*ʿābad*) has the basic sense of labour or service, with the larger context providing the specific meaning intended. Perhaps most noteworthy for our purposes is that from this root comes the most common term for 'servant' in the Hebrew Old Testament. This verb has already occurred in 2:5 to explain why there were no plants on the earth yet: 'there was no man to work the ground'. The play on words between 'man' (*ʾādām*) and 'ground' (*ʾădāmâ*) anticipates 2:7, where God forms the 'man' (*ʾādām*) of dust from the 'ground' (*ʾădāmâ*) and breathes life into him. The word for 'ground' (*ʾădāmâ*) is used as a rough synonym for 'earth' (*ʾereṣ*), which of course is exactly what humanity is supposed to subdue and have dominion over (1:28). In 2:15 the object of the verb 'work' (*ʿābad*) is the third-person feminine singular pronominal suffix, whose antecedent is 'the Garden of Eden'. The nature of this work is not specified, but it is important to note that humanity's work in the garden is framed as a form of service, reinforcing the notion that humanity was created as Yahweh's servant.

The verb rendered 'keep' (*šāmar*) also has a broad range of meaning, with the root having the sense of 'pay careful attention' to someone or

39 Oswalt 1997: 3.57. The name Noah (*nōaḥ*) comes from this same root.

40 Beale 2004: 70.

something.[41] The next use of the verb in Genesis 3:24 sheds light on its meaning here: God places cherubim and a flaming sword 'to guard [*šāmar*] the way to the tree of life'. The sense here is clearly that of protection, such that the cherubim are to prevent unclean humanity from approaching something that is sacred (i.e. the tree of life). This verb also has connotations of caring for someone or something. Cain was expected to be Abel's 'keeper' (Gen. 4:9), which suggests both protection and provision. The same is true of Jacob vowing to keep Laban's flocks (Gen. 30:31). This dual sense of protection and provision is even clearer in God's promise to 'keep' Jacob in the midst of his sojourning (Gen. 28:15, 20). Also noteworthy are places where individuals are commanded to keep God's covenant, statutes, commandments or ways (Gen. 17:9–10; 18:19; 26:5), always in the context of a relationship with God. So Adam's commission to keep the garden carries with it notions of provision and protection within the context of a relationship with Yahweh.

As helpful as it is to consider each verb on its own, something more profound emerges when they are considered together. After appearing together here in Genesis 2:15, from this point forward these two verbs (as well as their nominal forms) are often found in contexts that describe priestly duties in the tabernacle or temple:

> They shall keep guard [*šāmar*] over him and over the whole congregation before the tent of meeting, as they minister [*ʿābad*] at the tabernacle. They shall guard [*šāmar*] all the furnishings of the tent of meeting, and keep guard over the people of Israel as they minister [*ʿābad*] at the tabernacle.
> (Num. 3:7–8)

> They minister to their brothers in the tent of meeting by keeping guard [*šāmar*], but they shall do no service [*ʿābad*]. Thus shall you do to the Levites in assigning their duties.
> (Num. 8:26)

> And you and your sons with you shall guard [*šāmar*] your priesthood for all that concerns the altar and that is within the veil; and

[41] Schoville 1997: 4.182.

> you shall serve [ʿābad]. I give your priesthood as a gift, and any outsider who comes near shall be put to death.
> (Num. 18:7)

> Thus they were to keep [šāmar] charge of the tent of meeting and the sanctuary, and to attend the sons of Aaron, their brothers, for the service [ʿăbôdâ] of the house of the Lord.
> (1 Chr. 23:32)

> Yet I will appoint them to keep [šāmar] charge of the temple, to do all its service [ʿăbôdâ] and all that is to be done in it.
> (Ezek. 44:14)

These parallels strongly suggest that the combination of these two verbs in Genesis 2:15 have a priestly connotation. Adam's role is more than that of a simple gardener in the modern sense: he is a priest serving in God's garden sanctuary.

Even more relevant for our purposes is another set of texts that specifically connect these two verbal roots (and their related nominals) to someone identified as a servant of Yahweh. Note the following texts from Joshua:

> Above all, be strong and very courageous to observe [šāmar] carefully the whole instruction *my servant* [ʿebed] *Moses* commanded you. Do not turn from it to the right or the left, so that you will have success wherever you go.
> (Josh. 1:7 CSB)

> You have kept [šāmar] all that Moses *the servant* [ʿebed] *of the Lord* commanded you and have obeyed my voice in all that I have commanded you. You have not forsaken your brothers these many days, down to this day, but have been careful to keep the charge of the Lord your God. And now the Lord your God has given rest to your brothers, as he promised them. Therefore turn and go to your tents in the land where your possession lies, which *Moses the servant* [ʿebed] *of the Lord* gave you on the other side of the Jordan. Only be very careful [šāmar] to observe the commandment and the law that *Moses the servant* [ʿebed] *of the Lord* commanded you, to love the

> LORD your God, and to walk in all his ways and to keep [*šāmar*] his commandments and to cling to him and to serve [*ʿābad*] him with all your heart and with all your soul.
> (Josh. 22:2–5)

We will return to these texts in later chapters. But for now it is important to note that the language of 'working/serving' and 'guarding/keeping' is explicitly linked to the work of Moses the servant of Yahweh. It would seem reasonable, then, to view Adam as a servant of Yahweh in his role as priest in the Garden of Eden.

Concluding that Adam has a priestly role in the garden is further confirmed by what happens in Genesis 2:16. Immediately after placing Adam in the garden, God commands him not to eat from the tree of the knowledge of good and evil. Just as later priests were given a *tôrâ* to obey and communicate to others, so too Adam is given a '*tôrâ*' that he must obey and pass on to others (i.e. Eve, who it seems knows this commandment [Gen. 3:3] based on Adam telling her). Beale notes a similar pattern in 1 Kings 9:1–7[42] as, after Solomon's temple is completed (9:1), God warns:

> But if you turn aside from following me, you or your children, and do not keep [*šāmar*] my commandments and my statutes that I have set before you, but go and serve [*ʿābad*] other gods and worship them, then I will cut off Israel from the land that I have given them, and the house that I have consecrated for my name I will cast out of my sight, and Israel will become a proverb and a byword among all peoples.

Not only does the language echo that of Genesis 2:15, but the punishment for disobedience is also similar: being cut off from the place where God's presence dwells.

These later Old Testament parallels are sufficient to show that we should understand Adam's role in the garden as priestly service to Yahweh. As Beale helpfully summarizes:

> While it is likely that a large part of Adam's task was to 'cultivate' and be a gardener as well as 'guarding' the garden, that all of his

[42] Beale 2004: 68.

> activities are to be understood primarily as priestly activity is suggested not only from the exclusive use of the two words in contexts of worship elsewhere but also because the garden was a sanctuary . . . If this is so, then the manual labour of 'gardening' itself would be priestly activity, since it would be maintaining the upkeep and order of the sanctuary.[43]

Interpreting the Garden of Eden as Yahweh's temple sanctuary and Adam as a priest fits well within the larger ancient Near Eastern context. I have already noted above several texts that describe the creation of humanity as a means to relieve the gods of burdensome toil. Now I add to that picture by noting that such service to the gods is often described in priestly terms. Note, for example, the following excerpt from the *Enuma Elish*:

> He [Marduk] shall be the shepherd of the black-headed folk,[44]
> his creatures.
> They shall tell of his ways, without forgetting, in the future.
> He shall establish for his fathers great food offerings,
> (110) He shall provide for them, he shall take care of their
> sanctuaries.
> He shall cause incense burners to be savored, he shall make their
> chambers rejoice.
> He shall make on earth the counterpart of what he brought to pass
> in heaven,
> He shall appoint the black-headed folk to serve him.
> Let the subject peoples be mindful that their gods should be
> invoked,
> (115) At his command let them heed their goddess(es).
> Let their gods, their goddesses be brought food offerings;
> Let (these) not be forgotten, let them sustain their gods.
> Let their holy places be apparent (?), let them build their
> sanctuaries.
> (*COS* 1.111: 401)

43 Ibid.

44 In this context, the expression 'black-headed folk' appears to be a poetic term for humanity in general, possibly as 'a contrast to the fair-haired people living beyond the bounds of ancient Mesopotamia' (*COS* 1.111: 401, n. 14).

The priestly nature of humanity's role is also seen in an Akkadian prayer for the dedication of a temple's foundation stone:

> When Anu, Enlil, and Ea had a first idea of heaven and earth,
> They found a wise means of providing support for the gods:
> They prepared, in the land, a pleasant dwelling,
> And the gods were installed in this dwelling: their principal
> temple.
> Then they entrusted to the king the responsibility of assuring
> them their regular choice offerings.
> And for the feast of the gods, they established the required food
> offering!
> The gods love this dwelling![45]

These parallels make it likely that Genesis 2 is also describing Adam's role in priestly terms, albeit with important differences.

Later Jewish and early Christian texts also interpret Adam's role as a priestly one.[46] *Targum Neofiti Genesis* 2.15 asserts that Adam was placed in the garden 'to toil in the Law and to observe its commandments' (cf. *Tg. Ps.-J. Genesis* 2.15); several verses later it notes that Adam used the language of the sanctuary in naming the animals. According to *Midrash Rabbah Genesis* 16.5, the expression 'to work it and keep it' refers to Adam's responsibility to offer sacrifices that were later prescribed in the Mosaic law. Although fragmentary, 4Q265 describes the responsibilities of priests in the temple; in the midst of these descriptions it mentions Adam's being placed in the garden and notes that the garden was holy (frag. 7, col. II, lines 1–14).[47] In the *Epistle of Barnabas* (late first/early second century AD), believers are called a temple of God who must 'cultivate' the fear of God and 'keep' his commandments, language that echoes Genesis 2:15.

The cumulative weight of the evidence from Genesis, later Old Testament texts, ancient Near Eastern texts, later Jewish texts and even early Christian texts demonstrates that Adam was placed in the garden as a

---

45 Clifford 1994: 61, cited in Beale 2004: 90.

46 With the exception of the Qumran texts, this paragraph follows Beale (2004: 67–68).

47 In another fragmentary text, 4Q504 frag. 8 describes Adam's being made in the image of God's glory, being placed in the garden of Eden, and put there to govern (see similarly 4Q423 frag. 2).

priest. He was created to be a servant of Yahweh, functioning as a priest who mediated God's presence and protected the purity of God's garden sanctuary.

Summary

Genesis 1 – 2 presents human beings as servants in the image of Yahweh their creator, even though these chapters (or the rest of the OT for that matter) do not explicitly apply the title 'servant of Yahweh' to humanity in general or Adam as an individual. They serve Yahweh by living out their identity as image-bearers. To be an image-bearer means that human beings (1) *reflect* who God is and what he is like; (2) *represent* God and his purposes by mediating his presence; and (3) *rule* over creation by exercising benevolent authority as an extension of God's own rule over the universe. Human beings live out this identity in the context of a *relationship* with God that is rooted in the abundance of his own love for both humanity and creation. Thus, human beings function as image-bearers by serving Yahweh in both a royal and priestly capacity.

The servant fails

Unfortunately, the idyllic picture of Genesis 1 – 2 does not endure long. Although the text does not specify how long it was before the serpent entered the Garden of Eden to tempt humanity, the text gives the impression it happened rather quickly. The servants of Yahweh are faced with their first test, and they fail miserably. At the heart of their failure are intertwined questions of identity and authority.

The contest (Gen. 3:1–7)

The first hint of trouble comes in describing the serpent as 'more crafty than any other beast of the field the LORD God had made' (3:1). Although the Hebrew adjective *ʿārûm* can have the positive sense of prudence or wisdom (e.g. Prov. 12:16, 23; 13:16, 14:8, 15, 18), the context clearly shows the negative sense of cunning with connotations of deception (cf. Job 5:12; 15:5).[48] The serpent begins by questioning God's word. He deliberately

[48] There is likely an intentional wordplay between the serpent being 'crafty' (*ʿārûm*) in 3:1 and the man and the wife being 'naked' (*ʿārôm*) in 2:25. The point seems to be that craftiness of the serpent is about to undo the nakedness of the man and woman.

distorts God's command to not eat from the tree of the knowledge of good and evil into a prohibition against eating from any tree in the garden (3:1). When the woman 'corrects' the serpent, she herself makes two tweaks to the original command: (1) the tree of the knowledge of good and evil becomes 'the tree in the midst of the garden' and (2) the prohibition extends to even touching the tree (3:2–3). But the serpent focuses on the claim that touching the tree leads to certain death, instead claiming that 'You will not surely die. For God knows that when you eat of it your eyes will be opened, and you will be like God, knowing good and evil' (3:4–5). In these brief words the serpent challenges three attributes of God.

First, the serpent calls into question God's truthfulness. God stated in the most emphatic fashion possible the certain death that awaited anyone who ate from the tree (2:16).[49] The serpent claims this is a flat out lie: eating from the tree will not lead to death. In fact, as the narrative continues the serpent in essence promises that eating from the tree will lead to life.

Second, the serpent calls into question God's goodness. Far from trying to shield humanity from certain death, the serpent claims the real reason for the prohibition is that God is holding back something good from them. Instead of having their best interests in mind, God is the great cosmic killjoy, holding humanity back from being all that they could be. The serpent claims that God wants to keep humanity wandering in the darkness rather than living with their eyes opened to the true nature of the world they live in.

Third, the serpent calls into question God's authority. The serpent tells the woman that if they eat from the forbidden tree 'you will be like God, knowing good and evil' (3:5). To know good and evil in this sense is not mere awareness: it means to determine for themselves what is good and what is evil.[50] In contexts such as here the verb 'know' (*yāda'*) has the sense of discern. Thus, children are said not to know their right hand from their left (Jon. 4:11) or good from evil (Deut. 1:39; Isa. 7:15). Although using a different verb, Solomon prays 'Give your servant therefore an understanding mind to govern your people, that I may discern between good and evil, for who is able to govern this your great people?' (1 Kgs 3:9). As Yahweh's servant, Solomon asks for the ability to 'discern' (*bîn*) good

---

[49] In Hebrew the construction is an infinitive absolute followed by the imperfect of the same verb; see further Waltke and O'Connor 1990: 584–586; Gesenius 2006: 342; Joüon and Muraoka 2006: 392–393.

[50] The definitive study that demonstrates this conclusion remains Clark 1969 (266–278).

and evil. In 2 Samuel 14:17, the king is said to be 'like the angel of God to discern good and evil'. Even though a different verb is used (*šāma'*), the idea is the same – the king discerns and determines the difference between good and evil. Thus, when the serpent says the man and the woman will be able to know good and evil, he is inviting them to reject God's authority and autonomously determine it for themselves. The woman's first autonomous exercise of moral judgment is to note that 'the tree was good for food, and that it was a delight to the eyes, and that the tree was to be desired to make one wise' (3:6).

In addition to questioning God, the serpent strikes at the woman's identity. The serpent attempts to entice the woman to eat the fruit by claiming that when they eat the fruit, 'you will be like God' (3:5). As we have just noted, by this the serpent means determining for themselves good and evil. But Genesis 1:26–31 has already gone to great lengths to explain that the man and the woman were created in the image and likeness of God. The serpent, then, is implying that the man and the woman are not in fact like God, or that there is some sense in which they are not like God but should be. An appropriate response from the woman might have been something along the lines of 'I am already like God in every way that God intends me to be like him, no more and no less!'

At this point we should note that when the woman finally does take fruit from the tree, she gives it 'to her husband who was with her, and he ate' (3:6). It would seem, then, that the man was present with the woman while the serpent was tempting her, a conclusion confirmed by the consistent use of second-person plural forms in 3:1–5. Thus, part of Adam's failure in this contest with the serpent was in not exercising his dominion as king over creation and in not preserving the purity of God's garden sanctuary as a priest.

The effect of the fruit appears to have been immediate. Part of what the serpent said turned out to be true: their eyes were indeed opened (3:7a; cf. 3:5), but not in the way they expected. Although they had been 'naked and unashamed' (2:25), now 'they knew that they were naked' and by implication were ashamed (3:7). Just as Satan had promised the man and woman would know (i.e. determine) good and evil (3:5), now they 'know' (i.e. determine) that they are naked. Left to their own autonomous wisdom the man and woman decide to cover themselves with fig leaves (3:7), a pathetic attempt to hide their shame before each other and ultimately God himself.

The confrontation (Gen. 3:8–13)

When the time comes for Yahweh to take his stroll in 'the cool of the day' the man and the woman play the first game of hide and seek in human history (3:8). As we have already noted, the language used here portrays God walking in his sanctuary (cf. Deut. 23:14; 2 Sam. 7:6–7). But instead of eagerly greeting him as his faithful servants, the man and woman hide themselves, recognizing Yahweh's holiness and their own impurity are incompatible (3:8). God asks where Adam is not because he does not know, but rather to draw out the man to explain his actions (3:9). When Adam states he is afraid and hid himself because he was naked (3:10), Yahweh focuses on Adam's acknowledgment that he is naked. The issue here is not physical nakedness (after all, the man and woman had been naked from their creation, 2:25), but rather the entrance of sin and guilt that makes their physical nakedness a visible representation of being exposed before each other and God as guilty. So God asks two questions that he once again already knows the answer to: 'Who told you that you were naked? Have you eaten of the tree of which I commanded you not to eat?' (3:11). By asking Adam who told him he is naked, Yahweh highlights the source of this knowledge. No one told Adam he was naked (i.e. exposed and guilty); he determined it for himself, which in itself is an act of knowing/determining good and evil. The second question seems to confirm this conclusion, as Yahweh identifies the source of Adam's knowledge – eating from the forbidden tree.

The response of the man and woman to Yahweh's confrontation is peppered with blame shifting. Not only does Adam blame the woman for giving him the fruit to eat (even though he was present during the entire exchange between the woman and the serpent), but also blames God when he refers to her as 'the woman whom you gave to be with me' (3:12). The subtext of Adam's description seems to be that everything was just fine before God gave him the woman, and would still be that way if God had not given him the woman in the first place. In a similar fashion, the woman blames the serpent for deceiving her (3:13), which at one level is of course true. She portrays herself as a victim rather than taking responsibility for her actions.

Underlying this entire interaction are the issues of identity and authority. The man and the woman had rejected their identity as servants of Yahweh and asserted their own authority to determine for themselves good and evil. By confronting them God reasserts his authority and in doing so re-establishes their identity as his servants who must give an account to him. And because they have defied their sovereign and holy Lord, there must be consequences.

The consequences (Gen. 3:14–24)

Yahweh announces judgment on the three agents involved in the rebellion. In the confrontation God began with the man, who blamed the woman, who in turn blamed the serpent. Yahweh reverses that order in declaring judgment, moving from the serpent to the woman to the man. In each announcement of judgment God addresses the issues of identity and authority.

He begins with the serpent (3:14–15). The serpent is cursed 'above all livestock / and above all beasts of the field', which is pictured by the serpent moving on its belly and eating dust (3:14). This last expression vividly portrays the serpent's humiliation; thus later texts describe God's enemies being brought so low they lick the dust (Ps. 72:9; Isa. 49:23; Mic. 7:17). The nature of this humiliation is further explained in the next verse:

> I will put enmity between you and the woman,
>   and between your offspring and her offspring;
> he shall bruise your head,
>   and you shall bruise his heel.
> (Gen. 3:15)

The constant hostility between the serpent, the woman, and their respective offspring will eventually culminate in the serpent being brought into subjection. That defeat will come through an offspring of the woman, but in accomplishing this victory he will suffer. We will shortly return to this important text, but here we should note that this judgment re-establishes the identity of the serpent as one who is under the ultimate authority of God.

Next Yahweh turns to the woman (3:16). God will 'multiply' (*rābâ*) her pain in childbirth as she seeks to be fruitful, multiply (*rābâ*) and fill the earth (1:28). Living out her identity as an image-bearer serving God will now be complicated by the intensified pain of childbirth. In addition, Yahweh states: 'And towards your husband [will be] your desire, but/and he will rule over you' (Gen. 3:16b AT). This wooden translation hints at two key issues of interpretation: (1) is the sense of the phrase 'towards your husband' positive or negative? And (2) does the vav conjunction that begins the second clause communicate continuation or contrast?[51] The answer to both questions comes from an almost identical sentence in Genesis 4:7, where after God warns Cain that sin is crouching at the door he says: 'And towards you [is] its desire, but/and you must rule over it' (Gen. 4:7b AT). In the context of Genesis 4:7 sin's desire is clearly against or hostile towards Cain, which sets up the second clause as a contrasting action. The same, then, is true of the parallel expression in Genesis 3:16. The woman's desire will be against the man in the sense that she will seek to undermine his leadership, but nonetheless the man will rule over her, likely with the connotation that he will exercise this authority in a domineering rather than loving manner.

At last Yahweh turns to the man (3:17–19). He begins by reminding Adam that he listened to the voice of his wife rather than the explicit commandment of God. Because of his failure to submit himself to God's authority, Yahweh announces a curse on the ground (3:17). As part of being an image-bearer Adam was called to exercise dominion over the earth (1:28), but now that task will be significantly complicated by the earth itself producing thorns and thistles (3:18). Instead of subduing the earth, man will ultimately return to the ground from which God made him (2:7). Living out his identity as a servant will now be exponentially more difficult than it originally was.

In addition to these specific pronouncements, there are judgments that apply to both the man and the woman. Yahweh exiles humanity from his garden sanctuary and cuts off their access to the tree of life (3:22–24). Whereas before Adam and Eve were called to protect the purity of the place where God's presence dwelled, now it is the cherubim and a flaming sword that keep out anything unclean. The clean priest has become the unclean idolater.

Yet not all hope is lost. In the midst of judgment God makes several provisions for his fallen creatures. The man and the woman did not immediately experience physical death (though they did die spiritually); Adam even goes so far as to name the woman Eve 'because she was the mother of all the living' (3:20). Yahweh also addresses the nakedness of

[51] For a helpful discussion of the issues involved, see Foh 1974/1975: 376–383.

Adam and Eve by making 'garments of skins' to clothe them (3:21). Instead of Adam and Eve dying for their sin, God provides a substitute, taking the skins from the killed animals and covering the man and woman. This act is far more than providing them protection from the elements: it introduces the idea of a substitutionary sacrifice to atone for sin, paving the way for the sacrificial system and anticipating the ultimate sacrifice of the serpent-crushing servant.

That leads us back to the promise embedded within the judgment on the serpent. The ultimate hope of the man and the woman is the promise that one day a serpent-crusher will come. This offspring of the woman will be the servant who obeys where Adam and Eve failed. He will also be the servant who suffers for the failure of his people.

Summary

Adam and Eve's sin in the garden undermines each aspect of their identity as servants who bear God's image. By disobeying God's command, they display a distorted *reflection* of who God is and what he is like. By rejecting God's command, they fail to *represent* God and his purposes by embracing their own agenda. By listening to the voice of the serpent rather than God's command, they attempt to *rule* in a selfish way that disregards God's authority as the great king. No wonder this act of treachery and rebellion fundamentally alters their *relationship* with him!

God calls a servant

Despite the disastrous rebellion of Adam and Eve in Eden, God promised that a descendant of Eve would one day crush the head of the serpent (Gen. 3:15). Despite this promise, sin, death and the curse begin to spread throughout creation seemingly unchecked. The image of God in humanity was not erased in the fall (Gen. 5:1–3), but had become deeply tarnished. Instead of living as servants of God, humanity plunged deeper and deeper into rebellion and idolatry. Yet God remains committed to his original purpose of humanity serving him as royal priests who reflect who he is, represent his purposes and rule over creation under his authority, all in the context of a close relationship. As a result, God begins to raise up individual servants to play key roles in advancing God's purpose and plan in this world.

Noah

The first such servant outside Eden is Noah. In his days 'The LORD saw that the wickedness of man was great in the earth, and that every intention of the thoughts of his heart was only evil continually' (Gen. 6:5). He decides to 'de-create' by flooding the earth and begin anew with a man named Noah (Gen. 6:8). His father Lamech gave him this name because 'Out of the ground that the LORD has cursed this one shall bring us relief from our work and from the painful toil of our hands' (Gen. 5:29).[52] Noah is marked off as a recipient of divine grace (6:8), yet is also described as 'a righteous man, blameless in his generation. Noah walked with God' (6:9; 7:1). This combination of divine grace and human faithfulness play out in the flood narrative.

Noah's faithfulness finds primary expression in the repeated statements that he does everything God commands with respect to building the ark and taking in the animals (6:22; 7:5, 16). When Noah and his family are finally able to exit the ark, he builds an altar to sacrifice some of the clean animals and offer burnt offerings (8:20–21). These actions mark Noah as a man of piety and devotion to the Lord.

The most obvious expression of God's grace shown to Noah is God's promise that he will establish his covenant with Noah (6:18). God does not explain the nature of that covenant until after Noah emerges from the ark after the flood (8:20 – 9:17). After promising never to destroy the earth with a flood again (8:21–22), God addresses Noah in terms reminiscent of God's commission to Adam in Genesis 1:28–30. A careful comparison reveals both similarities and key differences (see Table 2 on p. 34).

The similarities begin with God blessing and then issuing to Noah the first three commands (be fruitful, multiply, fill the earth) he gave Adam in the garden. Yet a key difference emerges in that God does not issue the final two imperatives (subdue it and have dominion) from the garden; instead, he states that the animal kingdom will experience fear and dread towards humanity. What had been a command to exercise dominion has become a statement of something God has done.

So in one sense Noah is given a modified version of God's original commission to Adam, making him at one level a second Adam figure.

---

[52] The name Noah (*nōaḥ*) comes from the same root as the verb 'comfort' (*nāḥam*), which also appears in the niphal stem in Gen. 6:6–7, where it expresses God's grief at making humanity.

Table 2 Noah as a second Adam figure

Genesis 1:28–31	*Genesis 9:1–7*
God blessed them (1:28) Be fruitful, and multiply and fill the earth (1:28)	God blessed Noah and his sons (9:1) Be fruitful and multiply and fill the earth (9:1)
subdue it and have dominion over the fish of the sea and over the birds of the heavens and over every living thing that moves on the earth (1:28)	The fear of you and the dread of you shall be upon every beast of the earth and upon every bird of the heavens, upon everything that creeps on the ground and all the fish of the sea. Into your hand they are delivered. (9:2)
I have given you every plant yielding seed that is on the face of all the earth, and every tree with seed in its fruit. You shall have them for food (1:29)	Every moving thing that lives shall be food for you. And as I gave you the green plants, I give you everything. But you shall not eat flesh with its life, that is, its blood. (9:3–4) And for your lifeblood I will require a reckoning: from every beast I will require it and from man. From his fellow man I will require a reckoning for the life of man. (9:5) Whoever sheds the blood of man, / by man shall his blood be shed, / for God made man in his own image (9:6)
Be fruitful and multiply and fill the earth (1:28)	And you, be fruitful and multiply, teem on the earth and multiply in it.

Humanity's identity as image-bearers is reaffirmed. Noah and his descendants are servants of the Lord who are commanded to be fruitful, multiply and fill the earth. As with Adam, God raises up an individual servant to produce a servant people. But the absence of the commands to subdue the earth and have dominion over creation suggests that those elements of God's original commission to his servants await a future fulfilment.

Whatever hope the reader might have had that this second Adam figure would fare better than the first quickly dissipates. Instead of multiplying and filling the earth, Noah's descendants group together in rebellion against God (Gen. 11:1–9). In response God confuses their languages and scatters them.

Abraham

In the aftermath of confusing the languages and scattering humanity at Babel, God introduces the servant through whom he will bring his purposes to fulfilment. God makes Abram the following promise:

> Now the LORD said to Abram, 'Go from your country and your kindred and your father's house to the land that I will show you. And I will make of you a great nation, and I will bless you and make your name great, so that you will be a blessing. I will bless those who bless you, and him who dishonours you I will curse, and in you all the families of the earth shall be blessed.'
> (Gen. 12:1–3)

Within the context of Genesis, this promise expresses the means by which God will bring forth the serpent-crusher (Gen. 3:15) and ultimately bring to fruition humanity's commission as a servant who rules over creation and mediates God's presence (Gen. 1:26–31; 2:15). But rather than taking the form of a command, God's words to Abram are in the form of a promise stating what God himself will do. This conclusion is confirmed as God further expands this promise as Genesis unfolds.

God's original command to be fruitful, multiply and fill the earth (Gen. 1:28) now takes the form of his promise to make Abram a great nation (12:1). That promise expands into Abram's offspring, as numerous as the dust of the earth (Gen. 13:16) and the stars of the sky (Gen. 15:5; cf. 22:17). Indeed, a multitude of nations will come from Abram such that God must change his name to Abraham (exalted father) to reflect this promise (Gen. 17:5). This will happen because God will make Abram 'exceedingly fruitful' (Gen. 17:6). Even though Abraham's son Ishmael is not in the line of promise, because he is Abraham's son God promises to bless Ishmael by making him fruitful and multiplying him greatly into a great nation (Gen. 17:20).

God's original command to subdue the earth also finds expression in the promise of Genesis 12:1–3. God sends Abram to a land he will show him (Gen. 12:1). Here it is helpful to recall that in Hebrew it is the same word (*'ereṣ*) rendered 'earth' in Genesis 1:28. Initially, the land is Canaan

(Gen. 12:7; 13:14; 15:7) but over time God expands this beyond the borders of Canaan (Gen. 15:18–21).[53] It would seem, then, that Abraham and his descendants possessing the land is a first step towards humanity subduing the earth.

God's original command to have dominion over the earth and its inhabitants finds expression in Genesis 12:1–3, though admittedly in nascent form that requires later iterations of the promise to flesh out. God promises that all the families of the earth will be blessed in/by Abram (12:3), which in itself is ambiguous. Though again it should be noted that God's blessing of humanity in Genesis 1:28–30 is specifically linked to their commission to have dominion over the earth and its creatures. The development of the Abrahamic promise leaves no doubt that some form of dominion is in view. God promises that kings will come forth from Abraham (Gen. 17:6) and that his offspring will have the land as 'an everlasting possession' (17:8); such language suggests having dominion over that territory and its inhabitants. Genesis 22:17b–18 makes clear the connection between blessing the nations and exercising dominion: 'And your offspring shall possess the gate of his enemies, and in your offspring shall all the nations of the earth be blessed, because you have obeyed my voice.' There is hardly a more definitive way of expressing the idea of having dominion than to possess the gates of one's enemies. And the singular reference ('his enemies') should not be overlooked.[54] The text envisions an individual offspring who will have dominion over his enemies, and it is through this exercise of dominion that all the nations of the earth will be blessed.

These connections between God's promise to Abraham and his commission to humanity confirm that Abraham should be viewed as a servant figure who in some sense carries forward God's original purpose for humanity. Through this individual servant Yahweh will create a servant people. This conclusion may find further confirmation in Genesis 18, where Yahweh appears to Abraham through three mysterious men who visit the patriarch. Servant language peppers the narrative. Abraham refers to himself as a servant several times (18:3, 5), but most noteworthy is what Yahweh says in his self-deliberation: 'Shall I hide from Abraham

53 This point is made especially well by Martin (2015: 71–74).

54 Despite several English translations rendering this 'their enemies' based on the context, the third-person masculine singular suffix is best understood as referring to a singular offspring; see Alexander 1997: 363–367 and Williamson 2000: 248–250.

what I am about to do?' (18:17). The LXX, however, has an interesting addition: 'Surely I shall not hide from *my servant* Abraam what I am about to do?' (NETS). This is the first time in Scripture that Yahweh explicitly refers to someone as 'my servant' and in the context it is clearly linked to Abraham's special role in redemptive history. The following verses make this clear by reiterating the promise Yahweh made to him and his choice of Abraham and his descendants to keep the way of Yahweh (18:18–19).

Admittedly, the absence of the phrase 'my servant' in the MT warrants caution in making too much of this identification. But when God reaffirms the covenant promises to Isaac, he asserts his commitment to fulfil them 'for my servant Abraham's sake' (Gen. 26:24). As Goldingay rightly notes, this is the first place in the Old Testament where God refers to someone as 'my servant'.[55] This identification is further confirmed in Psalm 105, where the psalmist refers to Israel as:

> offspring of Abraham, his servant,
> children of Jacob, his chosen ones!
> (105:6)

Near the end of the psalm the writer explains that God brought forth water from the rock for his people in the wilderness because:

> he remembered his holy promise,
> and Abraham, his servant.
> (105:42)

So even though within Genesis itself Abraham is only explicitly referred to as a servant of Yahweh once in the Hebrew text (twice in the LXX), Psalm 105 confirms the legitimacy of identifying Abraham as a servant of Yahweh.

Patriarchs

Once Abraham steps off the stage, God's promise moves forward through Isaac, his son Jacob and Jacob's twelve sons. Nowhere in Genesis does God refer to any of these figures as his servant. However, in Genesis 32:9–12

---

55 Goldingay 1994: 39.

Jacob does refer to himself as 'your servant' when praying to Yahweh on the eve of encountering his brother Esau:

> And Jacob said, 'O God of my father Abraham and God of my father Isaac, O LORD who said to me, "Return to your country and to your kindred, that I may do you good," I am not worthy of the least of all the deeds of steadfast love and all the faithfulness that you have shown to *your servant*, for with only my staff I crossed this Jordan, and now I have become two camps. Please deliver me from the hand of my brother, from the hand of Esau, for I fear him, that he may come and attack me, the mothers with the children. But you said, "I will surely do you good, and make your offspring as the sand of the sea, which cannot be numbered for multitude."'

In the context Jacob's reference to himself as a servant of Yahweh seems to be tied to the promise that God made to his grandfather, Abraham, and his father, Isaac. As the heir to the promise made to them Jacob sees himself as yet another 'servant' in this line. That status is directly linked to the 'steadfast love' (*ḥesed*) and 'faithfulness' (*'ĕmet*) of Yahweh, a pairing of terms regularly linked to God's identity and covenant promises (e.g. Exod. 34:6). Jacob focuses on the promise of numerous offspring likely because Esau's presence threatens its fulfilment.

Although none of the other key figures in Genesis are specifically designated as a servant of Yahweh, the continuation of the promise through these generations demonstrates that Abraham's descendants are functioning as servants of Yahweh. Each reiteration of the promise reinforces the elements of numerous offspring, gaining possession of land and exercising authority over enemies that are God's means of realizing his purpose of humanity living out their identity as image-bearing servants who rule over creation and mediate God's presence to the world. The promise of producing a servant people through Abraham the individual servant is coming to fruition.

Conclusion

Genesis 1 introduces Adam as an image-bearer who serves God by ruling over creation under the authority of God (Gen. 1:26–31). Genesis 2 adds to that portrait by portraying Adam as a priest who is charged with serving and protecting Eden, the sanctuary of God (Gen. 2:15). But when Adam fails to fulfil these roles in Genesis 3, sin and death are unleashed into creation. Yet a promise is given that God will raise up a new servant, a serpent-crusher who obeys where humanity failed and takes upon himself the punishment humanity deserves for its disobedience (Gen. 3:15). God expresses his intention to create a servant people by raising up key individual servants such as Noah and Abraham. It is through the latter that God's purposes for creation and redemption will be realized. By the end of Genesis, however, that serpent-crushing servant seems to be nowhere in sight. Jacob, his twelve sons, and their families are living as sojourners in the land of Egypt. Yet God is preparing to introduce a new servant, one who will lead a people out of their bondage.

3
Moses: the servant prophet

> And he said, 'Hear my words: If there is a prophet among you, I the LORD make myself known to him in a vision; I speak with him in a dream. Not so with my servant Moses. He is faithful in all my house. With him I speak mouth to mouth, clearly, and not in riddles, and he beholds the form of the LORD. Why then were you not afraid to speak against my servant Moses?'
> (Num. 12:6–8)

We live in an age of almost constant and instant gratification. Waiting even just a few minutes for something that we really want can provoke frustration and even anger. So it can be hard for us to imagine what the descendants of Jacob and his twelve sons went through during the 400 years between their arrival in Egypt and their exodus. From generation to generation the stories of their ancestors and the promises God made to them were passed down. But as the years passed and their slavery in Egypt intensified, those promises must have seemed like a distant dream. How would they ever be free to return to the land that God had promised them?

So imagine the buzz it must have created when Moses appeared before the elders of the people announcing that the God of their fathers had appeared to him, and that at last God was going to act to fulfil his promises. And at the centre of his plan was Moses his servant. But before we can explore Moses' identity and role as the servant, we first need to set the stage for his entrance into the redemptive drama.

Setting the stage

Exodus begins by restating the names of the sons of Israel, noting that the total number of family members was seventy (1:1–5). After noting the death of Joseph and that entire generation (1:6), the author provides an important summary statement: 'But the people of Israel were fruitful and increased greatly; they multiplied and grew exceedingly strong, so that the land was filled with them' (Exod. 1:7). The intentional repetition of language from God's commission to humanity (Gen. 1:28) and the promise to Abraham (Gen. 12:1–3) signal to the reader that God is accomplishing his purposes. God is making the descendants of Abraham into a great nation by multiplying them greatly. But for the people to truly become a great nation, they need land. And therein lies the problem – Israel lives as slaves in Egypt. This tension introduces the book of Exodus, as God takes action to begin the process of bringing them into the land originally promised to Abraham and his descendants.

Not everyone is happy about Israel's rapid multiplication, however. As the generations pass and Joseph's life-saving service is long forgotten, Egypt's leadership concludes Israel is a national security threat and puts them to forced labour (Exod. 1:8–14). But in yet another example of God using for good an act someone meant for evil (cf. Gen. 50:20), Israel continues to multiply: 'But the more they were oppressed, the more they multiplied and the more they spread abroad. And the Egyptians were in dread of the people of Israel' (Exod. 1:12). Egypt's dread of the people grows as Israel continues to multiply, which may be an ironic echo of the promise to Noah and his descendants that God would put the 'fear of you and the dread of you . . . upon every beast of the earth and upon every bird of the heavens, upon everything that creeps on the ground and all the fish of the sea' (Gen. 9:2). Acting on this fear Pharaoh doubles down, making the forced labour even worse:

> So they caused the sons of Israel to serve [*ʿābad*] as slaves with harshness and they made their lives bitter with hard service [*ʿăbôdâ*] in mortar and brick, and in all kinds of service [*ʿăbôdâ*] in the field. In all their service [*ʿăbôdâ*] which they served [*ʿābad*] with harshness.
> (Exod. 1:13–14 AT)

The difficulty of working the ground that resulted from the fall (Gen. 3:17–19) is intensified by the oppression of the Egyptians. Most noteworthy is the repeated use of words from the *ʿbd* root in this short description of Israel's bondage, which I have attempted to reflect in the wooden translation above. This is the same verb that Genesis 2:15 uses to describe

Adam's purpose in the garden: to serve [*'ābad*] and protect it. Yet whereas God's placement of Adam in the garden to serve it is an act of benevolent stewardship, here the Egyptians are forcing the Israelites (note the hiphil stem of *'ābad*) to serve with harshness.[1] The result is a life of service [*'ăbôdâ*] that instead of expressing their identity as divine image-bearers demeans them by treating them as subhuman.

It is into this context of Israel's forced servitude that God intervenes to raise up a servant who will lead them out of their bondage in fulfilment of God's promises to Abraham, Isaac and Jacob (Exod. 2:24–25). That servant is a man named Moses.

No other individual in Scripture is referred to as the servant of Yahweh more often than Moses. To help us understand why that is and its significance for understanding the broader theme of our study, we need to survey the various places Moses is referred to as a servant.

Moses as servant of Yahweh in the Torah

As one would expect, the primary place we see Moses described as the servant of Yahweh is in the Torah.

Exodus

I have already described the context leading up to Moses' introduction on to the stage of redemptive history. Exodus 2 briskly describes the first 40 years of Moses' life, taking us through his birth and childhood in Pharaoh's court (2:1–10), his flight from Egypt as an adult after standing up for a fellow Hebrew (2:11–15), and finding refuge and a wife with the family of a priest of Midian (2:16–22). It is against this backdrop that the Israelites cry out to God 'because of their slavery [*'ăbôdâ*]' and their cry for 'rescue from slavery [*'ăbôdâ*]' comes before God (Exod. 2:23). In response: 'God heard their groaning, and God remembered his covenant with Abraham, with Isaac, and with Jacob. God saw the people of Israel – and God knew' (Exod. 2:24–25). God's call of Moses as his servant is an outworking of God's covenant promises with Abraham and his

---

[1] All six occurrences of the noun rendered 'harshness' (*perek*) are used in contexts of slavery (Exod. 1:13–14; Lev. 25:43, 46, 53) or with reference to the abusive exercise of authority (Ezek. 34:4). Besides its use here in Exod. 1:13–14, Lev. 25:43 is especially noteworthy. God warns Israel not to treat a brother who sells himself into servitude (because of poverty) harshly because 'they are my servants [*'ăbāday*], whom I brought out of the land of Egypt' (Lev. 25:42).

descendants (Gen. 12:1–3), which as we have seen is the specific expression of the means by which God will bring the serpent-crusher who will obey where Adam failed and suffer the punishment for that failure (Gen. 3:15).

When God calls out to Moses from the burning bush, he identifies himself as 'the God of your father, the God of Abraham, the God of Isaac, and the God of Jacob' (Exod. 3:6). In response to the cries of his people and in fulfilment of the covenant he made to them, God is ready to bring them into the land of promise (Exod. 3:7–9). When Moses expresses hesitation at the prospect of God sending him to Pharaoh to lead Israel out of their bondage (Exod. 3:10–11), Yahweh responds: 'But I will be with you, and this shall be the sign for you, that I have sent you: when you have brought the people out of Egypt, you shall serve [*'ābad*] God on this mountain' (Exod. 3:12). The authenticating sign that the covenant God of Abraham, Isaac and Jacob has sent Moses to lead them out of their dehumanizing forced servitude in Egypt is that the Israelites will serve God on the very mountain where Moses is standing. A key component of the nature of this service is found several verses later in 3:18, where Moses is instructed to demand that Pharaoh allow the Israelites to journey into the wilderness 'that we may sacrifice to the Lord our God'. As such it echoes the priestly service that God placed Adam in the garden to perform (more on this below).

As part of this commission, God reveals his covenant name to Moses. He is to tell the Israelites that 'Yahweh, the God of your fathers, the God of Abraham, the God of Isaac, and the God of Jacob, has sent me to you' (Exod. 3:15 AT). But the fulfilment of this covenant promise will not come easily. Because Pharaoh will refuse to let the Israelites go, God will compel him 'by a mighty hand' (Exod. 3:19) and as a result the Israelites will plunder the Egyptians (Exod. 3:20–22). Despite these lofty promises, Moses remains reticent. So God performs a series of signs that Moses will perform before the Israelites 'that they may believe that the Lord, the God of their fathers, the God of Abraham, the God of Isaac, and the God of Jacob, has appeared to you' (Exod. 4:5). Yahweh even goes so far as to provide Moses' brother Aaron as a spokesman (Exod. 4:10–17).

As Moses prepares to return to Egypt, Yahweh once again warns Moses that Pharaoh will not release the Israelites because God himself will harden Pharaoh's heart (Exod. 4:21). Then Yahweh instructs Moses to say this to Pharaoh: 'Thus says the Lord, Israel is my firstborn son, and I say to you, "Let my son go that he may serve [*'ābad*] me." If you refuse to let him go, behold, I will kill your firstborn son' (Exod. 4:22–23). The sonship language immediately reminds the reader of Adam, whom Genesis portrays as a son of God (Gen. 5:1–3).[2] God specifically ties Israel's identity as his firstborn son with the goal of the exodus: serving Yahweh. Like Adam before them, Israel is a son commissioned to serve Yahweh. Throughout the following chapters, Exodus repeatedly notes that the purpose of God bringing Israel out of Egypt is so that they may serve him (Exod. 7:16; 8:1 [MT 7:26]; 8:20 [MT 8:16]; 9:1, 13; 10:3, 7–8, 11, 24, 26; 12:31). It appears, then, that a central purpose of Israel's exodus 'out of the house of slavery [*'ebed*]' (Exod. 13:3, 14) is to enable Israel to serve Yahweh in a fashion that in some sense is analogous to Adam serving him in the garden (Gen. 2:15).[3] Once again God is using an individual servant to create a servant people.

When Israel at last departs from Egypt after the ten plagues judging the Egyptians and their gods, they must experience one final threat from the Egyptians on the shores of the Red Sea. After Israel passes through on dry ground and the Egyptians are drowned when they try to follow, Exodus 14:30–31 provides a summary statement of this climactic event in Israel's history that is worth quoting in full:

> Thus the LORD saved Israel that day from the hand of the Egyptians, and Israel saw the Egyptians dead on the seashore. Israel saw the great power that the LORD used against the Egyptians, so the people feared the LORD, and they believed in the LORD and in his servant Moses.
> (Exod. 14:30–31)

For the first time Moses is referred to as the servant of Yahweh. But perhaps what is most striking is that he is an object of the people's faith along with Yahweh himself! The verb rendered 'believe' (the hiphil stem of *'āman*) played a prominent role in Exodus 4, where Moses worried that

---

[2] Although Genesis never identifies Adam as a son of God, that is a clear inference from Gen. 5:1–5. After reintroducing Adam as created 'in the likeness of God' (5:1), the text goes on to explain that Adam 'fathered a son in his own likeness, after his image' (5:3). Luke's genealogy confirms this inference, referring to Adam as 'the son of God' (Luke 3:38).

[3] This is not to say Israel serving Yahweh in fulfilment of his covenant promises is the only purpose of the exodus. Other clearly stated purposes include (1) the Israelites (Exod. 10:2), the Egyptians (Exod. 7:5) and Pharaoh (Exod. 8:10, 22) knowing that Yahweh is the true God; and (2) the display of God's power and glory to magnify his own name (Exod. 9:16).

the people would not believe him when he claimed that Yahweh had appeared to him (4:1). In response God enables Moses to perform signs that will cause the people to believe him (4:5, 8–9). These signs have their intended result – the people believed when Moses performed them (4:31).

But what is most noteworthy in Exodus 14:31 is the specific construction used – the hiphil stem of *ʾāman* with the preposition *bě* to indicate the object of one's trust/faith. As a general rule this construction has the sense of not merely accepting something as true intellectually but has 'the added sense of acting in response to what is heard with trust or obedience'.[4] The only previous use of this construction to this point in the biblical narrative is Genesis 15:6, where in response to God reaffirming his promise Abraham 'believed the LORD, and he counted it to him as righteousness'. Thus, the point of this summary statement here in Exodus 14:31 is to assert that putting one's trust in Yahweh is expressed by putting one's trust in Moses his servant. Put another way, failure to trust in Moses the servant of Yahweh is a failure to trust in Yahweh himself.

Since this summary statement occurs in the immediate aftermath of Egypt's crushing military defeat, it seems reasonable to conclude that the use of servant language here has royal overtones. Yahweh accomplishes his victory over the enemies of his people through his servant Moses. As the servant who trusts in Yahweh, Moses is exercising dominion over the hostile forces that threaten the accomplishment of Yahweh's purposes in the world.

Three months after their departure from Egypt, Israel reaches the foot of Mount Sinai (Exod. 19:1). As part of preparing the people to meet with the living God, Yahweh instructs Moses to tell the people:

> Now therefore, if you will indeed obey my voice and keep my covenant, you shall be my treasured possession among all peoples, for all the earth is mine; and you shall be to me a kingdom of priests and a holy nation.
> (Exod. 19:5–6)

To say that if Israel obeys the Lord by keeping his covenant they will be a 'kingdom of priests and a holy nation' is another way of saying that Israel as a nation is set apart to fulfil a modified version of God's original

---

[4] Moberly 1997: 1.431.

creation purposes for Adam. Just as Adam was given both royal (Gen. 1:26–31) and priestly (Gen. 2:15) responsibilities, so Israel as a nation is commissioned to exercise similar functions. God's promise to multiply Abraham and his descendants into a great nation as the means by which he will fulfil his purposes for all humanity is coming into clearer focus. And central to God's plan is the role of his servant Moses. Now that Moses the servant has led God's people out of their bondage in Egypt, they are ready to become a servant people. In response to Moses' report of Israel's commitment to do everything Yahweh has commanded, Yahweh says to Moses, 'Behold, I am coming to you in a thick cloud, that the people may hear when I speak with you, and may also believe you for ever' (Exod. 19:9). The use of the hiphil stem of *ʾāman* with the preposition *bĕ* to indicate the object of one's trust signals the importance of the people trusting in Moses the servant as an expression of their trust in Yahweh.

In the chapters that follow (Exod. 20 – 31), we see Moses the servant clearly exercising a *prophetic* role. We have already seen this in Exodus 19, where on three separate occasions God calls Moses up on to the mountain to receive revelation that he is then to communicate to the people (19:3–6, 9–13, 20–24). After the Lord speaks to the people directly from Mount Sinai (Exod. 20:1–17), the people are so terrified that they ask Moses to speak to them rather than hear from God directly, a request that Moses grants (Exod. 20:18–21). Moses then proceeds to enter the thick darkness surrounding Yahweh's presence to receive further revelation for the people (Exod. 20:21 – 24:2). Moses then speaks the words of the Lord to the people, which they commit to obeying in a covenant ratification celebration that culminates in Moses, Aaron, Nadab, Abihu and the seventy elders eating and drinking in the presence of God (Exod. 24:3–11). Yahweh then summons Moses back up on to the mountain to receive the stone tablets of the covenant as well as further revelation (Exod. 24:12–18). Over the next 40 days and nights Moses stays on the mountain, receiving both the stone tablets of the covenant stipulations already revealed as well as additional revelation from the Lord regarding the tabernacle and the priests (Exod. 25 – 31).

Unfortunately, while Moses is on the mountain with God, Israel breaks its covenant with Yahweh by making a golden calf to worship and by engaging in various pagan worship practices (Exod. 32:1–6).[5] It is in this

[5] In addition to making burnt and peace offerings, the verb rendered 'play' (*ṣāḥaq*) may have connotations of a sexual orgy; see Allen 1997: 3.797.

context that we see Moses the servant functioning in a *priestly* role. Yahweh refers to Israel as 'your people' in describing what they have done (Exod. 32:7) and tells Moses his intention to wipe out the people and make a great nation of Moses (Exod. 32:8–10). Moses begins his intercession for Israel by asking Yahweh why his anger burns against 'your people' (Exod. 32:11), and then makes an appeal to the damage it would do to the Lord's fame among the Egyptians (Exod. 32:12). But at the foundation of Moses' intercession are the covenant promises that God made to the patriarchs:

> Remember Abraham, Isaac, and Israel, your servants, to whom you swore by your own self, and said to them, 'I will multiply your offspring as the stars of heaven, and all this land that I have promised I will give to your offspring, and they shall inherit it for ever.
> (Exod. 32:13)

In the midst of his intercession Moses the servant pleads with Yahweh to keep his covenant promises to his previous servants so that Israel may live out their identity as a servant people.

After Moses descends the mountain to rebuke the people for their idolatry (Exod. 32:15–30), he returns to the Lord to continue his plea for mercy. During this second round of intercession, Moses begins by acknowledging the magnitude of the people's sin and offering his own life in place of the people to make atonement (Exod. 32:31–32). Yahweh refuses Moses' gesture, but relents from his previously stated intention of completely destroying the people. He even promises to send his angel before them (Exod. 32:33–34). After noting that the Lord sends a plague upon the people as punishment (Exod. 32:35), the dialogue between Moses and Yahweh resumes. Yahweh instructs Moses:

> Depart; go up from here, you and the people whom you have brought up out of the land of Egypt, to the land of which I swore to Abraham, Isaac, and Jacob, saying, 'To your offspring I will give it.' I will send an angel before you, and I will drive out the Canaanites, the Amorites, the Hittites, the Perizzites, the Hivites, and the Jebusites. Go up to a land flowing with milk and honey; but I will not go up among you, lest I consume you on the way, for you are a stiff-necked people.
> (Exod. 33:1–3)

Note that Yahweh again seems to distance himself from the Israelites, referring to them as the people Moses brought up from the land. Yet in fulfilment of his promise to the patriarchs, he agrees to send his angel before them to drive out the current inhabitants of the land. But Yahweh refuses to go with the stiff-necked Israelites lest he destroy them along the way.

For a third time Moses intercedes on behalf of the people before the Lord (Exod. 33:12–23). This time Moses bases his appeal on two grounds: (1) he has found favour before Yahweh, and (2) Israel is his people (33:12–13). In response, Yahweh promises to go with his people (33:14). Moses pushes a bit harder, stressing that Yahweh's presence is what distinguishes Israel from the rest of the nations (33:15–16). After the Lord agrees to grant his request (33:17), Moses humbly pushes even further, asking to see Yahweh's glory (33:18). Yahweh responds by agreeing to make his goodness and glory pass before Moses (33:19–23).

Yahweh fulfils this promise the next morning (Exod. 34:1–7), passing before Moses and proclaiming his name:

> The LORD, the LORD, a God merciful and gracious, slow to anger, and abounding in steadfast love and faithfulness, keeping steadfast love for thousands, forgiving iniquity and transgression and sin, but who will by no means clear the guilty, visiting the iniquity of the fathers on the children and the children's children, to the third and the fourth generation.
> (Exod. 34:6–7)

This key statement of Yahweh's identity stresses his eagerness to show mercy, grace, steadfast love and faithfulness, while at the same time not in any way compromising his justice.[6] In response to this staggering self-revelation, Moses makes one final plea:

> If now I have found favour in your sight, O Lord, please let the Lord go in the midst of us, for it is a stiff-necked people, and pardon our iniquity and our sin, and take us for your inheritance.
> (Exod. 34:9)

6 On the importance of this summary statement of God's identity for OT theology, see Boda 2017: 27–51.

Yahweh agrees to this final plea by renewing the covenant with his people (Exod. 34:10–28). Moses is the servant of the Lord who mediates God's presence to the people and intercedes on their behalf.

Thus, in Exodus we see that Moses is explicitly identified at the servant of Yahweh. While there is a very clear sense in which Israel as a corporate entity is a servant formed to carry a modified form of God's original commission to Adam as both king and priest, Moses is singled out as the servant of the Lord set apart to lead Yahweh's servant people. He carries out his servant role by functioning as a king who leads God's people, a prophet who speaks God's words, and a priest who mediates God's presence. Through him God creates a servant people.

Numbers

The same threefold presentation of Moses as the servant of Yahweh runs throughout the narrative of Numbers, even though the explicit label shows up only twice. Both times the surrounding context involves challenges to Moses' special role as the leader of God's people.

The first appearance is in Numbers 11, where the people complain about their misfortunes and the manna from heaven that Yahweh is providing (11:1–9). In response to Yahweh's burning anger, Moses asks him, 'Why have you dealt ill with your servant? And why have I not found favour in your sight, that you lay the burden of all this people on me?' (Num. 11:11). Moses goes on to complain that he cannot carry the burden of leading this people by himself (Num. 11:12–15), so in response Yahweh instructs Moses to gather seventy elders from the people to help share the leadership mantle with Moses (Num. 11:16). To mark them off as leaders the Lord says:

> And I will come down and talk with you there. And I will take some of the Spirit that is on you and put it on them, and they shall bear the burden of the people with you, so that you may not bear it yourself alone.
> (Num. 11:17)

Although the text does not use this explicit language, it is as if Moses the servant is asking Yahweh to provide additional servants to help him carry the burden of leading God's corporate servant Israel.

What should not be overlooked is the connection between Moses' identity as the servant of the Lord and the work of God's Spirit. The way that God relieves some of Moses' burden is to take 'some of the Spirit that is on you and put it on them' (Num. 11:17). That connection is reinforced when the Lord does it. Once the Spirit comes upon the elders they begin to prophesy (Num. 11:25–26). When a concerned Joshua asks Moses to make them stop, God's servant responds: 'Are you jealous for my sake? Would that all the LORD's people were prophets, that the LORD would put his Spirit on them!' (Num. 11:29). The connection between the Spirit, prophesying and leading God's people confirms my earlier conclusion that as the servant of Yahweh Moses exercises a prophetic role. Furthermore, this passage establishes a connection between the role of Yahweh's servant as leader of God's people and the presence/empowerment of the Spirit that anticipates the work of future servants of the Lord.

The second explicit reference to Moses' identity as the servant of Yahweh occurs in the very next chapter. Perhaps emboldened by the apparent democratization of leadership, Miriam and Aaron criticize Moses for having a Cushite wife, asking: 'Has the LORD indeed spoken only through Moses? Has he not spoken through us also?' (Num. 12:2). After noting Moses' exemplary humility (Num. 12:3), the Lord confronts Miriam and Aaron in the tent of meeting (Num. 12:4–5). The Lord says:

> Hear my words: If there is a prophet among you, I the LORD make myself known to him in a vision; I speak with him in a dream. Not so with my servant Moses. He is faithful in all my house. With him I speak mouth to mouth, clearly, and not in riddles, and he beholds the form of the LORD. Why then were you not afraid to speak against my servant Moses?
> (Num. 12:6–8)

Even though God has taken 'some of the Spirit' resting upon Moses and placed him upon the seventy elders to help him lead the people, he still singles out Moses from everyone else. As the servant of Yahweh, Moses is in a distinct category.

Two specific things distinguish Moses from even a prophet. First, as the servant of Yahweh he is 'faithful in all my house' (Num. 12:7).[7] The

[7] The importance of v. 7 is further signalled by the chiastic structure of 12:6–8, in which 12:7 is at the centre; see further Cole 2000: 202–203. There is some debate regarding the exact meaning of the initial clause of the verse. Instead of rendering the initial phrase *lōʾ-kēn* 'not so', it is possible to read *l'* as an emphatic particle with the qal participle of *kûn*, resulting in a

Hebrew verb rendered 'is faithful' is the same verb (*'āman*) used in Exodus 14:31, where the people are said to believe in Yahweh and his servant Moses. By demonstrating his faithfulness to Yahweh Moses demonstrates he is a worthy object of the people's faith. The use of household imagery portrays Moses as the one to whom God has entrusted the oversight of his people. Second, Yahweh speaks to Moses 'mouth to mouth' and Moses 'beholds the form of the LORD'. Exodus 33:11 has already noted that Yahweh 'used to speak to Moses face to face, as a man speaks to his friend'. Although God had told Moses that no one could see his face and live (Exod. 33:20), he allows Moses to see his back (Exod. 33:21 – 34:10). Both expressions stress the unparalleled personal intimacy that Moses the servant has with Yahweh. By contrast, the Lord speaks to prophets in the form of visions, dreams and riddles. The picture is of direct and intimate communication. As the servant, Moses has direct and intimate access to Yahweh himself, rather than the mediated forms of communication that God uses with his prophets.

Before moving on from Numbers, we should note that another individual is called a servant of the Lord. In the aftermath of Israel refusing to enter the Promised Land (Num. 14:1–4), Moses, Aaron, Joshua and Caleb plead with the people not to rebel against the Lord (Num. 14:5–10), but when they remain intransigent Yahweh once again expresses his intent to wipe out the people (Num. 14:11). In response to Moses interceding for the people (Num. 14:13–19), the Lord agrees to exclude all the men of the current generation from entering the Promised Land (Num. 14:20–23). The lone exception is 'my servant Caleb, because he has a different spirit and has followed me fully, I will bring into the land into which he went, and his descendants shall possess it' (Num. 14:24). While there is no indication that Caleb is a servant of Yahweh in the same sense that Moses is, the bestowal of this title recognizes Caleb's faithfulness to the Lord even in the face of overwhelming enemies in the land and fierce opposition from his own people.

Deuteronomy

Servant language is not frequently applied to Moses in Deuteronomy. With the exception of referring to himself as Yahweh's servant when

(note 7 *cont.*) translation such as 'surely'; see further Kselman 1976: 502–503. But as Ashley (1993: 226–227) notes, the surrounding context suggests a contrast is in view.

recounting his request to enter the Promised Land despite his sin (Deut. 3:24), there is only one passage that refers to Moses as the servant. When the time comes to record the death of Moses, once again servant language resurfaces (Deut. 34:1–12). The Lord takes Moses up on to Mount Nebo to give him a panoramic view of the Promised Land, describing it as 'the land of which I swore to Abraham, to Isaac, and to Jacob, "I will give it to your offspring"' (Deut. 34:4). Then the text states: 'So Moses the servant of the LORD died there in the land of Moab, according to the word of the LORD' (Deut. 34:5). Of all the possible epitaphs the author could have chosen for Moses in summarizing his death, the author chooses 'servant of the LORD'. Moses' role as the servant is again linked to the fulfilment of the covenant promises God made to Abraham, Isaac and Jacob. The final words of Deuteronomy give further insight into Moses' significance:

> And there has not arisen a prophet since in Israel like Moses, whom the LORD knew face to face, none like him for all the signs and the wonders that the LORD sent him to do in the land of Egypt, to Pharaoh and to all his servants and to all his land, and for all the mighty power and all the great deeds of terror that Moses did in the sight of all Israel.
> (Deut. 34:10–12)

Although we have seen that as the servant of Yahweh Moses exercises royal and priestly roles, Deuteronomy closes with a focus on his prophetic role in the fulfilment of God's purposes. What sets Moses apart are 'the signs and the wonders . . . and . . . all the mighty power and all the great deeds of terror' that Yahweh sent him to do *to* the Egyptians *in the sight of* all Israel. The greatness of Moses does not rest in himself, as it was the Lord who sent him to do these miraculous signs. By specifically mentioning Pharaoh's servants, there may be a subtle contrast at play. In the contest between Yahweh and Pharaoh, both have servants, but it is Yahweh's servant who carries the day and demonstrates the superiority of Yahweh over Pharaoh. Echoing the promise that God will raise up a prophet like Moses that they must listen to (Deut. 18:15, 18–19), the book closes with a categorical statement that this promise has yet to be fulfilled (Deut. 34:10–12). This observation gives the book a distinctively eschatological conclusion, inviting the reader to wonder when and in whom that promise will be fulfilled.

Moses as servant of Yahweh in the Prophets and the Writings

No other individual in the Old Testament is referred to more frequently as the servant of Yahweh than Moses, and this remains the case even outside the Torah. Because the next chapter will discuss the repeated occurrences in the book of Joshua, this section will survey the numerous texts in the rest of the Old Testament that refer to Moses as the servant of Yahweh. These references can helpfully be organized into three categories.

Giver of the law or specific commands

Perhaps the most general category of references to Moses as the servant are those that describe certain actions or commands that are in accordance with the law Moses the servant gave. Embedded within the lengthy genealogies of 1 Chronicles 1 – 9, the author notes that Aaron and his sons made atonement for Israel 'according to all that Moses the servant of God had commanded' (1 Chr. 6:49 [MT 6:34]). Shortly after taking the throne, Solomon went to 'the tent of meeting of God, which Moses the servant of the LORD had made in the wilderness' (2 Chr. 1:3) that was in Gibeon. During the repairs to the temple commissioned by Josiah, the king asks the chief priest: 'Why have you not required the Levites to bring in from Judah and Jerusalem the tax levied by Moses, the servant of the LORD, and the congregation of Israel for the tent of testimony?' (2 Chr. 24:6; cf. v. 9). When Nehemiah recounts Israel's history that eventually led to exile, he notes the various laws Yahweh commanded 'by Moses your servant' (Neh. 9:14). In response to this prayer of confession the people make a covenant: they swear an oath 'to walk in God's Law that was given by Moses the servant of God, and to observe and do all the commandments of the LORD our Lord and his rules and his statutes' (Neh. 10:29).

In one sense this category provides the foundation for the two categories that follow.

Connection with exile

More significant than the seemingly straightforward references in the previous section are those places where Moses' identity as the servant of Yahweh is tied in some way to Israel being sent into exile. According to 2 Kings 18:12, the northern kingdom of Israel was carried away in exile to Assyria 'because they did not obey the voice of the LORD their God but transgressed his covenant, even all that Moses the servant of the LORD commanded'. Several chapters later – this time with reference to the southern kingdom of Judah – the author recounts a modified version of God's promise to David:

> In this house, and in Jerusalem, which I have chosen out of all the tribes of Israel, I will put my name for ever. And I will not cause the feet of Israel to wander anymore out of the land that I gave to their fathers, if only they will be careful to do according to all that I have commanded them, and according to all the Law that my servant Moses commanded them.
> (2 Kgs 21:7–8)

The initial portion of these verses is a modified version of God's promise to David (which found a measure of initial fulfilment in Solomon) in 2 Samuel 7:9–16. The wrinkle, however, is the specific link to doing all that is in the Law that Moses the servant of Yahweh commanded. Of course, since they did not in fact obey, the ultimate result was exile in Babylon.

It was near the end of this exile that Daniel mentions Moses the servant of God in his prayer of confession. After noticing that the 70 years of exile were coming to a close (Dan. 9:1–2), Daniel addresses God as the covenant-keeping God who justly poured out his wrath on his disobedient people (Dan. 9:3–10). Twice in these verses he mentions their failure to listen to 'your servants the prophets' (9:6, 10) before noting eventually that:

> All Israel has transgressed your law and turned aside, refusing to obey your voice. And the curse and oath that are written in the Law of Moses the servant of God have been poured out upon us, because we have sinned against him.
> (Dan. 9:11)

The work of Yahweh's servants the prophets is ultimately rooted in the covenant mediated through Moses the servant of God, who wrote in the law the curse and oath that Israel was experiencing.

Nearly a century after Daniel prayed his prayer of confession, Nehemiah prays a similar prayer. In doing so he too makes a clear connection between Moses' identity as Yahweh's servant and exile. As part of confessing the sins of the people, Nehemiah prays:

> We have acted very corruptly against you and have not kept the commandments, the statutes, and the rules that you commanded your servant Moses. Remember the word that you commanded your servant Moses, saying, 'If you are unfaithful, I will scatter you among the peoples, but if you return to me and keep my commandments and do them, though your outcasts are in the uttermost parts of heaven, from there I will gather them and bring them to the place that I have chosen, to make my name dwell there.
> (Neh. 1:7–9)

Israel's state of exile stems from their disobedience to the commandments Yahweh gave them through Moses his servant. Beyond this generalized statement Nehemiah recounts a combination of several warning texts in Leviticus and Deuteronomy. The promise to scatter them among the people is likely drawn from several texts (e.g. Lev. 26:33; Deut. 4:27; 28:64), and the same is likely true of the promised restoration (e.g. Lev. 26:39–42; Deut. 4:29–31; 30:1–10). Regardless of which text(s) may or may not be in view,[8] none of them use servant language to refer to Moses.

Fulfilment of covenant promises

We have already seen in my brief discussion of 2 Kings 21:8 that Moses' role as the servant of Yahweh was linked to God's covenant promises, though in that context it was linked to Israel's failure to keep the covenant and therefore ending up in exile. Three additional texts explicitly link the fulfilment of God's covenant purposes with Moses his servant.

The first is found in Solomon's lengthy prayer of dedication when the temple was completed (1 Kgs 8:12–61). Solomon asks that Yahweh's eyes and ears always be open to the pleas of his people Israel: 'For you separated them from among all the peoples of the earth to be your heritage, as you declared through Moses your servant, when you brought our fathers out of Egypt, O Lord God' (1 Kgs 8:53). Solomon likely has in view Exodus 19:5–6, where at the foot of Mount Sinai God promised that Israel would be his 'treasured possession among all the peoples' if they kept his covenant. As Solomon brings his prayer to a close, he calls the people to join him in praying: 'Blessed be the Lord who has given rest to his people Israel, according to all that he promised. Not one word has failed of all his

[8] Of the various texts listed, Deut. 30:1–10 has the most overlap.

good promise, which he spoke by Moses his servant' (1 Kgs 8:56). The rest that God had promised his people in the Promised Land was now being realized. In asserting that not one word of promise was spoken through 'Moses his servant' Solomon echoes Joshua 21:45 and 23:14, which make a similar assertion. Neither of those texts, however, refers to Moses as the servant.

Psalm 105 recounts at length Israel's history from God's promise to Abraham to the entry into Canaan. The opening section (105:1–6) calls the people to sing Yahweh's praises and remember the wondrous works that he has done for them, concluding by calling the Israelites:

> offspring of Abraham, his servant,
>   children of Jacob, his chosen ones!
> (105:6)

Israel's history begins with God's covenant promise to give Abraham and his descendants the land of Canaan (105:7–11). After summarizing Israel's early history to their Egyptian bondage (105:12–25), God 'sent Moses his servant, / and Aaron, whom he had chosen' to deliver them (105:26). Not only did Moses lead them out of Egypt; he provided for them in the wilderness (105:27–41) because Yahweh:

> remembered his holy promise,
>   and Abraham, his servant.
> (105:42)

As a result, Israel entered the land God had promised to them in order to keep Yahweh's laws (105:43–45). Thus, this retelling of Israel's history is bracketed by God fulfilling the promise he made to Abraham his servant, with Moses standing at the centre as God's servant to bring this promise to realization.

The final passage to consider comes from what is likely the last Old Testament book to be written. Malachi lived at a time when God's people were struggling to maintain their faith in God's promises. So, in addition to calling the people to repent of their covenant-breaking ways, Yahweh points them to the future realization of his promises. After announcing the coming day when he will act to trample down the wicked and bring healing (Mal. 4:1–3), Yahweh says this:

> Remember the law of my servant Moses, the statutes and rules that I commanded him at Horeb for all Israel.
>
> Behold, I will send you Elijah the prophet before the great and awesome day of the Lord comes. And he will turn the hearts of fathers to their children and the hearts of children to their fathers, lest I come and strike the land with a decree of utter destruction. (Mal. 4:4–6)

As we have seen previously, Moses' identity as the servant of Yahweh is tied to his role as the mediator of God's covenant. What is distinctive here is that God's people are called to pursue faithfulness to the covenant mediated through Moses as they await the 'great and awesome day of the Lord'.

Regardless, then, of whether Moses the servant is mentioned in connection with specific commandments, the threat of exile or the fulfilment of God's promises, the underlying thread that connects all three variations is covenant. It would seem, then, that Moses' identity as the servant of Yahweh is inextricably tied to God's covenant purposes.

Conclusion

As we saw in Genesis, God's covenant promises to Abraham were the means by which he would realize his original intention for humanity to serve him as royal priests ruling over creation and mediating his presence. In fulfilment of these covenant promises to Abraham, God multiplies Jacob and his twelve sons into a great nation. Yet this great nation lives as slaves in Egypt, labouring in a house of slavery. In order for this enslaved nation to live out their divine purpose as Yahweh's firstborn son, they must be freed from their slavery so they can serve Yahweh.

That is why God raises up Moses to be his servant. As a result of the signs that Yahweh performs through Moses, culminating in their crossing of the Red Sea, Israel comes to believe not only in Yahweh, but also in Moses his servant. When Israel arrives at Mount Sinai, God establishes a covenant with its people, setting them apart as a kingdom of priests and a royal nation to live out a modified version of God's original commission to Adam the servant. God has used Moses the servant to create a servant people.

As the servant of the Lord, Moses exercises royal, priestly and prophetic roles. As a kinglike figure he rules over the people under the authority of

Yahweh, leading them to freedom and enabling them to live out God's purpose for them. As a priestly figure, Moses repeatedly intercedes on behalf of the people, mediating between Yahweh and the people so they can experience God's presence among them without being consumed. As a prophetic figure, Moses speaks God's words to the people to enable them to understand who God is and how they should live as his covenant people. In his capacity as the servant, Moses holds a role that exceeds that of any 'ordinary' prophet or priest. His access and interaction with Yahweh are direct rather than mediated – Yahweh speaks with him face to face and allows Moses to behold his form. He has God's Spirit resting upon him in a way that no one else does.

Moses' identity as the servant of the Lord continues beyond his death. Throughout the remainder of the Old Testament Moses is referred to as the servant of Yahweh at several points. While in some cases this identification is merely a reminder of his role as the giver of God's law, it is more significantly linked to the warnings about exile and the fulfilment of God's covenant promises. The final mention of Moses the servant even has an eschatological orientation (Mal. 4:4–6), calling God's people to covenant faithfulness as they await the fulfilment of his covenant promises.

When Moses dies, the Lord has not finished raising up servants. In order to lead God's people through the next phase of fulfilling his covenant promises, he must raise up a new servant. That new servant is a man named Joshua, and in the next chapter I will tell his story.

4
Joshua: the servant conqueror

> After these things Joshua the son of Nun, the servant of the LORD, died, being 110 years old . . . Israel served the LORD all the days of Joshua, and all the days of the elders who outlived Joshua and had known all the work that the LORD did for Israel.
> (Josh. 24:29, 31)

Replacing a legend is never easy. In the realm of sports, it is often said that you never want to be the coach who follows the legend, but the person who follows the person who replaces the legend. The same is true in the realm of politics or even church history. Many Christians have at least heard the name Augustine, and perhaps even know that he served as the bishop of Hippo in the late fourth and early fifth century. Yet very few (perhaps not even some experts in church history!) know the name of the man who replaced him.[1] Some figures in history are so transcendent that they leave shoes that are seemingly impossible to fill.

Imagine how difficult it must have been to replace Moses as the leader of God's people. In recounting the death of Moses, Deuteronomy 34:10–12 makes it clear that Moses stands alone in Israel's history:

> And there has not arisen a prophet since in Israel like Moses, whom the LORD knew face to face, none like him for all the signs and the wonders that the LORD sent him to do in the land of Egypt, to Pharaoh and to all his servants and to all his land, and for all the mighty power and all the great deeds of terror that Moses did in the sight of all Israel.

[1] About three years before his death, Augustine had selected a man named Heraclius to replace him, who subsequently did when Augustine died; see Bray 2015: 28–29.

Those are the sandals that Joshua was called to fill. Right before noting the uniqueness of Moses, however, Deuteronomy 34:9 notes that 'Joshua the son of Nun was full of the spirit of wisdom, for Moses had laid his hands on him. So the people of Israel obeyed him and did as the LORD had commanded Moses.' Well before this moment Joshua had been commissioned by Yahweh as Moses' successor, but the transition from being second in command to the primary lead could not have been easy for Joshua. Perhaps that is why Yahweh tells Joshua three times 'be strong and courageous' (Josh. 1:6, 7, 9) when he passes the baton of leadership to Joshua.

Although the biblical text never mentions it, perhaps the Israelites had their own concerns about the transition from Moses to Joshua. After all, Moses had been the servant of Yahweh who had at last led the people out of their Egyptian bondage, performing countless signs and wonders. And even despite these miraculous acts, Israel often grumbled and rebelled against Moses' leadership. How would Joshua fare in similar situations?

The book of Joshua answers that question by portraying Joshua as another servant of Yahweh. To demonstrate this claim, we will look first at the transition from one servant (Moses) to another (Joshua). Then I will show that the book of Joshua portrays Joshua as the servant of Yahweh. It does so by (1) highlighting Joshua's obedience to all that Moses the servant commanded and (2) showing Yahweh performing similar acts through Joshua that he did through Moses. Only then can we fully appreciate the significance of the book concluding by noting the death of Joshua the servant of Yahweh.

The transition from one servant to another

The opening chapter of Joshua begins where the final chapter of Deuteronomy left off. Now that the rebellious generation that refused to enter Canaan the first time around has died off, the people of Israel stand on the verge of entering the Promised Land. But they must enter the land under new leadership, since God put Moses to death (Deut. 34:1–8) for his breach of faith (Num. 20:10–13). As noted in the previous chapter, Deuteronomy 34:5 states simply that 'Moses the servant of the LORD died there in the land of Moab, according to the word of the LORD.' The opening lines of Joshua 1 resume the narrative:

> After the death of Moses the servant of the LORD, the LORD said to Joshua the son of Nun, Moses' assistant, 'Moses my servant is dead. Now therefore arise, go over this Jordan, you and all this people, into the land that I am giving to them, to the people of Israel. Every place that the sole of your foot will tread upon I have given to you, just as I promised to Moses. From the wilderness and this Lebanon as far as the great river, the river Euphrates, all the land of the Hittites to the Great Sea towards the going down of the sun shall be your territory. No man shall be able to stand before you all the days of your life. Just as I was with Moses, so I will be with you. I will not leave you or forsake you.'
> (Josh. 1:1–3)

From this opening paragraph we should note three key observations.

First, Moses is twice referred to as the servant of Yahweh. Not only is he given this title by the author of the book, but Yahweh's first words spoken to Joshua are to inform him that 'Moses my servant is dead.' The use of this title is consistent with what we saw from Numbers 12:6–8, where Moses was singled out as the servant of Yahweh who had a special, intimate relationship that transcended that of any prophet.

Second, Joshua is reintroduced as Moses' 'assistant' (*šārat*), a word that often refers to someone who offers personal service to an important person such as a ruler (e.g. Gen. 29:4; 40:4; 2 Sam. 13:17–18; 1 Kgs 10:5).[2] But this word is also used in connection with the worship of Yahweh, whether with reference to priests (1 Kgs 8:11), Levites (1 Chr. 6:32 [MT 6:17]) or others (1 Sam. 2:11, 18).[3] Already to this point in the biblical narrative *šārat* has referred to Joshua three times (Exod. 24:13; 33:11; Num. 11:28). But even beyond the use of this specific word Joshua has been singled out as Moses' successor. In addition to his role as a military leader (Exod. 17:8–16) and scout/spy (Num. 13:16; 14:6, 30, 38), Joshua regularly accompanied Moses when he met with Yahweh (Exod. 24:13; 32:17; 33:11). So it comes as no surprise when God instructs Moses to appoint Joshua as his successor. Moses asks that Yahweh appoint someone 'who shall go out before them and come in before them, who shall lead them out

---

[2] Austel 1980: 958.

[3] Fretheim 1997: 4.256. Fretheim makes the interesting observation that 'The idea of serving God with one's whole self and life is not implied in this vb. as it is with *'ābad*' though he goes on to note the use of this verb in parallel with *'ābad* in Isa. 56:6.

and bring them in, that the congregation of the LORD may not be as sheep that have no shepherd' (Num. 27:17). In response, Yahweh selects Joshua, 'a man in whom is the Spirit' (Num. 27:18; cf. Deut. 34:9) and instructs Moses to:

> invest him with some of your authority, that all the congregation of the people of Israel may obey . . . At his word they shall go out, and at his word they shall come in, both he and all the people of Israel with him, the whole congregation.
> (Num. 27:20–21)

Under the leadership of Joshua, God will give his people the land he promised to Abraham and his offspring (Deut. 1:38; 3:21, 28).

Third, God stresses that Joshua's role as the newly appointed leader of God's people is the continuation of what God did through Moses. The land they are about to enter they are inheriting according to the promise that God had made to Moses. Even more significantly, God promises never to leave or forsake Joshua; indeed, Yahweh will be with Joshua 'just as I was with Moses' (Josh. 1:5).

These opening verses, then, begin to lay the foundation for a central theme in Joshua, and the main focus of our interest in Joshua: *Joshua is the new servant of Yahweh appointed by God to give his people their promised inheritance in the land.* Because he is Moses' successor as the servant of Yahweh, we should expect to see his role as servant through the lenses of prophet, priest and king that were evident in Moses' leadership as the servant.

That Joshua is the new servant raised up in place of Moses becomes even more evident from the remainder of what Yahweh says to Joshua:

> Be strong and courageous, for you shall cause this people to inherit the land that I swore to their fathers to give them. Only be strong and very courageous, being careful to do according to all the law that Moses my servant commanded you. Do not turn from it to the right hand or to the left, that you may have good success wherever you go. This Book of the Law shall not depart from your mouth, but you shall meditate on it day and night, so that you may be careful to do according to all that is written in it. For then you will make your way prosperous, and then you will have good success. Have I not

> commanded you? Be strong and courageous. Do not be frightened, and do not be dismayed, for the Lord your God is with you wherever you go.
> (Josh. 1:6–9)

Three times God calls Joshua to be strong and courageous, and each time the exhortation receives further elaboration.[4] The first is rooted in the promise that Joshua will lead the people into the land God promised their ancestors. The second is followed by the command to obey everything written in the law 'that Moses my servant commanded' Joshua and the people. If he does so, God promises to prosper Joshua in his role as his servant. The final call to be strong and courageous is rooted in Yahweh's promise that he will be with Joshua wherever he goes.

Joshua wastes no time in acting as the new servant of Yahweh. As part of his instructions to prepare the people to enter the land, Joshua reminds the tribes who received their inheritance east of the Jordan of their obligation to participate in the conquest (Josh. 1:12–15). He brackets these instructions with references to 'Moses the servant of the Lord', showing that he is in fact being careful to obey all that Moses the servant commanded. In response, these tribes reaffirm their original promise to take part in the conquest, proclaiming: 'Just as we obeyed Moses in all things, so we will obey you. Only may the Lord your God be with you, as he was with Moses!' (Josh. 1:17). By promising to obey Joshua in the same way they obeyed Moses, the people recognize that Joshua is the new servant and that Yahweh is with him in the same way he was with Moses.

But the careful reader will notice at this point that the text has not explicitly come out and referred to Joshua as the servant of Yahweh. Instead, the rest of the book will show the reader that Joshua is in fact the servant of Yahweh by showing that (1) Joshua does what Moses the servant commanded; and (2) Yahweh performs similar acts through Joshua as he did through Moses. Only when the author has shown that Joshua is the servant of Yahweh through his life of faithful service will the author at last call Joshua the servant of Yahweh when he finally dies.

---

[4] Yahweh's words here echo what Moses says to Joshua in Deut. 31:1–8. The similarities reinforce that Yahweh is now calling Joshua to assume his role as the successor to Moses and carry out what Moses commissioned him to do.

Joshua does what Moses the servant commanded

Central to the commission Yahweh gave to Joshua his servant was to do all that Moses his servant had commanded in the book of the law (Josh. 1:7–8). The first example is the covenant-renewal ceremony that takes place after Israel's breach of faith, their subsequent defeat at Ai (Josh. 7:1–26) and their eventual victory (Josh. 8:1–29). Joshua and the people build an altar on Mount Ebal, 'just as Moses the servant of the Lord had commanded the people of Israel, as it is written in the Book of the Law of Moses' (Josh. 8:31). Before entering the land, Moses instructed the people to gather at Mount Ebal and Mount Gerizim to worship Yahweh (Deut. 27:1 – 28:68). Half of them were to stand on Mount Gerizim reciting the blessings promised in the covenant for obedience, while the other half were to stand across the valley on Mount Ebal reciting the curses threatened for disobedience. Joshua orchestrates this ceremony 'just as Moses the servant of the Lord had commanded' (Josh. 8:33), functioning in both priestly and prophetic roles.[5] The ceremony culminates in the reading of 'all the words of the law, the blessing and the curse, according to all that is written in the Book of the Law' (Josh. 8:34). To reinforce Joshua's obedience to Moses the servant the passage concludes by noting: 'There was not a word of all that Moses commanded that Joshua did not read before all the assembly of Israel, and the women, and the little ones, and the sojourners who lived among them' (Josh. 8:35). Joshua lives out his identity as the servant of Yahweh by his meticulous obedience to the words of Moses the servant, and as a result Yahweh prospers him (Josh. 1:6–9).

Joshua allotting the land to the Israelites and conquering the inhabitants of the land are two acts that are repeatedly said to be done in accordance with the command of Moses the servant. Part of the reason the Gibeonites deceive the Israelites into making a treaty with them is that 'it was told to your servants for a certainty that the Lord your God had commanded his servant Moses to give you all the land and to destroy all the inhabitants of the land from before you' (Josh. 9:24). Joshua 11 recounts the conquest of northern Canaan and the distribution of the land

[5] The priestly nature of Joshua's actions are shown in that (1) he builds the altar for sacrifice (Josh. 8:30; cf. Exod. 20:24–26) and (2) leads the Levitical priests in the covenant-renewal ceremony (Josh. 8:33). In his prophetic role, Joshua (1) writes on stones a copy of the law of Moses (Josh. 8:32) and (2) reads all the words of the law to the people (Josh. 8:34).

to the various tribes. Four times in this lengthy section Joshua's actions are said to be the outworking of what God commanded Moses (11:12, 15, 20, 23). Two of these explicitly identify Moses as the servant of Yahweh. Look, for example, at Joshua 11:15: 'Just as the LORD had commanded Moses his servant, so Moses commanded Joshua, and so Joshua did. He left nothing undone of all that the LORD had commanded Moses' (cf. 11:12). When Joshua 12:1–6 recounts the various kings that God defeated through Moses, the text again identifies Moses as the servant of the Lord: 'Moses, the servant of the LORD, and the people of Israel defeated them. And Moses the servant of the LORD gave their land for a possession to the Reubenites and the Gadites and the half-tribe of Manasseh' (Josh. 12:6).

Even more consistent is the reminder of Moses the servant allotting land east of the Jordan to the tribes of Reuben, Gad and the half-tribe of Manasseh:

> With the other half of the tribe of Manasseh the Reubenites and the Gadites received their inheritance, which Moses gave them, beyond the Jordan eastwards, as Moses the servant of the LORD gave them. (Josh. 13:8)

> The Levites have no portion among you, for the priesthood of the LORD is their heritage. And Gad and Reuben and half the tribe of Manasseh have received their inheritance beyond the Jordan eastwards, which Moses the servant of the LORD gave them. (Josh. 18:7)

> At that time Joshua summoned the Reubenites and the Gadites and the half-tribe of Manasseh, and said to them, 'You have kept all that Moses the servant of the LORD commanded you and have obeyed my voice in all that I have commanded you . . . And now the LORD your God has given rest to your brothers, as he promised them. Therefore turn and go to your tents in the land where your possession lies, which Moses the servant of the LORD gave you on the other side of the Jordan. Only be very careful to observe the commandment and the law that Moses the servant of the LORD commanded you, to love the LORD your God, and to walk in all his ways and to keep his commandments and to cling to him and to serve him with all your heart and with all your soul.'
> (Josh. 22:1–2, 4–5)

Along a similar line, Caleb refers to Moses the servant when asking Joshua for the inheritance Caleb was promised:

> Then the people of Judah came to Joshua at Gilgal. And Caleb the son of Jephunneh the Kenizzite said to him, 'You know what the LORD said to Moses the man of God in Kadesh-barnea concerning you and me. I was forty years old when Moses the servant of the LORD sent me from Kadesh-barnea to spy out the land, and I brought him word again as it was in my heart. But my brothers who went up with me made the heart of the people melt; yet I wholly followed the LORD my God. And Moses swore on that day, saying, "Surely the land on which your foot has trodden shall be an inheritance for you and your children for ever, because you have wholly followed the LORD my God."'
> (Josh. 14:6–9)

As we would expect, Joshua blesses Caleb and grants this request (Josh. 14:13).

The clear emphasis of these passages is that Joshua is doing exactly what God commanded through Moses the servant, often with an emphasis on conquest and the division of the land. In accomplishing these feats Joshua acts in a kingly fashion as the servant of Yahweh. He is exercising an Adamic kind of dominion over the new Eden known as the Promised Land.

Yahweh performs similar acts through Joshua

Even more significant than Joshua's strict obedience to everything Moses the servant commanded are the acts that Yahweh performs through Joshua that are analogous to what he did through Moses. We see this point in at least four specific acts/events.

Parting the Jordan River

When the time comes for Israel to enter the land, they must first cross the Jordan River. So Joshua and the officers of the people prepare the Israelites for what is about to happen (Josh. 3:1–6). Notice what Yahweh says to Joshua shortly before the people set out to cross the Jordan: 'Today

I will begin to exalt you in the sight of all Israel, that they may know that, as I was with Moses, so I will be with you' (Josh. 3:7). So the Lord is doing more than simply getting his people across a physical boundary: he is about to perform an action that will confirm for the Israelites that he is with Joshua in the same way that he was with Moses. In response Joshua addresses the people as they prepare to cross the Jordan, preparing them for what is about to happen (Josh. 3:8–13). After the nation passes over the river on dry ground (Josh. 3:14–17), God instructs the people to have a man from each of the twelve tribes take the stones set up in the river and move them to the place where they set up camp (4:1–10).[6] When the people have finished crossing, the priests carrying the ark of the covenant exit the riverbed and the waters of the Jordan return (4:11–18). The people then set up the memorial stones taken from the river in Gilgal, as a testimony to future generations that Yahweh 'dried up the waters of the Jordan for you until you passed over, as the Lord your God did to the Red Sea, which he dried up for us until we passed over' (4:23).

At this point, a comparison of this account with the crossing of the Red Sea will help show the parallels between the two accounts (see Table 3 on p. 70).

The most noteworthy parallels are the last two rows. In response to Yahweh parting the Red Sea, the people 'believed in the Lord and in his servant Moses' (Exod. 14:31). The Lord twice states a similar purpose in parting the Jordan River for Joshua. In advance of the crossing, Yahweh says to Joshua: 'Today I will begin to exalt you in the sight of all Israel, that they may know that, as I was with Moses, so I will be with you' (Josh. 3:7). Once the Israelites have crossed the Jordan, the text notes: 'On that day the Lord exalted Joshua in the sight of all Israel, and they stood in awe of him just as they had stood in awe of Moses, all the days of his life' (Josh. 4:14). Exalting Joshua in the sight of the Israelites is not the only purpose of the dramatic river crossing: Yahweh wants the news to go viral. As part of explaining the memorial stones to future generations, the people are to say:

[6] The wording of Josh. 4:8–9 is initially confusing, giving the impression that there were two sets of stones – one in the middle of the river (4:8) and a second set on the shore (4:9). But it is more likely that only one set of stones is in view, with the sense being that the stones which had been in the middle of the river were then placed on the shore; see further Howard 1998: 135–136.

> For the LORD your God dried up the waters of the Jordan for you until you passed over, as the LORD your God did to the Red Sea, which he dried up for us until we passed over, so that all the peoples of the earth may know that the hand of the LORD is mighty, that you may fear the LORD your God for ever.
> (Josh. 4:23–24)

Table 3 Comparison of the Red Sea and the Jordan River crossings

Crossing the Red Sea (Exod. 14:1 – 15:21)	*Crossing the Jordan River (Josh. 3:1 – 4:24)*
God's presence (angel of the God) protects the people (14:19–20)	God's presence (the ark of the covenant) goes with the people through the waters (3:8, 10, 14, 17)
The waters divide and make the sea dry land, forming a wall on each side of them (14:21, 29)[7]	The waters are gathered into a heap, allowing the people to pass over on dry land (Josh. 3:16–17)
The people celebrate in song (15:1–21)	The people take memorial stones to celebrate (4:1–10)
The people believe in Yahweh and his servant Moses (14:31)	Yahweh exalts Joshua in the sight of the people, causing them to stand in awe of Joshua just as they did Moses (3:7; 4:14)
Yahweh acts so that the Egyptians will know that he is the Lord (14:4, 18)	Yahweh acts so all the peoples of the earth will know the hand of the Lord is mighty (4:24)

Just as the exodus had the purpose of spreading Yahweh's fame to the nations,[8] so too this river crossing has an international scope – the demonstration of the Lord's powerful hand to all the peoples of the earth. It does not take long for this purpose to be realized:

[7] The imagery of the waters being separated and gathered together so that dry land would appear when the Israelites crossed both the Red Sea and the Jordan River may echo God's work in creation on the second day (Gen. 1:9–10). If so, both crossings can be seen as acts of new creation.

[8] See e.g. Exod. 3:19; 13:3, 9, 14, 16; 14:30–31; 32:11; Deut. 3:24; 4:34; 5:15; 6:21; 7:8, 19; 9:26; 11:2; 26:8; 34:12.

> As soon as all the kings of the Amorites who were beyond the Jordan to the west, and all the kings of the Canaanites who were by the sea, heard that the LORD had dried up the waters of the Jordan for the people of Israel until they had crossed over, their hearts melted and there was no longer any spirit in them because of the people of Israel. (Josh. 5:1)

In the light of Israel's miraculous crossing of the Jordan, the peoples of the land realize their days are numbered.

These parallels portray Joshua as the servant of the Lord who, like Moses before him, is exalted in the sight of the people. Through this new servant Yahweh will make known his glorious power to the surrounding nations. So it comes as no surprise when in the aftermath of Jericho's conquest, the text notes: 'So the LORD was with Joshua, and his fame was in all the land' (Josh. 6:27). Not only is Yahweh's fame spreading; so too is the fame of his servant Joshua.[9] Through him God is mediating his presence to the nations, a role originally designated for Adam in the garden.

Appearing to Joshua

Once Joshua has led Israel across the Jordan, they begin to prepare for the conquest of the land. After circumcising the wilderness generation (Josh. 5:2–9) and celebrating the Passover (Josh. 5:10–12), Joshua has a startling encounter:

> When Joshua was by Jericho, he lifted up his eyes and looked, and behold, a man was standing before him with his drawn sword in his hand. And Joshua went to him and said to him, 'Are you for us, or for our adversaries?' And he said, 'No; but I am the commander of the army of the LORD. Now I have come.' And Joshua fell on his face to the earth and worshipped and said to him, 'What does my lord say to his servant?' And the commander of the LORD's army said to

[9] As to why the fame of Joshua rather than that of Yahweh is stressed here, Hess (1996: 149–150) notes that this is Joshua's first military campaign as the leader of God's people. In the ancient Near East, the outcome of a leader's first campaign 'was considered essential in establishing leadership. Such a victory on the part of Joshua would secure him respect, not only among the Israelites (who already had ample evidence) but also among the Canaanites. If, as seems likely, this text was designed to present the case for Joshua's leadership, it would make an effective argument in the context of the rulers of Canaan.'

> Joshua, 'Take off your sandals from your feet, for the place where you are standing is holy.' And Joshua did so.
> (Josh. 5:13–15)

The command to take his sandals off immediately evokes echoes of Moses' encounter with the Lord at the burning bush (Exod. 3:5). But unlike Moses' burning bush incident, this encounter is not a commissioning for service. Yahweh does not have to prevail upon Joshua to lead God's people. Instead, this encounter is more akin to a strategic planning session, with the Lord instructing Joshua how to conquer Jericho (Josh. 6:1–5). Nonetheless, by revealing himself to Joshua in a manner similar to that of Moses, Yahweh signals that Joshua is the new servant of the Lord.[10]

Joshua's response to the commander of the Lord's army seems to confirm this conclusion. After bowing down in worship, Joshua asks, 'What does my lord say to *his servant*?' (Josh. 5:14). This is the only place where Joshua refers to himself as a servant, and the context suggests it is more than simply a humble manner of responding. At the least it is suggestive, if not ultimately certain, that Joshua understands himself to be the servant of the Lord in a way analogous to Moses before him.

Answering prayer for victory in battle

After Israel's stunning and humiliating defeat at Ai and the subsequent punishment of Achan for breaking the covenant (Josh. 7:1–26), Yahweh sends Israel back for another crack at the city. He begins by informing

---

10 Scholars have debated the precise identity of this figure. When first introduced in v. 13, he is simply identified as a man. Yet when this figure speaks he identifies himself as 'the commander of the army of Yahweh' (5:14). The Hebrew expression rendered 'commander of the army' (*śar-ṣĕbāʾ*) regularly refers to a human military commander (e.g. Gen. 21:22, 32; 26:26; Judg. 4:2, 7; 1 Sam. 12:9; 14:50; 17:55; 2 Sam. 10:16, 18; 1 Kgs 1:19, 25; 2:5; 16:16; 2 Kgs 5:1). And the expression 'army of Yahweh' (*ṣĕbāʾ-yĕhwâ*) could be a reference to the Israelite army (cf. Exod. 12:41). Yet the army (*ṣābāʾ*) of Yahweh can also refer to the inhabitants of the spiritual realm (1 Kgs 22:19) and celestial bodies (Gen. 2:1; Ps. 33:6); furthermore, God is repeatedly called 'the LORD of hosts' (*yhwh ṣĕbāʾōt*), a title that stresses his authority not merely over the human armies of his people but the angelic forces as well; see the helpful summary in Hartley 1980: 750. On the whole the context of Josh. 5:14 suggests that the army in view is in fact the Israelites, though a possible reference to Yahweh's angelic warriors fighting for Israel cannot be ruled out; for this view see Howard 1998: 157–158. As for the identity of this commander, despite being initially identified as a man, the context suggests this figure is at the least an angelic messenger from Yahweh, perhaps akin to the angel of the Lord. The seamless transition from this 'man' commanding Joshua to remove his sandals because he is standing on holy ground (5:14–15) to Yahweh speaking directly to Joshua in 6:2–5 suggests that this is a direct manifestation of God's presence; see further Hess 1996: 139–140.

Joshua that he has given the king, the people, the city and its land into Israel's hand, and then instructs Joshua to take the city by ambush (Josh. 8:1–2). Joshua explains the strategy to the Israelite army (Josh. 8:3–9), and the next day they execute it (Josh. 8:10–23). Joshua places 5,000 men in position for an ambush, while leading another 25,000 to feign fleeing away from the city. Once the armies of Ai have been drawn away from the city, Joshua stands in a place where he is visible to the men lying in wait, and holds aloft a javelin to signal that the time has come for them to enter the city and set it on fire (Josh. 8:18–19). When the armies of Ai see the city is aflame, they realize they are caught in an ambush and are subsequently struck down (Josh. 8:20–23). After summarizing the complete annihilation of Ai and its army, the text notes: 'But Joshua did not draw back his hand with which he stretched out the javelin until he had devoted all the inhabitants of Ai to destruction' (Josh. 8:26). Although admittedly subtle, there seems to be an echo of Moses' intercession when fighting the Amalekites (Exod. 17:8–16).[11] While Joshua leads the Israelite armies in battle, Moses stands on top of a nearby hill and holds up his hands; as long as his hands remain raised the Israelites prevail in battle (Exod. 17:8–11). When Moses' hands grow weary, Aaron and Hur hold up Moses' hands, thus ensuring Israel's victory over the Amalekites (Exod. 17:11–13). Yahweh then instructs Moses: 'Write this as a memorial in a book and recite it in the ears of Joshua, that I will utterly blot out the memory of Amalek from under heaven' (Exod. 17:14). Like Moses before him, Joshua intercedes on behalf of God's people to lead them to victory in battle. Joshua exercises a priestly function, interceding for Israel before the Lord like Moses before him.

The account concludes by highlighting Joshua's obedience to the Lord's instructions. The people followed the restrictions on plunder that Yahweh had commanded Joshua (Josh. 8:2, 27). Joshua hangs the king of Ai, but takes his body down before sunset in order to avoid defiling the land (Josh. 8:29), just as Yahweh commanded the people through Moses the servant (Deut. 21:22–23).

Writing down God's words

At the conclusion of his life, Joshua gathers the people together at Shechem for a covenant-renewal ceremony (Josh. 24:1–28). Just as Moses did before

[11] By contrast, Hess (1996: 184–185) argues that this account shows significant parallels with the Red Sea crossing. There is no reason, however, that these two proposals must be mutually exclusive.

him, so now Yahweh through Joshua reminds the people of what God has done for them. Throughout this retelling of Israel's history, the central issue at hand is the question of service; in other words, whom will Israel choose to serve? God begins this version of redemptive history with Terah and his sons Abraham and Nahor, who 'lived beyond the Euphrates . . . and they *served* [*'ābad*] other gods' (Josh. 24:2). God promised Abraham the land of Canaan and many descendants, promises that began to be fulfilled through Isaac, Jacob and his twelve sons (Josh. 24:3–4). Jacob and his twelve sons settled in Egypt, where Moses and Aaron led their descendants out through the plagues (Josh. 24:4–5).

Whereas Yahweh quickly summarizes Israel's history from Terah through the exodus, the pace slows considerably when describing the period from the Red Sea crossing to the entry into the land (Josh. 24:6–13). Highlights include the Red Sea crossing (24:6–7; cf. Exod. 14:1–31), the victory over the Amorites (24:8; cf. Num. 21:21–35), the victory over Balaam and the Moabites (24:9–10; cf. Num. 22:1–24:25), and the conquest of the land beginning with the Jordan River crossing (24:11–13; cf. Josh. 1:1 – 12:24). This section culminates with Yahweh reminding the Israelites that they are now enjoying cities, vineyards and orchards that they did not build for themselves.

That brief summary of Israel's history sets the stage for Joshua to call the people to covenant faithfulness, with the central thrust being the issue of service:

> Now therefore fear the LORD and *serve* [*'ābad*] him in sincerity and in faithfulness. Put away the gods that your fathers *served* [*'ābad*] beyond the River and in Egypt, and *serve* [*'ābad*] the LORD. And if it is evil in your eyes to *serve* [*'ābad*] the LORD, choose this day whom you will *serve* [*'ābad*], whether the gods your fathers *served* [*'ābad*] in the region beyond the River, or the gods of the Amorites in whose land you dwell. But as for me and my house, we will *serve* [*'ābad*] the LORD. (Josh. 24:14–15)

Joshua's repeated charge to the people to serve Yahweh 'in sincerity and faithfulness' comes in the midst of a rebuke for serving the gods their fathers served (24:14). Indeed, the people must choose whether they will serve these false gods or Yahweh (24:15); they cannot do both. As the servant of the Lord Joshua makes it clear his loyalty is to Yahweh (24:15).

In response to this charge, the people say:

> Far be it from us that we should forsake the LORD to *serve* [*'ābad*] other gods, for it is the LORD our God who brought us and our fathers up from the land of Egypt, out of the house of *slavery* [*'ebed*], and who did those great signs in our sight and preserved us in all the way that we went, and among all the peoples through whom we passed. And the LORD drove out before us all the peoples, the Amorites who lived in the land. Therefore we also will *serve* [*'ābad*] the LORD, for he is our God.
> (Josh. 24:16–18).

The people swear their loyalty to Yahweh, who brought them out of the house of slavery in Egypt, preserved them in the wilderness, and brought them into the land (24:16–18a). That is why they will serve Yahweh (24:18b).

Joshua's response to the people is surprising:

> You are not able to *serve* [*'ābad*] the LORD, for he is a holy God. He is a jealous God; he will not forgive your transgressions or your sins. If you forsake the LORD and *serve* [*'ābad*] foreign gods, then he will turn and do you harm and consume you, after having done you good.
> (Josh. 24:19–20)

Despite the Israelites' confident assertion, Joshua insists they will not be able to carry out being faithful. Yahweh's holiness and his zeal to preserve the exclusivity of his relationship with his people will make it impossible for the people to avoid breaking this covenant. When the Israelites do eventually turn away to serve other gods, Yahweh will set his face against them to do them harm.

The remainder of Joshua's charge and the people's response is worth citing in full:

> And the people said to Joshua, 'No, but we will *serve* [*'ābad*] the LORD.' Then Joshua said to the people, 'You are witnesses against yourselves that you have chosen the LORD, to *serve* [*'ābad*] him.' And they said, 'We are witnesses.' He said, 'Then put away the foreign

> gods that are among you, and incline your heart to the LORD, the God of Israel.' And the people said to Joshua, 'The LORD our God we will *serve* [*'ābad*], and his voice we will obey.'
> (Josh. 24:21–24)

So despite the repeated warnings from Joshua, the Israelites swear they will in fact serve Yahweh and obey his voice. But the careful reader of the biblical storyline to this point is understandably sceptical.

Joshua's pointed warnings are reminiscent of Moses' efforts to warn the people about their impending covenant unfaithfulness on the eve of his death. After Moses had written the memorial song for Israel as a witness against them, he wrote the words of the law in a book that he commanded the Levites to place next to the ark of the covenant (Deut. 31:24). In a similar fashion, Joshua 'wrote these words in the Book of the Law of God' (Josh. 24:26). In receiving and writing God's words Joshua performs a prophetic role as Yahweh's servant.

The death of Joshua the servant

When the time comes for Joshua to pass from the stage of redemptive history, the author at last makes Joshua's identity as the servant of Yahweh explicit:

> After these things Joshua the son of Nun, the servant [*'ebed*] of the LORD, died, being 110 years old. And they buried him in his own inheritance at Timnath-serah, which is in the hill country of Ephraim, north of the mountain of Gaash. Israel served [*'ăbād*] the LORD all the days of Joshua, and all the days of the elders who outlived Joshua and had known all the work that the LORD did for Israel.
> (Josh. 24:29–31)

At last the author states clearly what the reader has already concluded – Joshua is the servant of Yahweh. Why the author waits until Joshua's death to make this explicit statement is not clear. Perhaps the author reserves this title until Joshua's death so that his track record of Moses-like leadership makes such an exalted claim seemingly obvious. Whatever the reason, by the time this epitaph is applied to Joshua, no one can dispute its truthfulness. And consistent with Moses' own experience, Israel serving Yahweh is linked to the faithful work of Joshua the servant of the Lord. Through his servant Joshua Yahweh has formed a servant people.

Conclusion

The book of Joshua opens with the death of Moses the servant of Yahweh and ends with the death of Joshua the servant of Yahweh his successor. Although not explicitly given the title until the announcement of his death, Joshua is clearly shown to be the new servant of Yahweh appointed by God to give the Israelites their inheritance in the land. Joshua lives out his identity as the servant of Yahweh by defeating the enemies of God's people and giving them rest. But rather than replacing Moses, Joshua fills the role of the servant. Of course, this was anticipated at several points during the life of Moses, with special emphasis on Joshua's having the Spirit of the Lord (Num. 27:18–23; Deut. 1:38; 3:28; 31:3, 14–23; 34:9). Yet despite Joshua's exemplary service, he does not attain the same status as Moses: there is no statement comparable to Deuteronomy 34:9–12, which stresses Moses' uniqueness.

Nevertheless, as the servant Joshua faithfully obeys all that Moses the servant commanded. Yahweh repeatedly promises to be with Joshua just as he was with Moses. To authenticate his status as the servant, Yahweh does through Joshua similar things to those he did through Moses, including parting the Jordan River, appearing to Joshua, answering prayer for victory in battle, and writing down God's words. As Joshua performs these actions the people stand in awe of him, just as they stood in awe of Moses. Thus, by the end of the book there is no question that Joshua is the servant of Yahweh.

Yet Joshua's role as the servant goes back further in the biblical storyline than that of Moses. As the servant of Yahweh, Joshua performs Adam-like actions. Through his conquest of the land Joshua exercises dominion over a new Eden – the Promised Land. As a priestly figure Joshua the servant mediates God's presence to the nations around and intercedes on behalf of the people. By receiving and writing down the words of God Joshua the servant exercises a prophetic role. Although Joshua does not rise to the level of Moses within the biblical storyline, he dies a faithful servant of Yahweh who played his part well in redemptive history. He leaves behind a servant people committed to being faithful to Yahweh, even though Joshua knew that Israel would not live up to that commitment.

But unlike when Moses dies, there is no clearly defined successor for Joshua, no clearly identified individual who fills the role of servant. Instead, Israel must endure hundreds of years of suffering through the sporadic and increasingly failed leadership of the judges. Only when God installs a king after his own heart will an individual emerge who fulfils the role of the servant of Yahweh.

5
David: the servant king

> And I will set up over them one shepherd, my servant David, and he shall feed them: he shall feed them and be their shepherd. And I, the Lord, will be their God, and my servant David shall be prince among them. I am the Lord; I have spoken.
> (Ezek. 34:23–24)

If we are honest, oftentimes God's timing confuses or even frustrates us. We do not understand why he seems to wait so long to do things that seem so obviously to us are consistent with his purposes and promises. No doubt at least some of the Israelites felt this way as generations passed without the Lord raising up a servant to fill the void left by the death of Joshua. Yet the Lord waited hundreds of years before bringing the next servant of the Lord on to the stage of redemptive history.

That servant is a man named David, and as the servant of the Lord he plays a crucial role not only during his lifetime but also in the eschatological hopes of God's people. But before we can explore David's significance as the servant of the Lord, I must first briefly summarize Israel's experience between Joshua the servant and David the servant.

Israel's need for a servant

After announcing the death of Yahweh's servant, the book of Joshua concludes by noting that 'Israel served [*ʿăbād*] the Lord all the days of Joshua, and all the days of the elders who outlived Joshua and had known all the work that the Lord did for Israel' (Josh. 24:31). But unlike the book of Joshua, there is no indication that Yahweh is raising up a new servant.

Judges opens where Joshua left off. Initially, Israel shows some promising signs of faithfulness to Yahweh. They ask the Lord who should lead them in battle against the Canaanites, and he responds by singling out the tribe of Judah (Judg. 1:1–2). In his final blessing of his sons, Jacob had promised that:

> The scepter shall not depart from Judah,
> nor the ruler's staff from between his feet,
> until tribute comes to him;
> and to him shall be the obedience of the peoples.
> (Gen. 49:10)

By singling out Judah to lead this next phase of the conquest, Yahweh is setting in motion his plan to bring his next servant David on to the stage of redemptive history.

So along with the tribe of Simeon, Judah marches throughout the land of Canaan gaining possession of large swathes of territory, including the key city of Jerusalem (Judg. 1:3–20). Yet despite these successes, there remain significant pockets of resistance from the Canaanites that the Israelites are unable to root out (Judg. 1:21–36). The reason for these remaining pockets of Canaanites is Israel's disobedience, and because of this unfaithfulness to the covenant made at Sinai the angel of the Lord announces to the Israelites: 'So now I say, I will not drive them out before you, but they shall become thorns in your sides, and their gods shall be a snare to you' (Judg. 2:3).

At this point the author of Judges repeats the concluding words of the book of Joshua (24:29–31), noting the death of Joshua the servant of Yahweh and that Israel served the Lord 'all the days of Joshua, and all the days of the elders who outlived Joshua, who had seen all the great work that the LORD had done for Israel' (Judg. 2:7). But after this generation died, 'there arose another generation after them who did not know the LORD or the work that he had done for Israel' (Judg. 2:10).

With the arrival of this generation who does not know Yahweh, the stage is set for the well-known cycle that permeates the book of Judges:

> *Rebellion*: Israel does what is evil in the sight of the Lord, serving the gods of the people around them and provoking Yahweh to anger.[1]

[1] The verb 'serve' (*'ăbād*) is repeatedly used in Judges to describe Israel's posture towards foreign gods and the surrounding peoples (e.g. 2:11, 13, 19; 3:6, 7, 8, 14; 10:6, 10, 13). With the exception of describing the generation of Israelites from Joshua's days (2:7), only once does Judges use this verb to describe Israel's posture towards Yahweh (10:16). Exodus was the

Retribution: God hands Israel over to their enemies, even fighting against his people.
Repentance: Israel cries out for deliverance from their enemies.[2]
Redemption: God raises up a judge to deliver them from their enemies.
Rest: Israel and the land experiences rest for a certain number of years.[3]

Once the judge dies the cycle starts over. This cycle is laid out in summary form in Judges 2:11–19, and then vividly illustrated in Judges 3:7 – 16:31. With each successive iteration, however, the cycle breaks down. The judges become less exemplary, the people stop crying out for deliverance, the deliverance accomplished by the judges becomes less definitive and decisive, and eventually the land is no longer said to experience rest. By the time that Samson kills the lords of the Philistines the cycle simply concludes by noting that he judged Israel 20 years.[4] No deliverance for Israel. No rest for the land. All that remains are the ruins of a Philistine worship site and his tragic life (Judg. 13:1 – 16:31). The remaining snapshots of Israel's unfaithfulness to the covenant that conclude the book (Judg. 17:1 – 21:25) reinforce the people's need for a king (Judg. 17:6; 18:1; 19:1; 21:25).

The opening chapters of 1 Samuel narrate the transition from Samuel the last judge to Saul the first king (1:1 – 15:35). Despite Samuel's largely faithful tenure as a judge over Israel, the immorality and corruption of his

account of Yahweh redeeming his people out of their service to Pharaoh so they could serve him. During the days of Joshua the people served Yahweh as they gained possession of the Edenic Promised Land, culminating with Joshua's challenge for the people to serve Yahweh. But just as Joshua had warned, the people during the period of the Judges prove unable to serve Yahweh and instead choose to serve the false gods of the surrounding peoples.

[2] Not every iteration of the cycle includes the mention of repentance. Several of the early cycles refer to Israel crying out because of their oppression (e.g. Judg. 3:9, 15; 4:3; 6:7; 10:10). But with the last example there is a noticeable shift. This time when Israel cries out for deliverance, Yahweh instructs them to cry out to the false gods they have been worshipping (10:11–14). Notably, he tells them he will no longer save them. But when Israel responds by putting away their foreign gods and 'serving' (*'ăbād*) Yahweh, he delivers them once again (10:16). Yet this is the final time in Judges where the people are said to cry out to Yahweh for deliverance, and it is the final time where the text states that Yahweh delivers Israel.

[3] Not every cycle concludes with the mention of Israel or the land experiencing rest; it is only a feature of the first few cycles (Judg. 3:11, 30; 5:31; 8:28).

[4] In passing it should be noted that in Judg. 15:18 Samson prays, 'You have granted this great salvation by the hand of *your servant* [*'ebed*], and shall I now die of thirst and fall into the hands of the uncircumcised?' But the larger context of Judges makes it clear that although God used Samson to some degree, he should not be considered in the same line of servants as Adam, Moses and Joshua before him.

sons lead the people to ask for a king (8:1–5). When Samuel brings this request before Yahweh, the Lord responds:

> Obey the voice of the people in all that they say to you, for they have not rejected you, but they have rejected me from being king over them. According to all the deeds that they have done, from the day I brought them up out of Egypt even to this day, forsaking me and serving other gods, so they are also doing to you. Now then, obey their voice; only you shall solemnly warn them and show them the ways of the king who shall reign over them.
> (1 Sam. 8:7–9)

This request is but the latest example of Israel's rejection of Yahweh and unfaithfulness to the covenant he made with them. Their request for a king so they can be like the other nations is a direct rejection of God's purpose of them being a 'treasured possession among all peoples . . . [and] a kingdom of priests and a holy nation' (Exod. 19:5–6). As a fitting response to Israel's request for a king like the other nations, Yahweh gives them Saul, who is tall and handsome (1 Sam. 9:1–2). Notwithstanding some early successes, Saul proves to be a king who refuses to submit himself to Yahweh.

So despite getting the kind of king they wanted, what Israel truly needs is more than simply a king: they need a new servant of the Lord.

The life of David the servant

With the anointing of David Israel enters a new phase of history. What the people asked for with sinful motives becomes the means by which the next servant of the Lord will enter the stage of redemptive history.

Pre-reign

The transition from Saul to David as king is marked both by Samuel's anointing (1 Sam. 16:1–13) and the Spirit of the Lord rushing upon him. After an initially successful stint in Saul's service, David eventually flees for his life from Saul and spends a number of years on the run, hiding from Saul's nearly relentless efforts to eliminate this threat to his throne. Like Israel before him, David must wander the wilderness before experiencing the fulfilment of God's promises. It is during these wilderness years that David first refers to himself as a servant of the Lord. While in the city of Keilah, David learns that Saul is plotting to capture him. So David borrows the ephod from Abiathar the priest and prays:

> 'O LORD, the God of Israel, your *servant* [*'ebed*] has surely heard that Saul seeks to come to Keilah, to destroy the city on my account. Will the men of Keilah surrender me into his hand? Will Saul come down, as your *servant* [*'ebed*] has heard? O LORD, the God of Israel, please tell your *servant* [*'ebed*].' And the LORD said, 'He will come down.' Then David said, 'Will the men of Keilah surrender me and my men into the hand of Saul?' And the LORD said, 'They will surrender you.' (1 Sam. 23:10–12)

Three times in this prayer David approaches Yahweh as a servant. At a minimum this is an act of humility and submission, but the prominence of this title in later key texts suggests something more. Even at this early stage David may see himself as a servant of Yahweh in the tradition of Adam, Moses and Joshua before him.

A second example of David referring to himself as the servant occurs in the aftermath of his encounter with Abigail and her foolish husband Nabal (1 Sam. 25:1–42). Despite David's men providing security for Nabal's flocks while they were in the wilderness, Nabal spurns David's request for provisions. Before David can execute his plan for vengeance at this slight, Nabal's wife Abigail brings provisions to David's camp and pleads for him to change his mind.[5] David relents, and less than two weeks later Nabal dies. In response to the news, David says: 'Blessed be the LORD who has avenged the insult I received at the hand of Nabal, and has kept back his servant [*'ebed*] from wrongdoing. The LORD has returned the evil of Nabal on his own head' (1 Sam. 25:39). Again, apart from later developments in the biblical narrative, David's self-designation could easily be seen as a posture of humility and nothing more. But these two examples before David assumes the throne seem to anticipate the fuller revelation of David's identity as the new servant of Yahweh.

One final example may suggest someone other than David himself recognized David's unique identity as the new servant. In the midst of

[5] In her plea to David, Abigail refers to herself as David's 'servant/handmaid' (*'āmâ*) five times.

consolidating his rule, Abner (former commander of Saul's army) decides to pledge his loyalty to David (2 Sam. 3:6–21). In his efforts to persuade the elders of Israel to join him in doing so, Abner says to them:

> For some time past you have been seeking David as king over you. Now then bring it about, for the LORD has promised David, saying, 'By the hand of my servant David I will save my people Israel from the hand of the Philistines, and from the hand of all their enemies.' (2 Sam. 3:17–18)

Abner justifies his changed loyalty by referring to a specific promise that the Lord has made to David. Although the content is consistent with promises that God had indeed made to this point, its specific wording is in fact different. Abner asserts that Yahweh has already referred to David as 'my servant' and promised to save Israel from the hands of their enemies. Taken at face value, then, this is the first time that Yahweh refers to David as 'my servant'.

As with the previous two examples, by itself this could be nothing more than a recognition that as the king David is a servant of Yahweh in a general sense. But in the light of later revelation it seems to anticipate David's identity as the new servant of Yahweh in the tradition of Adam, Moses and Joshua before him.

God's covenant with his servant

Once Saul dies and David assumes the throne, he acts rapidly to solidify his power. After the ark of the covenant is brought to Jerusalem, 2 Samuel 7:1 notes:

> Now when the king lived in his house and the LORD had given him rest from all his surrounding enemies, the king said to Nathan the prophet, 'See now, I dwell in a house of cedar, but the ark of God dwells in a tent.'

The theme of rest is important here, as it connects with earlier moments in the biblical storyline. When God finished his work in creation, he rested (Gen. 2:3). As God prepared the Israelites to enter the land, he repeatedly promised that when they entered they would experience rest (Deut. 3:20; 12:10; 25:19). Once Joshua accomplished his conquest of the land and allotted the inheritance to the people, the land had rest from war (Josh. 11:23; cf. 14:15; 22:4). When the initial judges redeemed Israel from their bondage to the surrounding nations, the result was that the land experienced rest (Judg. 3:11, 30; 5:31; 8:28). In each instance there is a faint echo of the rest that Adam and Eve experienced in the garden before their rebellion.

Just as in the garden, the notion of rest is linked to God's presence, which explains why once David has rest from his enemies his mind turns to where God's presence dwells.[6] Despite the prophet Nathan's initial blessing of David's intentions, the Lord sends Nathan back to David with a different message (2 Sam. 7:4–17). Yahweh sets the stage for his response to David's intentions by telling Nathan to address 'David my servant' (2 Sam. 7:5). At last Yahweh is commissioning a new servant!

Yahweh's message to David turns on the double meaning of the key term 'house'. The Lord explains that he has dwelt with his people for centuries and never once asked them to build a house for him (2 Sam. 7:6–7). Yahweh then turns to his personal history with David (2 Sam. 7:8–9a), once again telling Nathan to address 'my servant David' (2 Sam. 7:8). The Lord took David from the pastures to lead his people, and as a result Yahweh has been with him everywhere he went to cut off all his enemies. Based on this record of faithfulness, Yahweh turns to the future and promises the following:

> And I will make for you a great name, like the name of the great ones of the earth. And I will appoint a place for my people Israel and will plant them, so that they may dwell in their own place and be disturbed no more. And violent men shall afflict them no more, as formerly, from the time that I appointed judges over my people Israel. And I will give you rest from all your enemies. Moreover, the Lord declares to you that the Lord will make you a house. When your days are fulfilled and you lie down with your fathers, I will raise up your offspring after you, who shall come from your body,

[6] Beale (2004: 63–66) notes that in the ancient Near East there is a pattern of temple building that follows the overcoming of opposition. He claims, 'Israel's tabernacle may well have been conceived to be a travelling war headquarters from where the Lord directed the troops until all opposition was put down. When the enemies are defeated, then a more permanent dwelling can be built to signify God's sovereign "resting" from opposition, as happened during Solomon's reign' (64).

> and I will establish his kingdom. He shall build a house for my name, and I will establish the throne of his kingdom for ever. I will be to him a father, and he shall be to me a son. When he commits iniquity, I will discipline him with the rod of men, with the stripes of the sons of men, but my steadfast love will not depart from him, as I took it from Saul, whom I put away from before you. And your house and your kingdom shall be made sure for ever before me. Your throne shall be established for ever.
> (2 Sam. 7:9b–16)

Yahweh makes a number of staggering promises to David, and although the word 'covenant' is nowhere used in 2 Samuel 7, later Scripture makes it clear that God is in fact establishing a covenant with his servant David.[7] This covenant involves promises that will be fulfilled in David's lifetime (7:8–11a) and those that will be fulfilled after his death (7:11b–16).[8] Both sets of promises have their roots in God's promise to Abraham as well as his original commission to Adam in the garden.

During David's lifetime Yahweh promises David (1) a great name; (2) a place where he will plant his people Israel so they can dwell securely; and (3) rest from all his enemies. Just as God has promised to make Abram's name great (Gen. 12:2), so now it is David's name that will be great. It was the responsibility of Adam to reflect Yahweh's glory as an image-bearer ruling over creation, and the great name that David will be given as he rules is another way of expressing that he is reflecting the glory of the Lord.[9] The gift of land was central to God's promise to Abram; now to David Yahweh swears to give his people a place where he will plant them.[10] God had commissioned Adam to be fruitful, multiply and fill the

---

7 Gentry and Wellum (2012: 392–393) note that 'While 2 Samuel 7 does not specifically call the arrangement a covenant, the term (*bĕrit*) is in fact used in 2 Samuel 23:5; Jeremiah 33:21; Psalm 89:3, 28, 34, 39; 132:12 and 2 Chronicles 13:5. Moreover, (*ḥesed*), the term used of the Davidic covenant in Isa. 55:3, *is used* in 2 Samuel 7:15.'

8 This distinction is highlighted by the use of the messenger formula in 7:8a ('Thus says the Lord of hosts') and 7:11b ('the Lord declares to you'); see ibid. 394.

9 The interplay between David's desire to build Yahweh a 'house' (i.e. temple) and Yahweh's subsequent promise to make a 'house' (i.e. dynasty) for David is frequently noted. Less observed is David's intention to build a house for Yahweh's name (1 Kgs 8:16–18) and God's promise to make David a great name (2 Sam. 7:9). God makes David's name great as a means of magnifying his own name among the nations.

10 The use of the term 'place' (*māqôm*) rather than 'land' is interesting here. While it could simply be synonymous with land (e.g. Exod. 23:20; 1 Sam. 12:8; Jer. 16:2–3), the term was also used for the specific sites for acts of worship (Gen. 22:3; Deut. 12:5, 14; 14:23–25; 15:20; 16:2,

earth (Gen. 1:28), and the specific use of the agricultural term 'plant' may further suggest that God's promise to David here has its roots in Adam's commission.[11] Rest from David's enemies parallels God's promise to Abraham that his offspring would possess the gates of his enemies (Gen. 22:17–18). It is an outworking of Adam's commission to subdue the earth and exercise dominion over creation itself.

The promises that God will fulfil after David's lifetime display significant overlap with those during his lifetime, though in a significantly heightened sense. The great name for David during his lifetime intensifies into a 'house' (i.e. dynasty of kings) that come from David's line (2 Sam. 7:11). God promised Abraham that kings would come from his offspring, and the succession of Davidic kings envisioned here is at least a partial fulfilment of that promise. This line of kings also resonates with God's commission of Adam, who as the image-bearing servant king was to multiply and produce offspring who continue humanity's call to rule over and subdue the earth. After this initial promise of a line of kings, the focus shifts to one specific king from that line. Yahweh will establish the kingdom of this king for ever (2 Sam. 7:12–13, 16). The promise of a line of kings yet with a focus on one particular king is analogous to God's promise to Abraham in Genesis 17, where after promising multiple offspring (Gen. 17:1–8) he singles out Isaac as the individual offspring through whom the promises will be fulfilled (Gen. 17:15–21). This specific king from David's line will build a 'house' (i.e. temple) for the name of the Lord. In a sense this is a heightened version of the actions of Abraham, who built altars at various places during his sojourn in the land of promise in order to worship Yahweh (e.g. Gen. 12:7–8; 13:4, 18; 22:9). The act of building this temple by a Davidic descendant is analogous to Adam's role in the garden, who served in a priestly role not only in his commission to protect the purity of Yahweh's garden sanctuary but also by expanding the borders of that sanctuary.

6; 17:8; 18:6) or locations where God appeared (Gen. 28:11–19; Exod. 3:5), including Yahweh's sanctuary (e.g. 1 Kgs 8:29–30, 35; 2 Chr. 6:20–21, 26; Ps. 24:3; Isa. 18:7; 60:13; Jer. 27:22; Ezek. 43:7). The choice of this word here in 2 Sam. 7 may stem from the focus on the building of the temple within the context.

[11] In Gen. 2:8 God 'planted' (*nāṭa'*) the garden in Eden. In the Song of Moses, the people sing that Yahweh will 'plant' (*nāṭa'*) them in the mountain of his inheritance (Exod. 15:17). This verb often describes either the initial act of God's placing his people in the land (e.g. Pss 44:3; 80:9; Jer. 2:21; 11:17; 45:4) or the future act of God's planting his people when he restores them from exile (e.g. Jer. 24:6; 32:41; Ezek. 36:36).

Yet within this staggering promise of future blessings just noted is one that is even greater – the covenant promise that Yahweh will establish a father–son relationship with him (2 Sam. 7:14–15).[12] Yahweh promised to be the God of Abraham and his offspring (Gen. 17:8). He referred to Israel as his 'firstborn son' when redeeming them from their Egyptian bondage (Exod. 4:22–23). In his covenant with Israel God promised: 'I will walk among you and will be your God, and you shall be my people' (Lev. 26:12). But this promise to a Davidic descendant transcends even those lofty blessings; one must go all the way back to Eden to find an analog. As an image-bearer Adam was a son of God, commissioned by God to rule over creation as an extension of God's own rule over the universe.[13] God is now revealing that his original purpose of humanity ruling over creation will be realized through this Davidic descendant who will rule over an eternal kingdom.

The special nature of this promise is further highlighted by what Yahweh says next. This covenant relationship goes well beyond his arrangement with David's predecessor, Saul. When Saul failed to obey the Lord, he took the kingdom away from Saul (1 Sam. 13:13–14; 15:28–29). But when David's offspring sins, God will discipline him but not remove his steadfast love (*ḥesed*) from him.[14] The Lord further stresses the eternal nature of this covenant promise in the following verse, when he twice affirms that the throne of this Davidic descendant will be 'made sure for ever' and 'shall be established for ever' (2 Sam. 7:16).

Just as important, though often overlooked, is David's response (2 Sam. 7:18–29).[15] Perhaps the most striking feature of this response for our purposes is David's repeated references to himself as Yahweh's servant. Ten times in these twelve verses David refers to himself as 'your servant' (*'ebed*) when addressing Yahweh (2 Sam. 7:19, 20, 21, 25, 26, 27 [2×], 28, 29[2×]). At one level these repeated self-descriptions as Yahweh's servant

---

12 Gentry and Wellum (2012: 394–395) note that the chiastic structure of 7:11b–16 highlights this blessing as the pinnacle of the promises, with 7:14–15 being at the centre of the initial statement of the promises (7:11b–13) and their restatement (7:16).

13 On Adam as a son of God, see chapter 2.

14 The parallel account in 1 Chr. 17:13 omits the expression 'When he commits iniquity, I will discipline him with the rod of men, with the stripes of the sons of men' but retains the promise of not removing his steadfast love. Since this account was almost certainly written in exile or perhaps even afterwards, this editorial decision may reflect an intentionally messianic reading of the promise.

15 Bergen (1996: 342) notes that in the Hebrew text vv. 18–29 are 'literarily shaped so as to make David's response as thematically important as the divine words themselves'.

are an expression of David's humility at the staggering nature of the promises being made to him. And it is also true that kings in the ancient Near East often referred to themselves as the servant of a deity. But the context of 2 Samuel 7 and the larger biblical narrative suggest David has more in mind than mere humility or formality. The repeated self-designation as Yahweh's servant suggests that David understands himself to be in the line of key figures in redemptive history before him such as Adam, Abraham, Moses and Joshua. A second notable feature of this prayer is David repeatedly addressing God as 'Lord Yahweh' (*'ădōnāy yĕhwih*).[16] To this point in the biblical narrative this collocation is rare, occurring a mere nine times (Gen. 15:2, 8; Exod. 23:17; 34:23; Deut. 3:24; 9:26; Josh. 7:7; Judg. 6:22; 16:28); David uses it seven times in this prayer (2 Sam. 7:18, 19 [2×], 20, 22, 28, 29).[17] The fact that this significant title for God appears on the lips of key figures such as Abraham (Gen. 15:2, 8), Moses (Deut. 3:24; 9:26), Joshua (Josh. 7:7), Gideon (Judg. 6:22) and Samson (Judg. 16:28) further suggests that David understands himself to be a key figure within salvation history.[18]

A closer look at the content of David's prayer bears this observation out. David begins by expressing his wonder at the promises God has made to him (2 Sam. 7:18–21). He marvels at what God has done for him so far, while at the same time acknowledging that 'this was a small thing in your eyes' (2 Sam. 7:18–19). According to David, Yahweh's promise of building a house (i.e. dynasty) for him is (woodenly translated) 'torah of humanity' (*tôrat hā'ādām*). As Walt Kaiser has argued, this expression is best understood as 'charter for humanity'.[19] Understood this way, David understands that God's covenant promises to him are not merely for his own benefit or even the benefit of Israel. God's purpose is to bless all humanity through this covenant with his servant David, and in doing so fulfil his promises to Abraham and bring to realization his original purpose of humanity

[16] The importance of this title is helpfully noted by ibid. 343–344.

[17] Overall in the OT, this expression occurs 309×, with most occurrences in the major prophets Isaiah (31×), Jeremiah (14×) and Ezekiel (231×).

[18] Several uses of this title occur at key points in redemptive history: Abraham querying God about the fulfilment of his promise and being counted righteous because of his faith (Gen. 15:2, 8); Moses interceding for Israel in the aftermath of the golden calf (Deut. 9:26); Joshua crying out for understanding after Israel's defeat at Ai (Josh. 7:7). The link to Abraham's conversation with Yahweh seems especially significant in the light of the connections between God's covenant promises to Abraham and the covenant promises he is making to David (noted above).

[19] See Kaiser 1974: 310–315.

ruling over creation under his authority. Yahweh has 'known' (i.e. chosen) David and revealed his heart/will to him so that David will 'know' (i.e. experience) Yahweh's greatness (2 Sam. 7:20–21).[20] Because David now has an even deeper experience of Yahweh's greatness through this covenant promise, he confesses the unique greatness of the Lord (2 Sam. 7:22). Part of what makes Yahweh so uniquely great are the 'great and awesome things' he did to redeem Israel from Egypt to be his own people (2 Sam. 7:23–24). He did this not only to make Israel his people, but even more significantly to make a name for himself. David sees the covenant promises to him and his offspring as the next phase in redemptive history, beginning with the commission to Adam/humanity, progressing through the covenant promises made to Abraham on through God's work of redemption through the exodus.

In the light of God's unique greatness revealed in both history and the covenant promises he has just received, David asks Yahweh to confirm (i.e. fulfil) them (2 Sam. 7:25–29). Just like God's servant Moses before him – who prayed for God to forgive Israel and keep his promises to his servants Abraham, Isaac and Jacob for the sake of Yahweh's reputation among the nations (Exod. 32:11–13) – so now David the servant prays for God to fulfil these covenant promises to him so that Yahweh's name 'will be magnified for ever' (2 Sam. 7:26). The glory of Yahweh's name will be seen in his relationship with Israel and in particular the establishment of David's house for ever (2 Sam. 7:26–27a). Indeed, it is on the basis of who God is and the staggering nature of the promises that David prays for God to fulfil them (2 Sam. 7:27b–29).

This brief survey of God's covenant promises to David and his response leave little doubt that Yahweh raises David up as his next servant in the line of men such as Adam, Moses and Joshua before him, and that David saw himself as such.

The singing servant

As the servant of Yahweh, David wrote a large number of psalms. In two of those psalms David is identified as the servant of Yahweh in the superscription. Psalm 18, which is taken nearly word for word from 2 Samuel 22,

20 Bergen (1996: 343) suggests that David's reference to Yahweh's promise at the beginning of v. 21 may hearken back to Gen. 49:10, where God promised: 'The scepter shall not depart from Judah'.

is in essence David's celebration song for Yahweh defeating his enemies. In the context of 2 Samuel the psalm functions as a summary statement of David's praise for numerous victories as the anointed servant king. The superscription of Psalm 18 makes this more explicit by referring to this as 'a psalm of David, the servant of the LORD' (Ps. 18:1). The psalm concludes with a reference to the steadfast love that Yahweh shows 'to his anointed, / to David and his offspring for ever' (Ps. 18:50), a clear allusion to the covenant made in 2 Samuel 7. Psalm 36 also identifies its author as 'David, the servant of the LORD' (Ps. 36:1). Although this psalm is less explicit about David's role as king, he does make repeated mention of Yahweh's steadfast love shown not only to him, but to creation (36:5), humanity in general (36:7) and his covenant people (36:10).

Even more significant are the number of psalms written by David in which he refers to himself as a servant of the Lord. Broadly speaking these references fall into three categories. The first is in connection with sin, whether it is a warning about its dangers (19:11), a prayer to be kept from it (19:13) or not to be judged for it (143:2). A second category is in prayers that Yahweh will not turn away or hide his face from his servant (27:9; 69:17). A third category is those places where David requests or give thanks for deliverance from danger or enemies (31:16; 34:22; 35:27; 86:2, 4, 16; 143:12; 144:10). Each of these categories has their roots in the covenant promises of 2 Samuel 7. God warned that when a Davidic king committed iniquity he would 'discipline him with the rod of men, with the stripes of the sons of men' (2 Sam. 7:14). The prayers for God not to hide his face connect to his promise of his presence with David his servant (2 Sam. 7:9). God's promise to give David rest from all his enemies (2 Sam. 7:11) undergirds David's requests and thanksgiving for deliverance from his foes. These repeated self-references as the servant of Yahweh make it clear that David understood himself to be a servant who played a key role in God's redemptive plans.

This conclusion is further bolstered by other psalms written by David where he does not refer to himself as a servant of the Lord, but clearly articulates an understanding of his own role within redemptive history. The starting point is Psalm 2, which, although not explicitly ascribed to David, is attributed to David in Acts 4:25.[21] The psalm vividly portrays

---

[21] Together Pss 1 – 2 introduce the entire collection, setting both their theological foundation and the eschatological trajectory; see further Cole 2013; Robertson 2015: 53–61.

human rebellion against the Lord and his anointed, as the nations and their kings plot to overthrow their authority (Ps. 2:1–3). Such rebellion is no genuine threat to Yahweh's rule because he has installed his king on Zion (Ps. 2:4–6). Yahweh's anointed king then announces what the Lord has said to him: he is Yahweh's son who has been given the nations as an inheritance and will crush all opposition from his enemies (Ps. 2:7–9). The psalm closes with a warning and a call to the kings of the earth to take refuge in the Son by serving the Lord with fear and submitting to the rule of his anointed royal son (Ps. 2:10–12).

The theological foundations of this psalm are clearly rooted in Genesis 1 – 3 and 2 Samuel 7. The rebellion of these nations and their rulers has its origins in Adam's sin in the garden, and manifests itself throughout human history, including in the life and reign of David. The royal son whom Yahweh appoints to rule over the nations and decisively defeat his enemies is rooted in the Adamic commission to rule over creation and subdue it, as well as in his promise of serpent-crusher who will obey where Adam failed. The promise to David gives more specific shape to these promises, identifying the royal son as one who will come from David's line and rule over an eternal kingdom. Thus, the theological framework of this psalm demonstrates that David understood himself to have a pivotal role in God's plan for creation stretching back all the way to the garden and finding particular expression in the covenant promises God had made to him.

Psalm 8 bears this conclusion out further. It is bracketed with the refrain 'O LORD, our Lord, / how majestic is your name in all the earth!' (Ps. 8:1a, 9). David extols the wonders of creation, from the heavens above to the creation of humanity (Ps. 8:1b–2). Given humanity's 'smallness' in comparison to the vastness of the heavens, David marvels that God even bothers to pay attention to humanity (Ps. 8:3–4). But not only does Yahweh pay attention to humanity; he has made them only slightly lower than God and given them the honour of ruling over creation (Ps. 8:5–8).[22] David is doing more here than merely reflecting on God's commission to Adam in

22 In Ps. 8:5 it is unclear whether God has made humanity a little lower than 'the heavenly beings' (ESVUK, NIV; KJV; cf. LXX 'angels' [*angelous*]) or 'God' (CSB; NASB). The Hebrew word *'ĕlōhîm* regularly refers to the God of Israel, but can also refer to gods (as in the gods of the nations) or angelic beings; see the range of uses in *HALOT* s.v. *'ĕlōhîm*. Given that *'ĕlōhîm* does not frequently refer to angels and that David is clearly alluding to Gen. 1:26, rendering it 'God' here in Ps. 8:5 seems preferable; see similarly Goldingay 2006: 159; Ross 2011: 296. But further complicating matters is that Heb. 2:7 quotes this text and follows the LXX in rendering it 'angels'; see further Kidner 2008: 84–85.

Genesis 1: he is doing so as the one through whom God has promised to bring the king who will finally realize Adam's original commission to rule over creation and bring glory to the divine name as the perfect image-bearer.

A final indication of David's self-understanding as a servant in God's redemptive purposes is Psalm 110. It begins with Yahweh saying to David's Lord 'Sit at my right hand, / until I make your enemies your footstool' (Ps. 110:1), which is followed by another command: 'Rule in the midst of your enemies!' (Ps. 110:2). After confidently asserting that God's people will freely offer themselves in service to David's Lord (Ps. 110:3), he explains that Yahweh has sworn to his Lord 'You are a priest for ever / after the order of Melchizedek' (Ps. 110:4). David then expresses his confidence that his Lord will shatter his enemies in such a decisive way that he will be able to drink from the brook of water along the way (Ps. 110:5–7).

As with the previous two psalms, the connections to Genesis 1 – 3 and 2 Samuel 7 are evident. The command to rule over his enemies echoes the Adamic commission to rule over and subdue creation, while at the same time resonates with the promise of a serpent-crusher who will obey where Adam failed. The fact that David refers to this figure as his Lord suggests that he has in view the promised descendant from his line who will rule over an eternal kingdom. The assertion that this promised king will also be 'a priest for ever after the order of Melchizedek' further reflects a background in Genesis 1 – 2, where Adam was commissioned not merely as a king but consecrated as a priest.

A final line of evidence from the Psalms comes from places where authors other than David refer to him as Yahweh's servant.[23] In most cases, the reference to David as a servant of the Lord comes in the context of reciting redemptive history. For example, Psalm 78 recounts Israel's story, beginning with God's covenant at Sinai. It culminates with the assertion:

He chose David his servant
  and took him from the sheepfolds;

[23] In passing, it should be noted that other figures besides David are referred to as servants of the Lord in the specialized sense being discussed here. For example, Ps. 105 – which recounts Israel's history from God's covenant with Abraham through their possession of the land – contains references to Abraham as Yahweh's servant near the beginning (105:6) and the end (105:42), with a mention of Moses the servant of the Lord in the middle (105:26).

from following the nursing ewes he brought him
to shepherd Jacob his people,
Israel his inheritance.
With upright heart he shepherded them
and guided them with his skilful hand.
(Ps. 78:70–72)

David's identity as the servant also forms the basis of pleas for God not to abandon his people, as seen in Psalm 132:10:

For the sake of your servant David,
do not turn away the face of your anointed one.
(Ps. 132:10)

But by far Psalm 89 is the most developed example of a retelling of redemptive history that situates God's covenant promises to David his servant within the larger scope of God's purposes for creation. The psalmist (Ethan the Ezrahite) begins by announcing his intent to sing of Yahweh's steadfast love and faithfulness (Ps. 89:1–2). The specific expression of these foundational attributes of God is the covenant Yahweh made with 'David my servant' (Ps. 89:3–4). The scene then shifts to the heavenly realm, where Yahweh's faithfulness exalts him above all other angelic creatures (Ps. 89:5–8). Yahweh's uniqueness is then extolled through his work in creation, with emphasis on his power to bring order from chaos and the steadfast love and faithfulness that go before him (Ps. 89:9–14). After extolling the blessedness of Israel because they are the people of God (Ps. 89:15–18), the psalmist returns to the Davidic covenant promises at length (Ps. 89:19–37). This section is worth quoting in full:

Of old you spoke in a vision to your godly one, and said:
'I have granted help to one who is mighty;
I have exalted one chosen from the people.
I have found David, my servant;
with my holy oil I have anointed him,
so that my hand shall be established with him;
my arm also shall strengthen him.
The enemy shall not outwit him;
the wicked shall not humble him.

I will crush his foes before him
  and strike down those who hate him.
My faithfulness and my steadfast love shall be with him,
  and in my name shall his horn be exalted.
I will set his hand on the sea
  and his right hand on the rivers.
He shall cry to me, 'You are my Father,
  my God, and the Rock of my salvation.'
And I will make him the firstborn,
  the highest of the kings of the earth.
My steadfast love I will keep for him for ever,
  and my covenant will stand firm for him.
I will establish his offspring for ever
  and his throne as the days of the heavens.
If his children forsake my law
  and do not walk according to my rules,
if they violate my statutes
  and do not keep my commandments,
then I will punish their transgression with the rod
  and their iniquity with stripes,
but I will not remove from him my steadfast love
  or be false to my faithfulness.
I will not violate my covenant
  or alter the word that went forth from my lips.
Once for all I have sworn by my holiness;
  I will not lie to David.
His offspring shall endure for ever,
  his throne as long as the sun before me.
Like the moon it shall be established for ever,
  a faithful witness in the skies.' *Selah*

Within this reflection Yahweh's steadfast love and faithfulness remain central. The starting point for this reflection is God's choice of David from among the people to be his servant (Ps. 89:19–20). The stated purpose of God choosing David as the servant is 'so that my hand shall be established with him; / my arm also shall strengthen him' (Ps. 89:21).[24] The parallelism

[24] V. 21 (MT v. 22) begins with the Hebrew particle *'ăšer*, which here indicates purpose; on this usage see BDB s.v. *'ăšer* 8.b.

of hand and arm echoes verse 10, where similar language describes Yahweh's work in creation. The promise that 'the enemy shall not outwit him; / the wicked shall not humble him' (Ps. 89:22) can plausibly be seen as a reversal of what happened in the garden, where the serpent outwitted Adam and brought him into a state of humiliation.[25] Just as Yahweh's steadfast love and faithfulness were expressed in his work in creation (Ps. 89:9–14), so too they are inseparably bound to his covenant promises to David (Ps. 89:24). In promising to extend David's rule the psalmist describes the span of that authority as being from the sea to the rivers (Ps. 89:25), which is a modified form of Adam's commission to rule over creation. Given the close connection between being made in the image of God and being a son of God we have already noted, the Davidic king crying out to God 'You are my Father, / my God, and the Rock of my salvation' (Ps. 89:26) can be understood as an affirmation that through this covenant God will accomplish his purpose of an image-bearing son who accomplishes the Adamic reign over creation. This reign of this Davidic king will be so extensive that he will be 'the firstborn, / the highest of the kings of the earth' (Ps. 89:27). The fulfilment of this covenant is certain, as it rests on Yahweh's steadfast love and faithfulness (Ps. 89:28). The command to be fruitful and multiply and fill the earth (Gen. 1:28) as well as the promise to multiply Abraham's offspring (Gen. 12:1–3) finds its fulfilment in the promise to establish David's 'offspring for ever, / and his throne as the days of the heavens' (Ps. 89:29). Even when David's descendants are unfaithful, Yahweh will punish but not ultimately remove his steadfast love and faithfulness from them (Ps. 89:30–34). By comparing the certainty and duration of this covenant to the permanence of the sun and moon the psalmist further connects the Davidic covenant with God's purposes for creation (Ps. 89:35–37). In the light of these covenant promises, Ethan the Ezrahite spends the rest of the psalm trying to reconcile the certainty of these promises with his experience of God's judgment being poured out on Israel (Ps. 89:38–52).

So, regardless of whether it is the psalms of David himself or those written by others, it is clear from the Psalms that David understood himself to be the new servant of Yahweh, raised up with a special role in

---

25 Further confirmation of a reversal of Eden may be found in v. 23, where God promises to 'crush' (*kātat*) David's foes before him. Although using a different verb, God promised a descendant from the line of Eve who would 'bruise' (*šûp*) the serpent's head.

God's redemptive plan stretching from Eden to the promise to Abraham and now taking even more specific shape in God's covenant promises to David and his offspring.

Solomon the servant's son

In a very clear sense the covenant promises to David find their initial and partial fulfilment in his son Solomon. This conclusion becomes apparent when Yahweh appears to Solomon shortly after 'the kingdom was established in the hand of Solomon' (1 Kgs 2:46b). Yahweh appears to Solomon and invites him to ask for whatever he wants (1 Kgs 3:5). Solomon's response is worth quoting in full:

> You have shown great and steadfast love to your *servant* David my father, because he walked before you in faithfulness, in righteousness, and in uprightness of heart towards you. And you have kept for him this great and steadfast love and have given him a son to sit on his throne this day. And now, O Lord my God, you have made your *servant* king in place of David my father, although I am but a little child. I do not know how to go out or come in. And your *servant* is in the midst of your people whom you have chosen, a great people, too many to be numbered or counted for multitude. Give your *servant* therefore an understanding mind to govern your people, that I may discern between good and evil, for who is able to govern this your great people?
> (1 Kgs 3:6–9)

Solomon begins by referring to his father David as the servant of the Lord, connecting this identity with Yahweh's steadfast love and the covenant promise (1 Kgs 3:6). Because Solomon sees his reign as an initial fulfilment of that promise, he refers to himself as 'your servant' in addressing the Lord in prayer (1 Kgs 3:7). He repeats this title in the very next verse as he juxtaposes his identity as servant with the great multitude of the people of Israel (note again the echoes of God's promise to Abraham in Gen. 12:1–3). When Solomon finally makes his request of the Lord, yet again he refers to himself as the Lord's servant in order to govern the people of God wisely (1 Kgs 3:8). Such wisdom is necessary because he is in the midst of God's chosen people, whom he has multiplied beyond number (cf. Gen. 15:5). Notice the specific wording of Solomon's request: he asks for an understanding mind 'that I may discern between good and evil' (1 Kgs 3:9). The echoes of Genesis 3 are unmistakable. The serpent tempted Eve with the prospect of 'knowing good and evil'; that is, determining for herself good and evil rather than relying upon God's own declaration (Gen. 3:5). Solomon is asking for wisdom so that he does not repeat Adam's failure as he attempts to live out the modified version of Adam's commission contained within God's covenant promises to David.

After the Lord grants Solomon's request – along with the additional blessings of wealth, long life and victory over his enemies – for wisdom (1 Kgs 3:10–15), the text provides several initial examples of these blessings on display in Solomon's life, with a particular emphasis on wisdom (1 Kgs 3:16 – 4:34). He settles a challenging dispute between two mothers (1 Kgs 3:16–28) and establishes administrative structures to govern his kingdom (1 Kgs 4:1–19, 22–28). His reign becomes so successful that God's people 'were as many as the sand by the sea' and exercised dominion over nations stretching from the Euphrates to the Mediterranean Sea (1 Kgs 4:20–21), which is a partial fulfilment of God's promise to Abraham of numerous offspring and possessing the gates of his enemies (Gen. 22:17–18). These examples culminate in this summary paragraph:

> And God gave Solomon wisdom and understanding beyond measure, and breadth of mind like the sand on the seashore, so that Solomon's wisdom surpassed the wisdom of all the people of the east and all the wisdom of Egypt. For he was wiser than all other men, wiser than Ethan the Ezrahite, and Heman, Calcol, and Darda, the sons of Mahol, and his fame was in all the surrounding nations. He also spoke 3,000 proverbs, and his songs were 1,005. He spoke of trees, from the cedar that is in Lebanon to the hyssop that grows out of the wall. He spoke also of beasts, and of birds, and of reptiles, and of fish. And people of all nations came to hear the wisdom of Solomon, and from all the kings of the earth, who had heard of his wisdom.
> (1 Kgs 4:29–34)

Language that previously described the people of God is now applied to Solomon's wisdom ('like the sand on the seashore'). His wisdom extends to the natural world, echoing language from the creation account in

Genesis 1. People and kings from all the nations stream to hear his wisdom. As the new servant Solomon is exercising an Adamic role over creation, as he is being fruitful, multiplying, ruling over and subduing the Promised Land and expanding that authority into the surrounding regions.

Just as in Genesis the Adamic commissioning (Gen. 1) is followed by the creation of Yahweh's garden sanctuary (Gen. 2), so here in 1 Kings the building of the temple follows Solomon's Adamic rule. After a lengthy section detailing the construction of the temple (1 Kgs 5:1 – 7:51), complete with Edenic imagery,[26] Solomon dedicates the temple by bringing the ark of the covenant into it (1 Kgs 8:1–11). He then pronounces a blessing in which he attributes the completion of the temple as God fulfilling his promise to David his father, while at the same time portraying this temple as the culmination of God bringing his people out of slavery in Egypt (1 Kgs 8:12–21).

What follows is a lengthy prayer of dedication, peppered with references to different servants of the Lord (1 Kgs 8:22–53). Solomon begins by praising Yahweh's uniqueness as the one 'keeping covenant and showing steadfast love to your servants who walk before you with all their heart' (1 Kgs 8:23). Thus, in bringing the temple to completion Yahweh has 'kept with your servant David my father what you declared to him. You spoke with your mouth, and with your hand have fulfilled it this day' (1 Kgs 8:24). Based on the fulfilment of this promise, Solomon now asks 'keep for your servant David my father what you have promised him' in regard to not lacking a man to sit on his throne (1 Kgs 8:25), and then again asks that God confirm the word he spoke 'to your servant David my father' (1 Kgs 8:26).

In the next section of his prayer Solomon transitions from Yahweh's faithfulness to his servant David to asking the Lord to listen to his prayer as the new servant. After acknowledging that no structure can contain the presence of God (1 Kgs 8:27), Solomon nonetheless asks:

> Yet have regard to the prayer of your *servant* and to his plea, O Lord my God, listening to the cry and to the prayer that your *servant* prays before you this day, that your eyes may be open night and day towards this house, the place of which you have said, 'My name

[26] On the Edenic imagery of the temple, see especially Beale 2004: 66–80.

> shall be there', that you may listen to the prayer that your *servant* offers towards this place. And listen to the plea of your *servant* and of your people Israel, when they pray towards this place. And listen in heaven your dwelling place, and when you hear, forgive.
> (1 Kgs 8:28–30)

Four times in this brief paragraph Solomon refers to himself as Yahweh's servant. As the new servant following in the footsteps of his father David, the servant of the Lord, Solomon understands he has been raised up by God to play a key role in redemptive history. By offering this prayer Solomon is acting not merely as a king, but also in a priestly fashion, mirroring Adam's royal and priestly role in the garden. This dual role as king and priest was also anticipated in Psalm 110, where David foresaw a descendant of his who would be both his Lord and a priest in the line of Melchizedek (Ps. 110:1–4).

After a series of petitions for God to fulfil his promises to Israel, bless the nations and magnify his name (1 Kgs 8:31–51), Solomon concludes his prayer as follows:

> Let your eyes be open to the plea of your *servant* and to the plea of your people Israel, giving ear to them whenever they call to you. For you separated them from among all the peoples of the earth to be your heritage, as you declared through Moses your *servant*, when you brought our fathers out of Egypt, O Lord God.
> (1 Kgs 8:52–53)

As the new servant, Solomon pleads with God to hear the prayers of his people whom he has chosen as his heritage from among all the peoples of the earth. He roots this statement in what Yahweh himself declared to his servant Moses. In the benediction that follows (1 Kgs 8:54–61), Solomon asserts that Yahweh has given rest to his people (note again the echoes of previous promises to Israel!) and that 'Not one word has failed of all his good promise, which he spoke by Moses his servant' (1 Kgs 8:56). By echoing the words of Joshua 21:45 and 23:14, and calling Moses the servant of Yahweh, Solomon makes it clear he sees himself as the new servant of the Lord bringing to fulfilment what God promised the previous servants Adam, Moses, Joshua and his father David. He concludes the benediction by once again affirming his identity as Yahweh's servant:

> Let these words of mine, with which I have pleaded before the LORD, be near to the LORD our God day and night, and may he maintain the cause of his *servant* and the cause of his people Israel, as each day requires, that all the peoples of the earth may know that the LORD is God; there is no other. Let your heart therefore be wholly true to the LORD our God, walking in his statutes and keeping his commandments, as at this day.
> (1 Kgs 8:59–61)

Solomon links Yahweh's blessing of him as the servant with maintaining and advancing not only the cause of Israel, but also the glory of Yahweh among the nations. Solomon understands that as the servant God is working through him to fulfil his promises to Abraham's offspring and magnify Yahweh's glory among the nations as a divine image-bearer exercising dominion over the nations just as Adam was commanded to do. He also seems to understand that through him God is creating a servant people, as twice in his lengthy prayer he refers to Israel as Yahweh's servants (1 Kgs 8:32, 36).

After describing the staggering number of sacrifices offered to the Lord (1 Kgs 8:62–65), the account of Solomon's temple dedication concludes by noting the seven-day feast commemorating the event (1 Kgs 8:65). On the eighth day the people return to their homes 'joyful and glad of heart for all the goodness that the LORD had shown to David his servant and to Israel his people' (1 Kgs 8:66). The author leaves no doubt that the work of Solomon the servant is rooted in God's faithfulness to David the servant, which in turn stemmed from his faithfulness to Moses the servant.

Unfortunately, despite this strong start, Solomon the servant ultimately fails. He 'loved many foreign women' who turned his heart away from the Lord; as a result, he builds high places for the gods of his foreign wives (1 Kgs 11:1–8). Thus, in an ironic twist, the Lord says: 'Since this has been your practice and you have not kept my covenant and my statutes that I have commanded you, I will surely tear the kingdom from you and will give it to your servant' (1 Kgs 11:11). The servant of the Lord will have his kingdom given to one of his own servants. But Solomon's failure will not nullify God's covenant promise to his father, David, as the Lord promises: 'I will not tear away all the kingdom, but I will give one tribe to your son, for the sake of David my *servant* and for the sake of Jerusalem, which I have chosen' (1 Kgs 11:13). Yahweh makes similar statements through the prophet

Ahijah to Jeroboam, telling him that he will tear the kingdom from Solomon's hands but leave him one tribe 'for the sake of my servant David' (1 Kgs 11:32, 34, 36). The Lord also promises Jeroboam that if he walks in obedience 'as David my servant did, I will be with you and will build you a sure house, as I built for David, and I will give Israel to you' (1 Kgs 11:38).

These promises provide a natural transition to consider how David's identity as the servant of the Lord continues to play an important role in the unfolding of God's creational and redemptive purposes well beyond the deaths of both David and Solomon.

The eschatological hope in David the servant

David as the servant of the Lord casts a long shadow extending throughout the remainder of the Old Testament. This shadow takes a variety of different shapes.

The pattern of faithfulness for kings

As we have already seen in God's instructions to Jeroboam, David the servant becomes a paradigm for how a king should obey the commands and statutes of the Lord (1 Kgs 11:38). When Jeroboam fails to walk in obedience to the Lord, the prophet Ahijah returns with a message from the Lord rebuking him for not being 'like my servant David, who kept my commandments and followed me with all his heart, doing only that which was right in my eyes' (1 Kgs 14:8). Such a sweeping statement may seem surprising, given David's adultery with Bathsheba and the murder of her husband Uriah (2 Sam. 11:1–26). Perhaps recognizing this, the author of 1 Kings later acknowledges this, noting that 'David did what was right in the eyes of the LORD and did not turn aside from anything that he commanded him all the days of his life, except in the matter of Uriah the Hittite' (1 Kgs 15:5). As the history of both Israel and Judah unfolds, the character and actions of the various kings are regularly compared to the standard set by David,[27] though he is rarely explicitly referred to as the servant of the Lord. Presenting David as the paradigm of faithfulness

[27] Among the kings of Israel only Jeroboam is compared to the standard set by David (1 Kgs 14:8). Six kings of Judah are compared to David: Abijam (1 Kgs 15:3–5), Asa (1 Kgs 15:11), Amaziah (2 Kgs 14:3), Ahaz (2 Kgs 16:2), Hezekiah (2 Kgs 18:3) and Josiah (2 Kgs 22:2). All but one of these kings of Judah are 'good' kings.

for subsequent kings makes sense in the light of God's covenant promises of building David a house (2 Sam. 7:11).

The reason God will not destroy Judah/ Jerusalem

More prominent than David the servant as the paradigm for subsequent kings is the repeated promise not to destroy utterly the kingdom or Jerusalem based on David's identity as the servant. We have already seen the initial example of this in 1 Kings 11, where, in the midst of announcing the split of the nation and the appointing of Jeroboam over the northern kingdom, Yahweh insists four times he will not utterly do away with the line of David or destroy Jerusalem because of his servant David (vv. 13, 32, 34, 36).

Similar statements become more frequent as both Israel and Judah (along with their kings) spiral further downward into idolatry and covenant unfaithfulness. Despite the fact that King Jehoram of Judah:

> walked in the way of the kings of Israel . . . Yet the Lord was not willing to destroy Judah, for the sake of David his servant, since he promised to give a lamp to him and to his sons for ever.
> (2 Kgs 8:18–19)

In 702 BC, when the Assyrians threatened to conquer Judah and Jerusalem (2 Kgs 18:13 – 19:13), King Hezekiah prayed for God to save them from the hand of the Assyrians (2 Kgs 19:14–19). Through the prophet Isaiah, Yahweh announces that he will turn away the Assyrians (2 Kgs 19:20–33); indeed, they will not even enter the city of Jerusalem because 'I will defend this city to save it, for my own sake and for the sake of my servant David' (2 Kgs 19:34; cf. the parallel account in Isa. 37:35). In the very next chapter God promises both to heal Hezekiah of his illness and deliver Judah from the hand of the Assyrians 'for my own sake and for my servant David's sake' (2 Kgs 20:6).

The fulfilment of God's promises

Not only is David the servant a paradigm of faithfulness for future kings and the reason God refuses to destroy Jerusalem. Fulfilling the covenant promises made to David the servant is central to the eschatological hope of the prophets.

The place to begin is Jeremiah.[28] In the midst of the moral decay infesting Judah in the decades leading up to their exile, God promises that exile will not be the final word:

> Behold, the days are coming, declares the LORD, when I will raise up for David a righteous Branch, and he shall reign as king and deal wisely, and shall execute justice and righteousness in the land. In his days Judah will be saved, and Israel will dwell securely. And this is the name by which he will be called: 'The LORD is our righteousness.' (Jer. 23:5–6)

God will fulfil his covenant promises to David by raising up one of his descendants to exercise an Adamic dominion and allow his people to dwell securely in the land. Yahweh will magnify the name of this Davidic king along with his own name by calling him 'Yahweh is our righteousness.'

God fulfilling his promises to David his servant also plays a prominent role in the so-called Book of Comfort (Jer. 30 – 33). As part of restoring the fortunes of his people God insists that instead of his people serving foreigners, the foreigners 'shall serve the LORD their God and David their king, whom I will raise up for them' (Jer. 30:9). Central to this restoration will be the cutting of a new covenant in which God's law will be written on the hearts of his people, every member of the covenant community will know the Lord, and sin will be fully and finally forgiven (Jer. 31:31–34). As part of this new and everlasting covenant God will plant his people in the land and give them a united heart to fear him so they do not turn away from him (Jer. 32:36 – 33:13).

This new/everlasting covenant and the covenant promises to David converge in the culminating passage of the Book of Comfort (Jer. 33:14–26). Repeating language from Jeremiah 23:5–6, the Lord promises to raise up a righteous branch for David who will rule in righteousness and bring peace and security to Jerusalem (Jer. 33:14–16).[29] David will never lack a descendant to sit on the throne (Jer. 33:17–18). The fulfilment of these promises is so certain that Yahweh swears:

---

[28] The references to David in Isaiah will be dealt with in the following chapter.

[29] Whereas in Jer. 23:5–6 it is this king who is given the name 'The LORD is our righteousness', here in Jer. 33:16 it is the city (which figuratively refers to the restored people of God) that is given this title. This is a vivid picture of imputation in that the righteousness of the king is transferred to the people.

> If you can break my covenant with the day and my covenant with the night, so that day and night will not come at their appointed time, then also my covenant with David my *servant* may be broken, so that he shall not have a son to reign on his throne, and my covenant with the Levitical priests my ministers. As the host of heaven cannot be numbered and the sands of the sea cannot be measured, so I will multiply the offspring of David my *servant*, and the Levitical priests who minister to me.
> (Jer. 33:20–22)

The connection between God's covenant with creation and his covenant with David is no mere analogy, as the covenant promises to his servant David will be the means by which God fulfils his purposes for creation. As Gentry and Wellum note:

> There is an emphasis in Jeremiah 33:12–26 on the notion of servanthood, indicated by the Hebrew terms עֶבֶד ('servant') and מְשָׁרֵת ('minister'). David is called the servant of Yahweh in verses 21 and 22, and the Levites are described by the parallel term, ministers of God. In a way reminiscent of the servant, singular, becoming the servants, plural, in the last part of Isaiah, verse 22 says that the 'seed,' i.e., descendants, of David and the Levites, will be countless, and the language used is that of the Abrahamic covenant – the stars of the sky and the sand on the seashore.[30]

God's promise to make Abraham's offspring as numerous as the sand of the sea (Gen. 22:17–18) finds its fulfilment in multiplying the offspring of David the servant of the Lord. Indeed, this new/everlasting covenant will bring to realization all the promises made to the offspring of David as well as the offspring of Abraham, Isaac, and Jacob (Jer. 33:26). Through this new and everlasting covenant God will accomplish his original creational purpose of humanity ruling over creation under his universal authority.

The fulfilment of God's covenant promises to David his servant also plays a prominent role in Ezekiel. After condemning the wicked shepherds of Ezekiel's day (Ezek. 34:1–10), the Lord promises to seek out his scattered

[30] Gentry and Wellum 2012: 528.

sheep, restore and shepherd them (Ezek. 34:11–24). Notice the means by which he will do so:

> And I will set up over them one shepherd, my *servant* David, and he shall feed them: he shall feed them and be their shepherd. And I, the LORD, will be their God, and my *servant* David shall be prince among them. I am the LORD; I have spoken.
> (Ezek. 34:23–24)

In connection with this restoration Yahweh promises to establish with his redeemed people 'a covenant of peace' in which even creation itself will be transformed, as they dwell securely in the land (Ezek. 34:25–29). God's people will be a blessing to the nations and even creation itself (Ezek. 34:26; cf. Gen. 12:1–3). Most significantly, 'they shall know that I am the LORD their God with them, and that they, the house of Israel, are my people, declares the Lord GOD' (Ezek. 34:30).

The nature of this new/everlasting covenant of peace is further described in Ezekiel 36 – 37. God will cleanse his people of their sin and remove their heart of stone to give them a new heart of flesh and a new spirit (Ezek. 36:25–26). Yahweh will even put his own Spirit inside them to cause them to walk in obedience to his ways (Ezek. 36:27). He will plant them securely in the land and dwell with them as their God (Ezek. 36:28). In an act of new creation he will raise his people from the dead and settle them in the land (Ezek. 37:1–14). The Lord will reunite Judah and Israel into one nation with one king ruling over them (Ezek. 37:15–23). All these various threads come together in the culminating paragraph:

> My *servant* David shall be king over them, and they shall all have one shepherd. They shall walk in my rules and be careful to obey my statutes. They shall dwell in the land that I gave to my *servant* Jacob, where your fathers lived. They and their children and their children's children shall dwell there for ever, and David my *servant* shall be their prince for ever. I will make a covenant of peace with them. It shall be an everlasting covenant with them. And I will set them in their land and multiply them, and will set my sanctuary in their midst for evermore. My dwelling place shall be with them, and I will be their God, and they shall be my people. Then the nations will

> know that I am the Lord who sanctifies Israel, when my sanctuary is in their midst for evermore.
> (Ezek. 37:24–28)

God fulfilling his promises to his servant David will be the culmination of his creational and redemptive purposes and result in an everlasting covenant of peace. God's people will be multiplied and dwell in a new Eden where God dwells with them for ever. They will be ruled over by a Davidic king whose kingdom will be eternal. The coming of 'my servant David' is the linchpin for the fulfilment of these promises.

This hope of a Davidic servant king remains alive in the post-exilic prophets. In the midst of stirring the returned exiles to proceed with the rebuilding of the temple, God directly addresses Zerubbabel the governor of Judah, promising 'I will take you, O Zerubbabel my servant, the son of Shealtiel, declares the Lord, and make you like a signet ring, for I have chosen you, declares the Lord of hosts' (Hag. 2:23). Although Zerubbabel was not the promised servant king from David's line, he was a Davidic descendant whom God was using as his servant to move forward his purposes by rebuilding the temple.

During the same time frame, the Lord also spoke through the prophet Zechariah. As part of a vision Zechariah sees the high priest Joshua standing before Yahweh (Zech. 3:1–10). After cleansing Joshua of his sins (Zech. 3:1–5), the Lord speaks about the future (Zech. 3:6–10). He promises: 'behold, I will bring my servant the Branch . . . and I will remove the iniquity of this land in a single day' (Zech. 3:8–9). The promise of a Davidic servant king serves as motivation for action in the present for Joshua the high priest and provides hope for the people that the day is coming when the promises of a new covenant will result in the full and final forgiveness of sin.

Conclusion

After centuries without a servant, the Lord raises up David, a man after his own heart, to pick up the mantle of previous servants such as Joshua, Moses and even Adam himself. David is the king who serves the Lord by establishing a kingdom that anticipates the realization of God's creational purposes and the eschatological hopes of God's people.

As with previous servants, we see the threefold nature of David's role as the servant. He is the king through whom God is working to establish his original purpose of humanity ruling over creation under his ultimate authority. He exercises a priestly role making preparations for the building of the temple and leading the people in worship of the Lord. By receiving revelation from God and writing the words of God he functions in a prophetic capacity. As the servant of the Lord, David does all of this in anticipation of the day when one of his own descendants will bring to fulfilment God's creational and redemptive purposes. Through the son of David the servant, God will one day produce a servant people who will have God's law written on their hearts and be empowered by his Spirit to obey.

But no portrait of the servant of the Lord will be complete without an in-depth look at the book of Isaiah, where we find the most extended development of the servant theme in the Old Testament. That is the task for the next chapter.

6
The Isaianic servant: the suffering servant

> Behold, my servant shall act wisely;
> he shall be high and lifted up,
> and shall be exalted.
> (Isa. 52:13)

When most people think about the expression 'servant of the Lord' they tend to think of Isaiah, and in particular Isaiah 53. This is not without warrant, as Isaiah 53 is regarded by many as one of the most significant passages for understanding the identity and work of Jesus.[1] Yet too often discussion of Isaiah 53 (or, more precisely, Isa. 52:13 – 53:12) is isolated from the other servant passages in Isaiah 40 – 55. Furthermore, even when these other servant passages are taken into consideration, too often they are not treated within the larger literary context of Isaiah 40 – 55 or the larger book as a whole. Yet perhaps even more significantly, discussion of the Isaianic servant texts often fails to situate these texts within the larger biblical-theological stream we have been exploring to this point. As a result, the picture of the Isaianic servant is often incomplete.

To see how the servant figure is developed in Isaiah, we will look at the book in its three main sections.[2] Along the way we will see how the Isaianic servant texts incorporate God's promises to and the work of previous individual servants such as Adam, Moses and David. We will

[1] This conclusion is not shared by all, however; see further chapter 7.

[2] By dividing the book in this manner, I am not endorsing the common critical view of three different 'Isaiahs' (First Isaiah [chs 1–39]; Second Isaiah [chs 40–55]; Third Isaiah [chs 56–66]) written at three different time periods. Despite its common currency with academic study of Isaiah, there are good reasons for holding to single authorship by the eighth-century prophet; see e.g. Allis 1950; Margulies 1964; Oswalt 1986: 17–28; Motyer 1993: 25–30; Beale 2008: 123–159.

also see the pattern of God using an individual servant to create a servant people emerge even more clearly.

Servant references in Isaiah 1 – 39

Besides several general references to servants/slaves, there are three individuals that Yahweh refers to as 'my servant' in Isaiah 1 – 39.

The first is the prophet Isaiah himself.[3] The year is 711 BC, and the Assyrians have taken the city of Ashdod (20:1). Yahweh commands Isaiah, '"Go, and loose the sackcloth from your waist and take off your sandals from your feet", and he did so, walking naked and barefoot' (20:2). When the Lord explains to the people Isaiah's actions (20:3–6), Yahweh refers to the prophet as 'my servant Isaiah' (20:3). As the one commissioned by God to announce both judgment and salvation, Isaiah plays a special role in redemptive history.

The second figure identified as a servant of Yahweh is Eliakim. God's judgment is coming on Jerusalem (22:1–25), beginning with the valley of vision (22:1–14) and including the king's steward Shebna (22:15–25). In his arrogance Shebna carved for himself an elaborate tomb (22:15–16), but Yahweh promises a shameful death without burial and removal from his office (22:17–19). In his place the Lord 'will call my servant Eliakim the son of Hilkiah' (22:20) and give him authority and status within the house of David.[4]

The final servant figure is David, in an account that is parallel to 2 Kings 18 – 20. In 701 BC Sennacherib king of Assyria invaded Judah and captured every city but Jerusalem, which he surrounded (36:1–3). Sennacherib's Rabshakeh taunts the people of Jerusalem, warning them not to trust in Yahweh for deliverance from their inevitable destruction (36:4–20). Hezekiah's officials tear their clothes and repeat the words of the Rabshakeh to Hezekiah (36:21–22). Hezekiah tears his own clothes,

---

[3] Throughout the OT the prophets are referred to as servants of Yahweh (e.g. 2 Kgs 14:25; 17:13, 23; 21:10; 24:2; Isa. 20:3; Jer. 7:25; 26:5; 29:19; 35:15; 44:4; Ezek. 38:17; Dan. 9:6, 10, 17; Zech. 1:6).

[4] This text is cited in Rev. 3:7, where the risen Christ is described as the one 'who has the key of David, who opens and no one will shut, who shuts and no one opens'. The point of the citation is to indicate that 'Eliakim's temporary control of the kingdom as "prime minister" to the king of Israel was a prophetic historical pattern pointing forward to Jesus Christ's greater and eternal sovereignty over a greater kingdom' (Beale and Carson 2007: 1096–1097). On this citation see further Beale 1999: 283–285. Matt. 16:19 may also allude to Isa. 22:22.

puts on sackcloth, enters the temple, and sends servants to Isaiah (37:1–4). Isaiah assures Hezekiah that Sennacherib will not take Jerusalem, but return home based on a rumour (37:5–7). When the Rabshakeh reiterates his threat (37:8–13), Hezekiah responds with a prayer for deliverance based on the character and promises of God (37:14–20). Yahweh responds by taunting the Assyrian king and promising to use Sennacherib's own tactics to bring judgment on him (37:21–29). As a sign Yahweh promises that the people will eat the produce of the land and a remnant will be rooted and produce fruit (37:30–32). God's victory over Sennacherib will come without a single arrow fired or a siege mound constructed; he will not even set foot in the city (37:33–34).

Two separate, albeit closely related, reasons are given for defending Jerusalem (37:35). Yahweh is acting 'for my own sake'; in other words, he is protecting his own fame and reputation. The Lord is so closely identified with his people that their fate is inevitably tied to his own glory. But God is also acting 'for the sake of my servant David'. As we saw in the previous chapter, the fulfilment of God's goal to rule over creation through a servant will come through a descendant of David. Yahweh will accomplish his purpose through fulfilling his promise to David.

The servant in Isaiah 40 – 66[5]

Within Isaiah 40 – 66 the servant theme takes on special prominence. While most attention has been paid to the so-called servant songs (42:1–7; 49:1–12; 50:4–9; 52:13 – 53:12),[6] the significance of the servant theme extends well beyond these passages. One cannot understand these key passages properly without seeing how they fit within their larger context. So we will survey Isaiah 40 – 66, pausing at key points to note the

---

[5] The literature on this subject is enormous. For surveys of the various views, see e.g. Rowley 1952; North 1956; Kruse 1978: 3–27; Haag 1985; Janowski and Stuhlmacher 2004. For helpful bibliographies of works dealing with the identity of the servant in Isa. 40 – 66, see Blenkinsopp 2002: 166–174 and Janowski and Stuhlmacher 2004: 462–492. Oswalt (1998) organizes his commentary on Isa. 40 – 66 around the theme of servanthood: the vocation of servanthood (40:1 – 55:13) and the marks of servanthood (56:1 – 66:24); Knight 1984 even titled his commentary on Isa. 40 – 55 *Servant Theology*.

[6] Although I will use the expression 'servant songs' in our discussion of these texts, I will not treat them as isolated texts, an approach that began with Bernhard Duhm (see Duhm 1875 and 1892). Instead, we will explore their meaning within their context; for a similar approach, see North 1956: 156–160; Orlinsky 1967: 12–16; Knight 1984: 2–3; and Lindsey 1985: 1–34.

development of the servant theme and its relationship to other key themes in Isaiah and the rest of the biblical storyline.

The servant who fails (Isa. 40 – 48)

Isaiah 40 opens with God announcing comfort to his people because Yahweh's retribution for Israel's iniquity has been exhausted (40:1–3). God will prepare a way in the wilderness to reveal his glory to all flesh in accordance with his eternal word (40:3–8). God's people are called to announce the good news of Yahweh's powerful and yet compassionate rule (40:9–11), which extends over all creation (40:12–26). Rather than doubt or distrust, God's people must trust in Yahweh as the one who strengthens and sustains them (40:27–31).

Whereas the idolatrous nations must fear the arrival of Yahweh (41:1–7), God's people have been set apart for a special relationship with him (41:8–13). In contrast to these nations, Yahweh addresses his people as follows:

> But you, Israel, *my servant*,
> Jacob, whom I have chosen,
> the offspring of Abraham, my friend;
> you whom I took from the ends of the earth,
> and called from its farthest corners,
> saying to you, 'You are *my servant*,
> I have chosen you and not cast you off.'
> (Isa. 41:8–9)

God's people are described with three parallel monikers, each of which is then given an additional explanatory phrase:[7]

1 Israel, my servant
2 Jacob, whom I have chosen
3 offspring of Abraham, my friend

[7] Similar language is found in Ps. 105:6, where God's people are addressed as 'O offspring of Abraham, his servant, / children of Jacob, his chosen ones!' In fact, the terms *'ebed* and *bāḥar/bāḥîr* commonly occur together in parallelism: 1 Kgs 11:13, 32, 34; 1 Chr. 16:13; Pss 78:70; 89:4; 105:6, 26; Isa. 41:8–9; 42:1; 43:10; 44:1–2; 45:4; 49:7; 65:9, 15; Hag. 2:23 (Berlin and Knorina 2008: 144, n. 3). The roots for 'love' (*'ahab*) and 'choose' (*bāḥar/bāḥîr*) are parallel to each other in Deut. 4:37; 10:15; Pss 47:5 (Eng. 47:4); 78:68. The roots for 'serve/servant' (*'ebed*) and 'love' (*'ahab*) are parallel in Deut. 10:12; 11:13; Josh. 22:5; Ps. 69:37 (Eng. 69:36); Isa. 56:6; Jer. 8:2.

The names appear in reverse chronological order. God promised Abraham offspring as numerous as the stars of heaven and the sand of the seashore (Gen. 15:5; 22:17). Through Abraham's offspring would come the promised offspring of the woman who would crush the serpent's head and reverse the curse on creation (Gen. 3:15). As we have already seen, the Hebrew term for 'offspring' (*zera'*) can refer either to a plurality of descendants (Gen. 17:7–8) or an individual descendant such as Isaac (Gen. 17:19–21); in this context that ambiguity is also present.[8] The title 'offspring of Abraham' is further modified by the expression 'my friend',[9] which although never applied to Abraham in Genesis is found in 2 Chronicles 20:7 and James 2:23. Nonetheless, this term aptly reflects Yahweh's special relationship with Abraham.[10]

The second moniker is Jacob, a reference to Abraham's grandson, through whom God extended the promise to his twelve sons.[11] He is further described as the one whom Yahweh has chosen.[12] This designation has its roots in Genesis 25:19–26, where God announces to Rebekah that the older (Esau) of the twin boys she is pregnant with will serve the younger (Jacob). God regularly reaffirms that choice, repeating to Jacob the promise he made to his grandfather Abraham (Gen. 28:13; 32:9–12). Yahweh even changed Jacob's name to Israel to confirm his commitment to fulfilling the promise (Gen. 35:9–15).

That leads naturally to the final moniker 'Israel'. What began as a new name for the patriarch Jacob (Gen. 32:28; 35:9–15) eventually came to be the name for the nation that descended from him through his twelve sons (Exod. 1:1, 12; 4:22–23). Israel is further described as 'my servant', the first use of this term in Isaiah 40 – 55. This designation is then repeated when Yahweh says to his people:

---

[8] On the one hand, the next line referring to Jacob suggests an individual reference; yet the reference to Israel in the third line suggests a plural reference.

[9] The Hebrew expression rendered 'my friend' (*'ōhăbî*) is the qal participle of the verb that means 'to love' (*'ahab*). While the Hebrew expression could refer to Abraham's love for Yahweh, the parallelism with 'I have chosen' in the previous line along with the rendering of the LXX (which is not ambiguous) indicates that God's love for Abraham is in view; see further Goshen-Gottstein 1987: 101–104 and Höffken 2000: 17–22.

[10] As but one of many examples, Yahweh informs Abraham before destroying Sodom and Gomorrah, because he has chosen Abraham as the means by which he will bless all the nations (Gen. 18:17–19).

[11] Within Isaiah the name Jacob appears only five times (Isa. 14:1 [2×]; 41:8; 44:1–2), four of which occur in parallelism with Israel. All five occurrences refer to the nation of Israel, though here in 41:8 the primary referent is to the patriarch.

[12] Throughout Isaiah the verb rendered 'choose' (*bāḥar*) often describes the special relationship that God has with specific individuals or his people (14:1; 41:8–9; 43:10; 44:1–2; 49:7).

'you whom I took from the ends of the earth,
  and called from its farthest corners,
saying to you, "You are my servant,
  I have chosen you and not cast you off."'
(Isa. 41:9)

Reminding his people that they are his servant whom he has chosen serves as the basis for the exhortation not to fear that follows (Isa. 41:10–28). Israel as a nation, then, is clearly the servant of the Lord in view here.

That brings us to the initial 'servant song' in Isaiah 42:1–9, which because of its importance I will cite in full:

Behold *my servant*, whom I uphold,
  my chosen, in whom my soul delights;
I have put my Spirit upon him;
  he will bring forth justice to the nations.
He will not cry aloud or lift up his voice,
  or make it heard in the street;
a bruised reed he will not break,
  and a faintly burning wick he will not quench;
  he will faithfully bring forth justice.
He will not grow faint or be discouraged
  till he has established justice in the earth;
  and the coastlands wait for his law.
Thus says God, the Lord,
  who created the heavens and stretched them out,
  who spread out the earth and what comes from it,
who gives breath to the people on it
  and spirit to those who walk in it:
'I am the Lord; I have called you in righteousness;
  I will take you by the hand and keep you;
I will give you as a covenant for the people,
  a light for the nations,
  to open the eyes that are blind,
to bring out the prisoners from the dungeon,
  from the prison those who sit in darkness.
I am the Lord; that is my name;
  my glory I give to no other,

nor my praise to carved idols.
Behold, the former things have come to pass,
and new things I now declare;
before they spring forth
I tell you of them.'
(Isa. 42:1–9)

The parallelism in verse 1 between 'my servant' and 'my chosen' echoes the language of 41:8–9, which suggests that the servant in view here is still Israel as a nation. But Isaiah 42:1 goes beyond the description of Isaiah 41:8–9, adding that Yahweh has placed his Spirit on his servant. What follows is a series of statements regarding what the servant will do (Isa. 42:1d–4) with emphasis on establishing justice among the nations (42:1, 3, 4).

Verses 5–9 recount what Yahweh the creator says to the servant. He begins by stating what he has already done: 'called you in righteousness'. He then indicates three things that he will do: (1) take the servant by the hand; (2) keep/watch over the servant; and (3) give the servant as a covenant for the people and a light to the nations (Isa. 42:6). Yahweh has two purposes for doing these things for/to his servant: (1) open the eyes of the blind, and (2) bring out the prisoners sitting in the darkest of dungeons (Isa. 42:7). In verse 8 God repeats his covenant name Yahweh, stressing that he will not share his glory with any other, and in particular carved idols (Isa. 42:8). The song concludes with an assertion that the former things have come to pass and new things are being declared in advance of their happening (Isa. 42:9).

Who then is this servant? The parallels between Isaiah 42:1 and Isaiah 41:8–9 indicate that the servant is still the nation of Israel.[13] By describing himself as the one 'who gives breath to people' on the earth and 'spirit to those who walk in it' (Isa. 42:5), Yahweh sets the commission of his servant Israel against the backdrop of his creation of Adam and by implication his commission as a king who rules over creation (Gen. 1:26–31) and a priest who serves the Lord by mediating God's presence to the world (Gen. 2:15). The language of taking the servant by the hand

[13] Given that the immediate context of Isa. 42 indicates that the servant in view is Israel as a nation, what are we to make of Matthew's claim that Jesus is the fulfilment of Isa. 42:1–4 (Matt. 12:15–21)? While discussion of that text must await chapter 7, the brief answer is that Matthew presents Jesus as the one who relives Israel's experiences yet fulfils them through his life, ministry, death and resurrection.

recalls Yahweh's actions to deliver Israel from Egypt with a mighty hand (e.g. Exod. 3:20–21; 7:4–5; 13:3, 9, 14; 32:11; Deut. 3:24; 4:34; 5:15; 6:21; 7:8; 9:26; 26:8). At Sinai the Lord made a covenant with his people to be a kingdom of priests to display his glory to the nations (Exod. 19:5–6); here Yahweh makes the servant a covenant for the people and a light to the nations. Central to the exodus that formed Israel into a nation was God's intention to display his glorious name and demonstrate his uniqueness among the nations (Exod. 3:13–22; 9:16). By acting through the servant, Yahweh is displaying his unique glory.

Yet it should also be noted that the description of the servant in verses 1–4 bears striking affinities with the promised Davidic king portrayed in Isaiah 11:1–5. The Spirit of the Lord who rests on him (Isa. 11:2) also rests upon the servant (Isa. 42:1). The servant brings justice to the nations (Isa. 42:1, 3–4); the Davidic king judges all people with righteousness and brings the nations under his rule (Isa. 11:3–5). These similarities make sense when it is remembered that Israel's king was to be the personal embodiment of what Israel was supposed to be as a nation.

After a summons to sing about Yahweh's power over creation and the nations (Isa. 42:10–17), the focus shifts back to the servant:

> Hear, you deaf,
>   and look, you blind, that you may see!
> Who is blind but *my servant*,
>   or deaf as my messenger whom I send?
> Who is blind as my dedicated one,
>   or blind as *the servant of the Lord*?
> He sees many things, but does not observe them;
>   his ears are open, but he does not hear.
> (Isa. 42:18–20)

Despite their lofty calling, Israel as the servant has failed miserably. Instead of hearing the call of Yahweh to be a light for the nations and bring them out of their darkness (Isa. 42:6–7), Israel is instead deaf and blind (cf. Isa. 6:9–10). Yahweh warned that if Israel broke the covenant he would strike them with blindness such that they would grope in the darkness like someone blind (Deut. 28:28–29).[14] Their rebellion against the Lord has

[14] Isa. 42:18–20 uses the same word for 'blind' (*'iwwēr*) that occurs in Deut. 28:29.

prevented them from carrying out their mission as the servant. As the servant, Israel was God's messenger to the nations,[15] yet has become virtually indistinguishable from them in their idolatry (cf. Isa. 1:2–17). Yahweh also refers to Israel his servant as 'my dedicated one'; the underlying Hebrew is notoriously difficult, but the sense seems to be one who is reconciled or at peace with the Lord.[16] Instead of being the servant through whom Yahweh is working to overcome the blindness and deafness of the nations, Israel as a nation has instead become blind and deaf themselves. Despite the Lord giving Israel his law, they have been plundered by the very nations they are supposed to enlighten and are therefore handed over to the nations by Yahweh himself (Isa. 42:21–25; cf. Deut. 28:52–57).

Isaiah 43 – 44 contain several more references to the nation of Israel as Yahweh's servant. After calling his people not to fear because they have been made for his glory (Isa. 43:1–7), the Lord contrasts his people with the nations who worship false gods (Isa. 43:8–13). He says to Israel:

> 'You are my witnesses,' declares the LORD,
> 'and my servant whom I have chosen,
> that you may know and believe me
> and understand that I am he.
> Before me no god was formed,
> nor shall there be any after me.'
> (Isa. 43:10)

Here Israel's identity as the servant is further clarified as that of being witnesses. As in Isaiah 41:8–9 God's election of Israel the servant is stressed. But in contrast to the outward and missional description of Israel's purpose as the servant in Isaiah 42:6–7, here the purpose of their identity is more inward and relational – to know, trust and understand the unique greatness of Yahweh.

---

[15] In Isaiah the Hebrew term used here (*mal'āk*) primarily refers to messengers/officials from various nations (14:32; 18:2; 30:4; 37:9), including Israel (33:7). Twice it refers to an angelic being (37:36; 63:9). Only here and 44:26 is it parallel to 'servant'.

[16] The Hebrew expression *měšullām* is a pual masculine singular participle from the root *šlm*, which has the sense of 'peace', 'wholeness' or 'completeness'. The difficulty of this expression has led to various suggestions (including that it is a personal name, as it is in 2 Kgs 21:19, 22:3, or that an emendation is in order), but on the whole it seems most likely to describe the servant as one who is at peace or reconciled with Yahweh, or perhaps one who is in covenant with him (so Motyer 1993: 327–328).

Despite Israel's sin as the servant, and the subsequent judgment of exile, God promises restoration:

> But now hear, O Jacob *my servant*,
>   Israel whom I have chosen!
> Thus says the LORD who made you,
>   who formed you from the womb and will help you:
> Fear not, O Jacob *my servant*,
>   Jeshurun whom I have chosen.
> For I will pour water on the thirsty land,
>   and streams on the dry ground;
> I will pour my Spirit upon your offspring,
>   and my blessing on your descendants.
> They shall spring up among the grass
>   like willows by flowing streams.
> This one will say, 'I am the LORD's,'
>   another will call on the name of Jacob,
> and another will write on his hand, 'The LORD's,'
>   and name himself by the name of Israel.
> (Isa. 44:1–5)

Again Israel's identity as the servant is linked to God choosing them as his people (Isa. 44:1–2). Just as Yahweh made and formed his first servant Adam in the garden and then gave him a helper, so too he made and formed Israel as his chosen servant and helped him (Isa. 44:2).[17] The reason Israel the servant should not fear is that Yahweh will pour out his Spirit on the servant's offspring, resulting in their flourishing like willows by a flowing stream (Isa. 44:3–4). The gift of the Spirit is in some sense a fulfilment of God's promise to bless Abraham's offspring, resulting in even Gentiles being incorporated into the people of God (Isa. 44:3–5; cf. Gen. 12:1–3).[18]

Because Yahweh is the one true God in contrast to the vain idols worshipped by the nations (Isa. 44:6–20), he is able to redeem his people:

---

17 The verb 'made' (*ʿāśâ*) occurs repeatedly in Gen. 1 – 2 to describe God's creative activity (1:7, 11–12, 16, 25, 31; 2:2–4) and in particular refers to God making human beings in his image (1:26). Gen. 2:7–8 uses the verb 'formed' (*yāṣar*) to describe God's creation of Adam from the ground. Note the use of this verb in Isa. 43:7, describing the creation of Israel for Yahweh's glory. Gen. 2:18–20 uses this verb 'help' (*ʿāzar*) for the woman he provides Adam as his helper.

18 On this, see further Harmon 2010: 146–150.

Remember these things, O Jacob,
  and Israel, for you are *my servant*;
I formed you; you are *my servant*;
  O Israel, you will not be forgotten by me.
I have blotted out your transgressions like a cloud
  and your sins like mist;
return to me, for I have redeemed you.
(Isa. 44:21–22)

Only the Lord is able to forgive the transgressions of his servant Israel, and that is exactly what he has done. That is why Israel the servant should return to him in covenant faithfulness. So certain is this redemption that Israel is called to sing and shout it to the ends of the earth (Isa. 44:23). As Israel's creator and redeemer he frustrates the wise of this world (Isa. 44:24–25). Furthermore, he is the one:

who confirms the word of *his servant*
  and fulfils the counsel of his messengers.
(Isa. 44:26a–b)

Just as in Isaiah 42:19 Israel's role as the servant is cast in terms of a messenger, announcing in advance what the Lord will accomplish. Here it is the restoration of Jerusalem through the pagan king Cyrus (Isa. 44:26c–28). In using Cyrus as his anointed Yahweh will make himself known to this pagan king (Isa. 45:1–3). He will do this:

For the sake of *my servant* Jacob,
  and Israel my chosen,
I call you by your name,
  I name you, though you do not know me.
(Isa. 45:4)

Israel as the servant was called to be a light to the nations, yet ironically God raises up a pagan king to free his servant Israel from their bondage. Yahweh's purpose in doing so is to magnify his own name among the nations (Isa. 45:5–8).

There is one final reference to Israel the servant in Isaiah 40 – 48. In the concluding oracle, the Lord commands:

Go out from Babylon, flee from Chaldea,
declare this with a shout of joy, proclaim it,
send it out to the end of the earth;
say, 'The Lord has redeemed his servant Jacob!'
(Isa. 48:20)

On the day when Israel the servant is finally redeemed from Babylonian captivity, they will proclaim that good news to the ends of the earth.

Within Isaiah 40 – 48, then, there is little doubt that the nation of Israel is the servant of the Lord. Like Adam, Israel was created and formed to serve the Lord by exercising dominion over the earth and mediating God's presence to the nations. In fulfilment of God's covenant promises to Abraham they were to be a blessing to the nations. With a descendant of David on their throne, Israel the servant was to magnify the incomparable name of Yahweh as the one true God who both creates and redeems. Yet they failed spectacularly, becoming almost indistinguishable from the idolatrous nations. What would Yahweh do?

God raises up an obedient and suffering servant (Isa. 49 – 55)

The answer is raise up a new servant. This new beginning is signalled by the servant song (49:1–13) that opens Isaiah 49 – 55. The similarities to Isaiah 42:1–9 are striking:

Listen to me, O coastlands,
and give attention, you peoples from afar.
The Lord called me from the womb,
from the body of my mother he named my name.
He made my mouth like a sharp sword;
in the shadow of his hand he hid me;
he made me a polished arrow;
in his quiver he hid me away.
And he said to me, 'You are *my servant*,
Israel, in whom I will be glorified.'
But I said, 'I have laboured in vain;
I have spent my strength for nothing and vanity;
yet surely my right is with the Lord,
and my recompense with my God.'

And now the LORD says,
he who formed me from the womb to be *his servant*,
to bring Jacob back to him;
and that Israel might be gathered to him –
for I am honoured in the eyes of the LORD,
and my God has become my strength –
he says:
'It is too light a thing that you should be *my servant*
to raise up the tribes of Jacob
and to bring back the preserved of Israel;
I will make you as a light for the nations,
that my salvation may reach to the end of the earth.'
Thus says the LORD,
the Redeemer of Israel and his Holy One,
to one deeply despised, abhorred by the nation,
the servant of rulers:
'Kings shall see and arise;
princes, and they shall prostrate themselves;
because of the LORD, who is faithful,
the Holy One of Israel, who has chosen you.'
Thus says the LORD:
'In a time of favour I have answered you;
in a day of salvation I have helped you;
I will keep you and give you
as a covenant to the people,
to establish the land,
to apportion the desolate heritages,
saying to the prisoners, "Come out,"
to those who are in darkness, "Appear."
They shall feed along the ways;
on all bare heights shall be their pasture;
they shall not hunger or thirst,
neither scorching wind nor sun shall strike them,
for he who has pity on them will lead them,
and by springs of water will guide them.
And I will make all my mountains a road,
and my highways shall be raised up.
Behold, these shall come from afar,

and behold, these from the north and from the west,
and these from the land of Syene.'
Sing for joy, O heavens, and exult, O earth;
break forth, O mountains, into singing!
For the LORD has comforted his people
and will have compassion on his afflicted.
(Isa. 49:1–13)

The song can be divided into two smaller units: the servant's commission (Isa. 49:1–6) and Yahweh's confirmation (Isa. 49:7–13). The servant begins by calling the coastlands and peoples to listen as he recounts his commissioning from the womb and his preparation for the task at hand (Isa. 49:1–2). Yahweh calls him 'my servant, Israel, in whom I will be glorified' (Isa. 49:3). On an initial reading, it seems evident that the servant, then, is the nation of Israel, just as it has been throughout Isaiah 40 – 48. But the rest of the servant song will call that identification into question, as we will shortly see. The point to observe here is that God has commissioned the servant as the vessel in whom he will display his beauty and glory (cf. Isa. 44:23).[19] Despite this lofty calling, the servant worries that his efforts will be in vain; yet in the end he entrusts the outcome to Yahweh, who judges wisely (Isa. 49:4). The specifics of the servant's mission are laid out in verses 5–6. He will bring Jacob back to the Lord, cause Israel to be gathered back to the Lord, raise up the tribes of Jacob, and bring back the preserved ones of Israel. Yet the servant's mission goes beyond Israel; in fact, such a limited mission to Israel alone is 'too light a thing'[20] for someone as magnificent as the servant (Isa. 49:6). No, this servant is destined for an even greater accomplishment: Yahweh will appoint him 'as a light for the nations, / that my salvation may reach to the end of the earth' (Isa. 49:6).

Who, then, is this servant? The fact that the servant is identified as Israel (49:3) yet has a mission to restore Israel indicates that the servant of Isaiah 49 is not the nation. Nor can it be a faithful remnant within the

---

19 This Hebrew verb *pā'ar* has the sense of beautifying something, and occurs several times in Isaiah with the sense of God glorifying himself in saving his people (44:23; 49:3; 60:21; 61:3).

20 As used here, the niphal stem of the Hebrew verb (*qālal*) has the sense of something that is almost trivial or easy in comparison to something else. Thus, the wickedness of King Jeroboam is regarded as small or trivial in comparison to the sins of King Ahab (1 Kgs 16:31; cf. 1 Sam. 18:23; Ezek. 8:17).

nation, for the servant is restoring them ('the preserved of Israel' 49:6) as well. The servant, then, must be an individual, a person who as the servant embodies everything Israel was supposed to be but failed. No wonder Yahweh will display his glory in this servant![21]

In verses 7–13 the Lord describes what this new individual servant will do. Despite being despised by the nations and their rulers, the servant will one day receive their homage (Isa. 49:7). Yahweh will preserve the servant and give him as a covenant to his people; as a result, they will be restored to the land (Isa. 49:8). The servant will gather his people from the four corners of the earth and lead them in a new exodus that will transform creation itself (Isa. 49:9–12). When Yahweh comforts his people through the work of the servant, the appropriate response will be to sing with joy (Isa. 49:13).

Although I have hinted at this along the way, it will be helpful to note the numerous parallels between the description and mission of the respective servants in Isaiah 42:1–9 and Isaiah 49:1–13 (see Table 4).

Table 4 Israel and the individual servant

Israel the servant nation (Isa. 42:1–9)	*The individual servant (Isa. 49:1–13)*
Called in righteousness (42:6)	Called from the womb (49:1)
Yahweh will not give his glory to another (42:8)	Glorified in the servant (49:3)
A light for the nations (42:6)	A light for the nations (49:6)
Justice to the nations (42:1, 3–4)	Salvation to the end of the earth (49:6)
Chosen by Yahweh (42:1)	Chosen by Yahweh (49:7)
A covenant for the people (42:6)	A covenant for the people (49:8)
Bring prisoners out of darkness (42:7)	Bring prisoners out of darkness (49:9)
Singing as the proper response to the servant's work (42:10)	Singing as the proper response to the servant's work (49:13)

These parallels make it clear that the servant of Isaiah 49 shares a similar identity and mission with the servant of Isaiah 42: they are both in some sense Israel set apart as a light to the nations. Yet there are at least three

[21] See similarly Abernethy 2016: 147.

key differences. First, in addition to having a mission for the nations, the servant of Isaiah 49 has a mission to restore Israel as well. This leads to the second difference: the servant of Isaiah 49 is an individual. Thus, while there is obvious and strong continuity with the commission of the nation of Israel as the servant, the servant of Isaiah 49 also stands within the line of individual servants that includes Adam, Moses, Joshua and David before him. Third, the servant of Isaiah 49 obeys where the nation of Israel failed. Through this new servant Yahweh will establish his people in the land through a new exodus that transforms creation itself.

Because Isaiah 49 describes a new, individual servant, it is not surprising that we see language that connects his work to Adam in the garden, the promises to Abraham and the covenant with David. Like Adam, the servant is formed by Yahweh (Isa. 49:5) and given a commission that has the ends of the earth in view (Isa. 49:6). Through this servant all the nations of the earth will be blessed (Isa. 49:6). In fulfilment of God's commission to Adam and the covenant promises to David, nations and their rulers will bow before the servant (Isa. 49:7).[22] Through the servant God's people will live at peace in the land (Isa. 49:8) just as God promised David. In sum, it is through this individual servant that God will bring to fulfilment his creational and redemptive purposes.

The servant explicitly reappears in the very next chapter of Isaiah. Whereas the focus in Isaiah 49 was on the mission of the servant, in this third servant song the emphasis falls on the obedience of the servant:

> The Lord God has given me
>   the tongue of those who are taught,
> that I may know how to sustain with a word
>   him who is weary.
> Morning by morning he awakens;
>   he awakens my ear
>   to hear as those who are taught.

---

22 Further evidence that Adam's commission is in view may come from Isa. 49:23, where rulers who once oppressed God's people will bow down before them and 'lick the dust of your feet', an expression that may echo the curse placed on the serpent in the garden (Gen. 3:14). An additional link to the Davidic promises is found in Isa. 49:22, where Yahweh promises to 'raise my signal to the peoples'; Isa. 11:10 identifies this signal for the peoples as 'the root of Jesse' and asserts the nations will enquire of him.

The Lord GOD has opened my ear,
  and I was not rebellious;
  I turned not backwards.
I gave my back to those who strike,
  and my cheeks to those who pull out the beard;
I hid not my face
  from disgrace and spitting.
But the Lord GOD helps me;
  therefore I have not been disgraced;
therefore I have set my face like a flint,
  and I know that I shall not be put to shame.
  He who vindicates me is near.
Who will contend with me?
  Let us stand up together.
Who is my adversary?
  Let him come near to me.
Behold, the Lord GOD helps me;
  who will declare me guilty?
Behold, all of them will wear out like a garment;
  the moth will eat them up.
Who among you fears the LORD
  and obeys the voice of his servant?
Let him who walks in darkness
  and has no light
trust in the name of the LORD
  and rely on his God.
Behold, all you who kindle a fire,
  who equip yourselves with burning torches!
Walk by the light of your fire,
  and by the torches that you have kindled!
This you have from my hand:
  you shall lie down in torment.
(Isa. 50:4–11)

This passage divides into the servant's self-description (vv. 4–9) and a concluding call to heed the voice of the servant (vv. 10–11). Whereas Isaiah 49 has obvious parallels with Isaiah 42, the content of this servant song corresponds to the description of the servant's failure in Isaiah 42:18–20.

Whereas Israel the servant was a blind and deaf messenger, this individual servant has ears to hear what Yahweh says to him; therefore, he is able to speak a timely word to the weary (Isa. 50:4–5). This servant is obedient, even in the face of suffering humiliation (Isa. 50:5–6). Because Yahweh helps the servant he is not put to shame; instead, he remains focused on his God-given mission (Isa. 50:7). Verses 8–9 reveal why the servant is able to remain obediently on mission in the face of such suffering – he trusts in Yahweh to vindicate him against the accusations of all his adversaries. The proper response to this obedient servant is to obey his voice, which is equated with fearing, trusting in and relying upon Yahweh (Isa. 50:10). Those who refuse to do so will be consumed by their own sinful disobedience (Isa. 50:11).

Even though this servant song often flies under the radar, it establishes the two key elements of the servant's obedience and his suffering. The emphasis on his obedience reinforces our conclusion that the servant introduced in Isaiah 49 obeys where Israel had failed. Describing the suffering of the individual servant anticipates the much fuller exposition of that suffering in the final servant song.

Because that final servant song comes several chapters later, we need to survey the intervening chapters briefly. Because God was faithful to multiply Abraham and his descendants, he can be trusted not only to redeem his people from exile but transform creation itself through the revelation of his saving righteousness (Isa. 51:1–8).[23] In this new exodus God will display his power, turn away his wrath from his people and affirm his love for them (Isa. 51:9–23). In response God's people are called to wake up and prepare for their coming deliverance, because Yahweh is acting to make his name known to his people (Isa. 52:1–6). Heralds are being sent out to announce the good news that Yahweh is establishing his reign by redeeming his people and baring his holy arm in the sight of all the nations, so that Yahweh's salvation may extend to the ends of the earth (Isa. 52:7–10). Therefore, God's people are commanded to depart from Babylon and follow Yahweh, who goes before them (Isa. 52:11–12).

That brings us at last to the climactic servant song. At last it becomes clear how the servant will restore Israel and be a light of salvation to the nations – he will suffer for their sins and be vindicated by Yahweh.

23 The repeated references to God transforming creation throughout Isa. 40 – 66 demonstrate that the work of the servant extends far beyond Israel's restoration from exile: it is the consummation of his original purposes for creation.

Behold, *my servant* shall act wisely;
he shall be high and lifted up,
and shall be exalted.
As many were astonished at you –
his appearance was so marred, beyond human semblance,
and his form beyond that of the children of mankind –
so shall he sprinkle many nations;
kings shall shut their mouths because of him,
for that which has not been told them they see,
and that which they have not heard they understand.

Who has believed what he has heard from us?
And to whom has the arm of the LORD been revealed?
For he grew up before him like a young plant,
and like a root out of dry ground;
he had no form or majesty that we should look at him,
and no beauty that we should desire him.
He was despised and rejected by men,
a man of sorrows and acquainted with grief;
and as one from whom men hide their faces
he was despised, and we esteemed him not.
Surely he has borne our griefs
and carried our sorrows;
yet we esteemed him stricken,
smitten by God, and afflicted.
But he was pierced for our transgressions;
he was crushed for our iniquities;
upon him was the chastisement that brought us peace,
and with his stripes we are healed.
All we like sheep have gone astray;
we have turned – every one – to his own way;
and the LORD has laid on him
the iniquity of us all.
He was oppressed, and he was afflicted,
yet he opened not his mouth;
like a lamb that is led to the slaughter,
and like a sheep that before its shearers is silent,
so he opened not his mouth.

By oppression and judgment he was taken away;
and as for his generation, who considered
that he was cut off out of the land of the living,
stricken for the transgression of my people?
And they made his grave with the wicked
and with a rich man in his death,
although he had done no violence,
and there was no deceit in his mouth.
Yet it was the will of the Lord to crush him;
he has put him to grief;
when his soul makes an offering for guilt,
he shall see his offspring; he shall prolong his days;
the will of the Lord shall prosper in his hand.
Out of the anguish of his soul he shall see and be satisfied;
by his knowledge shall the righteous one, *my servant*,
make many to be accounted righteous,
and he shall bear their iniquities.
Therefore I will divide him a portion with the many,
and he shall divide the spoil with the strong,
because he poured out his soul to death
and was numbered with the transgressors;
yet he bore the sin of many,
and makes intercession for the transgressors.
(Isa. 52:13 – 53:12)

Despite the numerous exegetical and theological challenges this passage presents, there is broad consensus on the internal structure: a prologue that announces the exaltation of the servant and the astonishment of the nations (Isa. 52:13–15); an assessment of the servant and his suffering (Isa. 53:1–10); and Yahweh's vindication of the servant (Isa. 53:11–12). Thus, the song moves in a v-shaped pattern: the servant begins in a state of exaltation, descends into a state of humiliation, and then is vindicated to an even higher status than his initial exaltation.

The initial exaltation of the servant is linked to the fact that he 'acts wisely' (*śākăl*). Genesis 3:6 uses this same verb to describe the tree of the knowledge of good and evil as 'desired to make one wise'. More significantly, it describes the success of previous servants such as Joshua (Josh. 1:7–8), David (1 Sam. 18:14) and Solomon (1 Kgs 2:3), as well as Yahweh prospering Israel if they keep the covenant (Deut. 29:9).[24] To emphasize just how exalted the servant is, the author uses three different Hebrew verbs in an effort to capture it. Yahweh's exaltation of the servant (Isa. 52:13) is immediately contrasted with humanity's opinion of the servant (Isa. 52:14). They are astonished at the servant, or, perhaps more accurately, 'appalled'; this Hebrew verb (*šāmēm*) frequently describes a person's reaction when observing the results of divine judgment (1 Kgs 9:8; 2 Chr. 7:21; Job 17:8; Jer. 2:12; 18:16; 19:8; 49:17; 50:13; Ezek. 26:16; 27:35; 28:19), and in particular the reaction of the nations when they see God's judgment on Israel for breaking their covenant with Yahweh (Lev. 26:32). Here this reaction stems from the horrible disfigurement of the servant's appearance. What exactly the servant does to the nations in Isaiah 52:15a is unclear. If the sense of the verb *nāzā(h)* is 'sprinkle', the idea is that the servant purifies the nations (cf. Exod. 29:21). If the verb means 'cause to leap', the nations are instead startled. On the whole, 'sprinkle' seems the more likely sense, thus casting the work of the servant in priestly terms. In response the kings of the nations will be speechless and surprised (Isa. 52:15).

The astonished silence of the nations does not last long, as Isaiah 53:1 begins a section where those redeemed by the work of the servant tell his story.[25] The work of the servant is nothing less than the arm of the Lord being revealed (Isa. 53:1), the means by which God's people will be restored from exile and the nations will see Yahweh's salvation (Isa. 52:7–10).[26] Divine revelation is necessary to understand rightly the servant's story.

---

[24] The verb *śākăl* has a range of meanings: it describes 'the process of thinking through a complex arrangement of thoughts resulting in a wise dealing and use of good practical common sense. Another end result is the emphasis upon being successful'; see Goldberg 1980: 877. Thus, the difference between 'prosper' and 'act wisely' in English translations of Isa. 52:13 is not as significant as it may initially seem.

[25] Instead of translating the opening line of Isa. 53:1 'Who has believed what he has heard from us' (ESVUK), it is also possible to render it 'Who has believed what we have heard' (CSB). Either way, the identity of the speaker(s) is unclear. It could be the prophet himself; see e.g. Motyer 1993: 427. More common is the view that it is Israel (whether the community as a whole or an individual speaking on behalf of the community), now confessing their failure to recognize the servant; see e.g. Koole 1998: 2.276; Oswalt 1998: 381; Ekblad 1999: 194–195; Childs 2001: 413; Blenkinsopp 2002: 351. Another possibility is that it is the nations whom the servant has sprinkled (Isa. 52:15) who now proclaim the identity and work of the servant; see e.g. Melugin 1976: 167–168. Perhaps instead of seeing an either/or between Israel and the nations, a both/and works best. The 'we' is Israel and the nations together confessing their failure to assess the servant rightly initially, since the work of the servant applies not only to Israel but the nations as well.

[26] Mention of the arm of the Lord also recalls God's deliverance of Israel from Egypt 'with a mighty hand and an outstretched arm' (Deut. 26:8).

Describing the servant as a root out of dry ground casts the servant in a Davidic light (Isa. 53:2), taking up language from Isaiah 11:1–10, where the root of Jesse restores Israel, ushers in a new creation and becomes a signal for the nations. Yet, unlike David, whose handsome appearance is repeatedly noted (1 Sam. 16:12; 17:42), there is nothing about the appearance of the servant that attracts people to him. Just as Isaiah 49:7 had foretold, the servant is despised and rejected by people, marked by sorrow and grief; indeed, people go so far as to hide their faces from him (Isa. 53:3). The servant is one who knows 'sickness' (*ḥôlî*), a Hebrew term used to describe the sickness God poured out on the Egyptians that would come upon Israel as judgment for their sin (Deut. 28:59, 61). The disfigurement of the servant's face foretold in Isaiah 50:6 leads to people regarding him as insignificant.

Yet behind the disfigurement of the servant lies a shocking divine purpose: to take upon himself the punishment for the sins of his people. At one level the servant is a substitute for Israel the failed servant,[27] experiencing the curses (culminating in exile) Yahweh promised would come upon them if they broke the covenant.[28] These curses are detailed at various places in Scripture, but receive detailed discussion in Leviticus 26:14–39 and Deuteronomy 28:15–68. So it is not surprising that Isaiah 53 borrows language from these chapters (among others) to describe the servant's suffering. The griefs/sickness that the servant knows (Isa. 53:3) are actually those of his people (Deut. 28:59, 61), which he bears in their place (Isa. 53:4). The servant is struck by God (Isa. 53:4), just as God vowed to strike rebellious Israel for their covenant unfaithfulness (Deut. 28:22, 27–28, 35). Israel's transgressions and iniquities that led them into exile (Lev. 26:39–43) are what leads to the servant being pierced and crushed, verbs that accentuate the brutality of the servant's suffering and the mortal nature of the wounds.[29] The 'chastisement' (*mûsār*) that repeatedly fell

---

27 On the vicarious suffering of the servant, see Bailey 1998: 223–250; Spieckerman 2004: 1–15; Allen 2012: 171–189.

28 See similarly Ceresko 1994: 42–55 (esp. 47–50); Hugenberger 1995: 129–139; Watts 1998: 125–151. Although he does not draw connections between the specific sufferings of the servant and Deut. 28 – 30, Clements (1998: 39–54) does link the vicarious suffering of the servant to restoration from exile.

29 Both creation and the exodus are described as Yahweh having 'pierced [*ḥālal*] the dragon' (Isa. 51:9), while in Isa. 3:15 Yahweh condemns the leaders of Israel for 'crushing' (*dākā'*) his people by exploiting the poor. Ps. 89:10 (MT 89:11) brings these same two verbs together to describe the exodus: 'You crushed [*dākā'*] Rahab like a carcass [lit. 'as one pierced'; *ḥālal*]; / you scattered your enemies with your mighty arm.'

upon Israel for their disobedience (Deut. 11:2; Isa. 26:16; 30:32) now falls on the servant, so that his people can experience peace (i.e. the state of harmony that is the result of God fulfilling his promises and consummating his reign; cf. Isa. 32:17–18; 52:7). The peace promised through a Davidic king (Isa. 9:5–7) comes to pass through the suffering servant. The unhealable wounds that came as a result of Israel's rebellion (Deut. 28:27, 35; 32:39) and covered them from head to toe (Isa. 1:6) are now inflicted upon the servant, and it is through these wounds that the servant's people are healed (Isa. 53:5). Despite being set apart as the sheep of Yahweh's pasture (Num. 27:17), every individual sheep has turned 'to his own way' (Isa. 53:6),[30] a charge that resonates with the consistent description of rebellious Israel as failing to walk in the ways of Yahweh (Deut. 28:9, 29; 30:16; 31:29). The iniquities previously covered by two goats on the Day of Atonement (Lev. 16:1–34) are now being laid upon the suffering servant as a sacrificial lamb by Yahweh himself.

The servant's suffering is further explained in Isaiah 53:7–9. Like Israel before him (cf. Exod. 3:7; 5:6, 10, 13–14), the servant is oppressed and afflicted; unlike Israel, though, the servant does not even open his mouth in anguish. Just as God warned that he would expel Israel from the land for their disobedience (Deut. 28:64; 29:26–27), the servant is 'cut off out of the land of the living' (Isa. 53:8).[31] The 'transgressions' (*pĕšāʿîm*) atoned for on the Day of Atonement (Lev. 16:16, 21) are now inflicted upon the servant, who is struck for the transgression of his people (Isa. 53:8). Through his vicarious death (Isa. 53:8–9) the servant experiences the culminating curse of death that God promised Israel for breaking the covenant (Deut. 28:63–68) despite having done no violence or any deceit coming from his mouth.

But the servant does more than experience the curses that came from Adam's failure in the garden and Israel's repeated failure throughout their history: he also experiences their restoration and the blessings promised in connection with that restoration (Isa. 53:10–12). Mysteriously, Yahweh delights to crush the servant and put him to grief (Isa. 53:5), just as he delighted to magnify his law through Israel his servant for the sake of his

[30] This same language of sheep turning describes the Babylonians in Isa. 13:14; in essence, Israel has become just like the sinful nations around them, deserving judgment.

[31] There may be a subtle echo of Lev. 16:22 present here. The servant is 'cut off' (*gāzăr*) from 'the land [*ʾĕrĕṣ*] of the living' (Isa. 53:8); on the Day of Atonement the scapegoat bearing Israel's iniquities was driven 'to the land [*ʾĕrĕṣ*] of separation [*gĕzērâ*]' (i.e. an uninhabited area).

own righteousness (Isa. 42:21). That delight stems from the servant making himself 'an offering for guilt' (Isa. 53:10). The precise meaning of this Hebrew expression is debated,[32] but it seems most likely that the expression refers to the guilt offering, and perhaps specifically to its description in Leviticus 5:14–26.[33] According to Wenham, the basic idea of the guilt offering is reparation: it involves both the idea of substitutionary atonement (the ram dies in place of the sinner) and 'compensating God for the loss he has suffered as a result of sin'; as such it was applied to situations where God's holy things were defiled as well as sins against one's neighbour.[34] Based on Wenham's conclusions, Motyer summarizes that in Isaiah 53:10 'the death of the Servant satisfied both the needs of sinful people before God and the 'needs'/requirements of God in relation to his broken law and offended holiness'.[35] Yet regardless of the specifics, the general point is quite clear: the life of the servant is offered as a sacrifice that removes the guilt of his people.

The results of the servant offering himself as a sacrifice for the sins of his people are laid out in Isaiah 53:10c–11. But before enumerating these

32 There are three primary issues. The first is the force of the particle *'im* that introduces the clause. Although its use is wide ranging (see the lengthy entry in *DCH* s.v. *'im*), its most common use is to introduce the protasis (the 'if' clause) of a conditional statement. But in some contexts this particle can have the force of 'when' and that seems most likely here; for further discussion of the textual issues involved, see Sonne 1959: 335–342; Dahood 1960: 400–409; 1982: 566–570; Battenfield 1982: 485. The second issue is the unusual use of the verb *śîm* (typically translated 'make, place'). It rarely occurs in connection with sacrifice, though there are examples (Exod. 29:24; Lev. 2:15; 24:6; Deut. 26:2) where it describes the act of placing an offering somewhere (Koole 1998: 2.321). The unusual choice of this verb may stem from the fact that the servant does not bring the sacrifice but is himself the sacrifice (Motyer 1993: 439). An additional difficulty with this verb is that by form it can be understood as second-person singular masculine or third-person singular masculine. The former would indicate that Yahweh is the agent of the servant's death (i.e. 'you [Yahweh] make him a guilt offering' CSB), while the latter would make 'his soul' the subject and portray the servant as offering his life (i.e. 'his [the servant's] soul makes an offering for guilt' ESV). On the whole the latter option seems preferable; as such 'The Lord's pleasurable commitment to his will (10a) is thus matched by the Servant's "whole-hearted" involvement of what the Lord required of him' (ibid. 440). NT descriptions of Jesus willingly laying down his life for sin – which may draw on this very text – further support this conclusion (see e.g. Gal. 1:4). The final issue is the meaning of the noun *'āšām* (typically rendered 'guilt offering'), which is dealt with in the text above.

33 As Motyer (1993: 439) notes, in addition to the noun *'āšām* Lev. 5:17 also shares with Isa. 53:10 the particle *'im* (if/when) and the noun *něpěš* (soul). Oswalt (1998: 402) suggests that the guilt offering is referred to here because 'Of all the sacrifices, this one was for guilt that had knowingly been incurred by the individual, and had to be offered by the individual responsible.' If so, this makes it all the more shocking that the sinless servant offers himself as a sacrifice for the sins of his people.

34 See the lengthy discussion in Wenham 1979: 103–112 (quote is from 111) as well as Ross 2002: 146–154.

35 Motyer 1993: 439.

it should be noted that these results depend upon and assume the resurrection of the servant. Otherwise, how can the servant see his offspring or prolong his days? How else will he 'see and be satisfied'? What sense can be made of Yahweh dividing him a portion among the many or the servant dividing spoil with the strong? Further confirmation for the resurrection of the servant comes from the fact that the servant is not only suffering the Deuteronomic curses for Israel's covenant unfaithfulness but also experiencing their restoration – a restoration that Ezekiel 37 vividly describes as nothing less than the resurrection from the dead. When promising the resurrection of the righteous, Daniel 12:2–3 echoes Isaiah 53:11, showing that he understood that the servant was resurrected and thus vindicated. As Motyer summarizes, 'In the case of the Servant, however, death ushers him into sovereign dignity and power, with his own hand administering the saving purpose of the Lord, and as victor taking the spoil.'[36]

So the first result of the servant's self-sacrificial offering is that he 'will see his seed'. Although the exact expression is unusual,[37] the concept itself is not. In Isaiah 6:13 God concludes his commissioning of the prophet by promising that out of the devastating judgment 'the holy seed is its stump'.[38] Although widely disputed, this expression seems to be a reference to the remnant ('holy seed') that will be ruled over by the promised king from David's line, who in 11:1 is called a 'shoot from the stump of Jesse'.[39] As a nation Israel is the 'offspring of Abraham' (Isa. 41:8) and the seed of Jacob (Isa. 45:19) whom God called to be his servant who because of their idolatry (Isa. 48:19) must now be gathered from east and west

---

[36] Ibid. 440–441.

[37] Nowhere else in the OT is the noun 'seed' (*zera'*) the direct object of the verb 'see' (*rā'ā(h)*). There are two places where a pronoun whose antecedent is *zera'* is the direct object of *rā'ā(h)*. In Ps. 37:25 the psalmist asserts: 'I have not seen [*rā'ā(h)*] the righteous forsaken / or his children [*zera'*] begging for bread'. Closer to our context is Isa. 61:9, where Yahweh says to his restored people that 'Their offspring [*zera'*] shall be known among the nations, / and their descendants in the midst of the peoples; / all who see [*rā'ā(h)*] them shall acknowledge them, / that they are an offspring [*zera'*] the Lord has blessed.' Although not an exact parallel, it is worth noting that in Hannah's prayer (1 Sam. 1:11) she identifies herself as the Lord's servant and prays for God to look upon her affliction and give her seed (i.e. a son).

[38] This is a notoriously difficult verse and its interpretation is further complicated by its absence in the LXX. For a summary of the issues, see Emerton 1982: 85–118.

[39] Similarly, Motyer 1993: 80. By contrast, Beale (1991: 257–278) argues that this enigmatic expression portrays Israel as a nation that was supposed to be holy but has instead become the epitome of idolatrous practice. While this view is possible, the prominence of the remnant theme within Isaiah as well as the use of the term 'stump' to refer to the promised Davidic king in 11:1 both seem to weigh against Beale's conclusion.

(Isa. 43:5). It is in Yahweh that all the seed of Israel will be justified (Isa. 45:25), and Yahweh will even pour out his Spirit on Israel's seed (Isa. 44:3). And as I will discuss shortly, the seed of the servant are the ones who inherit what was promised to Abraham (Isa. 54:3), experience the covenant blessings sworn to David (Isa. 55:3–4) and live in a renewed creation where every last consequence of Adam's rebellion will be banished once and for all (Isa. 65:23; 66:22).

The second result of the servant offering himself as a sacrifice for sin is that 'he shall prolong his days' (Isa. 53:10c). God had promised to prolong the days of his people in the land if they kept the covenant requirements (e.g. Exod. 20:12; Deut. 4:40; 5:16, 33; 6:2; 11:8–9; 22:7; 25:15; 32:47; Ps. 91:16), and Yahweh made a similar promise to King David (Ps. 21:4) and King Solomon as well (1 Kgs 3:14). Especially noteworthy is Deuteronomy 30:19–20, where Yahweh exhorts Israel:

> I call heaven and earth to witness against you today, that I have set before you life and death, blessing and curse. Therefore choose life, that you and your offspring may live, loving the Lord your God, obeying his voice and holding fast to him, for he is your life and length of days, that you may dwell in the land that the Lord swore to your fathers, to Abraham, to Isaac, and to Jacob, to give them.

The length of days that God had promised to Israel and their seed if they kept the covenant requirements is granted to the servant for his obedient self-sacrifice.

The third result is that 'the will of the Lord shall prosper in his hand'. This second reference to Yahweh's will frames the entirety of the servant's work (both his death and his resurrection) as the expression of God's plan, regardless of how others perceive it. Through his death and resurrection, Yahweh's will 'prospers' (*śākăl*), recalling the announcement of the opening line of the song that asserted that Yahweh's servant will prosper (52:13). Whereas throughout Isaiah 40 – 52 there are repeated references to God performing various actions (especially with regard to creation and redemption) by his hand (40:2; 41:20; 42:6; 43:13; 45:11–12; 48:13; 49:22; 51:16–18), here it is the hand of the servant that accomplishes Yahweh's will.

Fourth, because of his anguished death the servant 'shall see and be satisfied'. According to Motyer, this slightly awkward expression means the servant will be 'satisfied with what he sees' – that is, the resulting pleasure of the Lord, his offspring and his authority.[40] But it should be noted that in several manuscripts from the Dead Sea Scrolls (4QIsa[a], 4QIsa[b] and 4QIsa[d]) and the LXX the servant sees 'light'.[41] If this is the original text, it would seem to connect to previous passages that identify the servant as a light to the nations (Isa. 42:6; 49:6), as well as Yahweh's promises to open the eyes of the blind (42:18–19). Because of the servant's obedience to the point of death, those who walk in darkness and have no light can trust in Yahweh by obeying the voice of the servant (50:10).

Fifth, the servant will 'make many to be accounted righteous'. Righteousness language occurs throughout Isaiah 40 – 55. Most notably, it is paralleled with salvation language at key points to refer to Yahweh's actions to bring about a state of well-being for his people by rescuing them from their unrighteousness and judging their enemies (45:21; 46:12–13; 51:5–6, 8).[42] In these contexts righteousness has a distinctively eschatological sense: it is something that God's people do not yet have and must wait for Yahweh to bring near and accomplish. Through his substitutionary self-sacrificial death the servant ensures that his people will be vindicated, declared not guilty before Yahweh despite their sinful rebellion (Isa. 53:4–6). He is able to accomplish this because he himself is 'the righteous one'. In the light of Yahweh's assertion in Isaiah 45:21 that 'there is no other god besides me, / a righteous God and a Saviour; / there is none besides me' it is all the more striking that the servant is given such a title. He brings about the righteous status of his people 'by his knowledge';[43] in contrast to Israel, who went into exile because of their lack of knowledge of God and his ways (Isa. 5:13), the servant knows Yahweh intimately and is thus able to accomplish his will. The reference to knowledge may also connect the servant to the promised Davidic king, who was described as having 'the Spirit of knowledge' (Isa. 11:2).[44]

---

40 Motyer 1993: 441.

41 For a helpful discussion of this variant, see Barthélemy 1982: 403–407.

42 See similarly Duhm 1892: 419, 430; Schmid 1968: 134–137; Scullion 1971: 341; Oswalt 1997: 186–187.

43 It is also possible that this phrase goes with the line before it instead; thus, 'he shall see [light] and be satisfied by his knowledge'; for discussion, see Koole 1998: 2.333–334.

44 See also Ekblad (1999: 253–254), who bases his argument in part on the connections between the two texts in the LXX.

In response to the servant's self-sacrificial death, Yahweh states that he 'will divide him a portion with the many' (Isa. 53:12). At one level this is the language of conquest. This same verb for 'divide' (*ḥālaq*) occurs in Isaiah 9:2, where it announces that when the promised Davidic king finally comes, the people will be glad 'when they divide the spoil' (Isa. 9:3).[45] Yet this is also the language of inheritance, which the LXX recognizes when it renders this clause 'he [i.e. the servant] shall inherit many' (Isa. 53:12a NETS). As such this expression connects to the promise made to Abraham, which will become even clearer in Isaiah 54:1–3 (see below). But the servant does not keep the spoil/inheritance to himself: in turn 'he shall divide the spoil with the strong' (Isa. 53:12). While the Hebrew noun rendered 'strong' (*'āṣûm*) can refer to powerful people such as kings (Ps. 135:10) or armies (Dan. 11:25), in the plural (as it is here) it can refer to a large number of people (e.g. Num. 14:12; Deut. 11:23), which makes good sense here. Thus, the spoil/inheritance that the servant is given because of his self-sacrificial and substitutionary death he then shares with all his numerous people. And these numerous people are not limited to Israelites; for the many that the servant shares his inheritance with include the many nations for whom he lays down his life (Isa. 52:15). As Motyer summarizes: '"the many" are the whole company of the redeemed; the "kings" fall silent because they are in the presence of the stronger than the strong, they are spoil at his disposal'.[46]

The passage closes with a final mention of the servant's self-sacrificial death. In saying that he 'poured out his soul to death' the servant is pictured as a vessel that empties itself for the benefit of his people.[47] In doing so the servant was 'counted among the rebels' (Isa. 53:12 CSB);[48] in other words, in his death he was identified with the sins of his people. Yet to make it crystal clear that the servant was not suffering for his own sin, the final two lines remind the reader that he was bearing 'the sin of many' and interceding 'for the rebels' (CSB). While the intercession described here likely includes prayer, it also has the broader sense of all

45 Of the eleven occurrences in Isaiah, six of them (9:3; 17:14; 33:23; 34:17; 53:12 [2×]) are in the context of dividing spoil from battle.

46 Motyer 1993: 443.

47 This same verb (*'ārâ*) occurs in Isa. 32:15 to describe the pouring out of the Spirit on God's people.

48 The LXX uses a form of the verb *logizomai* in this clause, which the NT authors regularly use in connection with God's reckoning or counting a person righteous (e.g. repeatedly in Rom. 4), a usage that likely stems from its appearance in Gen. 15:6 LXX.

that the servant does on behalf of his people through his death and resurrection.[49] The servant is both priest and sacrifice.

Isaiah 54 – 55 lays out the wide-ranging results of the servant's work. Within these chapters is an important result that could easily be overlooked. At the end of a long description of what the servant's self-sacrificial substitutionary death produces, Isaiah 54:17 concludes:

> This is the heritage of the *servants* of the LORD and their
> righteousness is from me, declares the LORD.
> (AT)

To this point in Isaiah 40 – 54, every use of the word 'servant' (*'ebed*) was in the singular, even when it refers to the nation of Israel. But the use of the plural here highlights an important insight: the work of the singular servant has produced a servant people.[50] 'Whatever their blessings, their chief dignity is to share his title.'[51] Now that the suffering servant has freed his people from their sin, they are free to serve Yahweh. They have a 'righteousness' (*ṣĕdāqâ*) that comes from the Lord, not themselves; they have been vindicated of the charges against them and been declared not guilty because of what the servant has done for them.[52] The various blessings that come to his servant people through work of the servant are summed up as their 'heritage' (*naḥălâ*) or their inheritance, language that encompasses the land promise to Abraham but goes far beyond it to

---

[49] The verb *pāga'* has the general sense of encountering someone, but the nature of that encounter can take a variety of forms. In numerous places it refers to pleading or making intercession with someone, whether another human being (Gen. 23:8; Ruth 1:16; Isa. 53:12; 59:16; Jer. 15:11; 36:25) or God (Job 21:15; Jer. 7:16; 27:18); see Grisanti 1997: 3.575. Isa. 53:6 uses this verb to assert that Yahweh 'laid on him the iniquity of us all', resulting in a subtle wordplay with Isa. 53:12. Yahweh laying the sin of his people on the servant is the means by which the servant in fact intercedes for his people (i.e. acts on behalf of them).

[50] This may be hinted at in Isa. 19:21–23, where in the promised day of the Lord 'the Egyptians will know Yahweh in that day and serve [*'ābad*] with sacrifice and offering . . . in that day . . . the Egyptians will serve [*'ābad*] with the Assyrians' (AT).

[51] Motyer 1993: 451. Cf. Koole (1998: 2.398), who summarizes that the inheritance in view here is that 'God's servants share in this promised glory'.

[52] Most English versions render *ṣĕdāqâ* as 'vindication', which as Oswalt (1998: 431) points out would make better sense if the verse were referring to the Lord's righteousness. But since it here refers to that of the servant's people, 'righteousness' makes better sense as a translation, since it focuses on the status of the people redeemed by the servant (cf. the conclusion of Motyer [1993: 451] that 'vindication' is 'an absurd mistranslation' here!). As Oswalt (1998: 431) goes on to note, 'It is not accidental that this is just what the first Christians understood the righteousness of faith to consist of: it is the inheritance of the servants of the Lord.'

express a renewed relationship transcending anything previous.[53] Thus, Koole is on the right track when he concludes that righteousness here refers to humanity's restored relationship with God, 'in which his original and ultimate purpose for man and the world is realized'.[54] The freedom to serve Yahweh unrestricted by the constraints of spiritual and political oppression is in one sense the ultimate goal of the suffering servant redeeming his people. Once again, we see the pattern of God producing a servant people through the work of an individual servant.

From this starting point we can now look at how the work of the servant fulfils God's promises to Abraham and David, which as we have seen will be the means by which God will realize his original purpose for creation. The Abrahamic promises are most prominent from the opening lines of Isaiah 54, which opens with a call for God's restored people to 'sing' (*rānan*) and 'break forth' (*pāṣaḥ*). These same verbs occur in Isaiah 49:13, here in response to what the servant will do. The 'barren one, who did not bear' (Isa. 54:1) hearkens back to Isaiah 51:2, where Abraham's wife, Sarah (who according to Gen. 11:30 was barren), is referred to as the one 'who bore you'. God's people are called to remember that despite her barrenness, Yahweh fulfilled his promise to bless and multiply Abraham's offspring through her; based on that previous faithfulness God's people can be assured that he will comfort Zion and transform creation itself (Isa. 51:2–3). When that happens, God's righteousness will finally be revealed, resulting in the salvation of God's people, including the Gentiles (Isa. 51:4–8). Through the work of the suffering servant, the promised eschatological people of God have come into existence (Isa. 54:1–3). They are so numerous that their habitations must be enlarged! The offspring of the servant will 'inherit the nations' (Isa. 54:3 AT; cf. LXX),[55] language that recalls God's promise to bless all the nations through Abraham (Gen. 12:3; 18:18) and that he would become the father of many nations (Gen. 17:5–6).

The work of the servant also fulfils the promises to David. The assertion that the servant will see his offspring and prolong his days (Isa. 53:11) may echo themes from God's promise to David in 2 Samuel 7:12–16 of an offspring who will reign over an eternal kingdom. Referring to the servant

53 Oswalt 1998: 431.

54 Koole 1998: 2.399.

55 Most English versions render this clause 'possess the nation', which has a connotation of conquest. But as ibid. (357) points out, the language here must be understood in the light of Isa. 49:17–23, where the nations are included within God's redemptive actions.

as 'the righteous one' recalls the description of the Davidic king in Isaiah 11:4–5, who judges the poor in righteousness and wears righteousness as a belt around his waist. Dividing a portion with the many and the spoil with the strong (Isa. 53:12) shows affinity to what will happen when the Davidic king comes; according to Isaiah 9:2 that will result in the nation being multiplied and experiencing the kind of joy that comes when one divides the spoil of battle. In Psalm 2:8 Yahweh promises that the promised Davidic king will inherit the nations, which is exactly what Isaiah 54:3 indicates has happened through the work of the servant.[56] The self-sacrificial and substitutionary death of the servant results in Yahweh's 'steadfast love' not departing and a 'covenant of peace' that 'shall not be removed' (Isa. 54:10).[57] That this refers to the Davidic covenant is confirmed by Isaiah 55:3–4, where Yahweh says to those who respond to his invitation to experience the benefits of the work of the servant:

> I will make with you an everlasting covenant,
>   my steadfast, sure love for David.
> Behold, I made him a witness to the peoples,
>   a leader and commander for the peoples.

The parallelism between 'everlasting covenant'[58] and 'steadfast sure love for David' mirrors the parallelism between 'covenant of peace' and 'steadfast love' in 54:10. Through his death and resurrection the servant will

---

[56] Helpfully noted by Motyer (1993: 446).

[57] The exact expression 'covenant of peace' occurs elsewhere in only three other places. In response to Phinehas's zeal to protect the purity of God's people from idolatry, God grants him his 'covenant of peace' (Num. 25:12). The other two occurrences are in Ezekiel. As a result of appointing his servant David to feed and shepherd his people (Ezek. 34:23–24), Yahweh promises 'I will make with them a covenant of peace' (Ezek. 34:25) that results in the transformation of creation (Ezek. 34:25–31). In a similar vein, God promises a day when his servant David will be king and shepherd over his people (Ezek. 37:24–25); in that day Yahweh says, 'I will make a covenant of peace with them. It shall be an everlasting covenant with them. And I will set them in their land and multiply them, and will set my sanctuary in their midst for evermore' (Ezek. 37:26).

[58] This exact expression is applied to the Noahic covenant (Gen. 9:16), the Abrahamic covenant (Gen. 17:7, 13, 19; 1 Chr. 16:15, 17; Ps. 105:8, 10), the Sabbath requirement of the Mosaic covenant (Exod. 31:16; Lev. 24:8), the food provision for the Levitical priests (Num. 18:19), the Davidic covenant (2 Sam. 23:5) and the new covenant (Isa. 61:8; Jer. 32:40; 50:5; Ezek. 16:60; 37:26). One interesting use of this expression is Isa. 24:5, where in the context of judgment on the whole earth its inhabitants are said to have 'broken the everlasting covenant'. The context provides little help in determining what is in view: the covenant (if there was one!) with Adam? The various covenants considered as a whole?

bring the Davidic covenant to fulfilment, a fulfilment that includes the Gentiles within his saving work.

Although less prominent in the immediate context of Isaiah 52:13 – 53:12,[59] the larger context of Isaiah 40 – 66 links the work of the servant to the fulfilment of God's original purpose for creation. Yahweh's promise to forgive the sins of his people and restore them from their exile is repeatedly linked to the transformation of creation (e.g. Isa. 42:15–16; 43:19–21; 51:3, 16). Given that the servant is the agent who accomplishes these realities, it is at least implicit that the servant is also the agent of the new creation. This conclusion is further supported by the connections between the servant and the promised Davidic king noted above. According to Isaiah 11:1–9, the final outcome of his righteous rule is the transformation of creation itself. But it is not until the closing chapters of Isaiah that the transformation of creation through the work of the servant comes into focus.

Isaiah 65:1–16 lays out a basic contrast between those who rebel against Yahweh and his servants. His servants (also referred to as offspring from Jacob) will possess/inherit the new creation (65:8–9); in that inheritance they will eat, drink, rejoice and sing with gladness of heart (65:13–14). Yahweh will even give them a special name (65:15). That description of the blessings that come to Yahweh's servants leads into a description of where the servants will dwell – the new heavens and new earth that the Lord is making (65:17–25). The assertion that the former things will no longer be remembered (65:17) recalls similar statements in connection with the work of the servant (Isa. 42:9; 43:18–19). The calls to rejoice and the emphasis on the joy of God's people in the new creation (65:18) echo the commands to rejoice in response to the work of the servant (49:13; 54:1). The claim that God's transformed people will not labour in vain (65:23) answers the concern of the servant that his labour will be in vain (49:4). The offspring who are blessed by Yahweh (65:23) are the offspring that the servant sees prosper as a result of his work (53:10), servants created by the suffering servant (54:17). The harmony within nature and among humanity promised as a result of the Davidic king (Isa. 11:6–7) has now come to pass through the work of the servant in the new creation

[59] It should be noted in passing that Isa. 54:11–12 describes different features of restored Zion with various precious stones, language that Rev. 21:19–21 uses to describe the New Jerusalem; see further Beale 1999: 1082–1085.

(65:25). Even the great enemy of humanity – the serpent – will be finally and eternally condemned (65:25; cf. Gen. 3:14). Yahweh's servants will dwell peacefully with him on his holy mountain (Isa. 65:25), which is another way of referring to the Lord's temple sanctuary (cf. Isa. 2:2–4).

Isaiah 66:7–24 extends the vision of the new creation even further. Using language that echoes Isa. 54:1–3, God's renewed people – brought into existence through the work of the servant – are called to rejoice (Isa. 66:7–11). The culminating blessing of this redemption (66:12–14) is that 'the hand of the LORD shall be known to his servants' (66:14). God will send out his servants to the nations to proclaim Yahweh's glory to those who have neither seen nor heard it (65:18–19), just as he commissioned the servant to be a light to the nations (49:6). They will stream to 'my holy mountain Jerusalem' and make offerings to the Lord; some will even serve Yahweh as priests and Levites (66:20–21)! The offspring of the suffering servant will endure for ever, just like the new heavens and new earth themselves (66:22–23; cf. 53:10). All flesh will worship before Yahweh (66:23), since God has bared his holy arm to the ends of the earth through the work of the servant (52:10; 53:1).

Conclusion

To this point in the biblical narrative each of the key servants we have identified – Adam, Moses, Joshua and David – were individuals who had already stepped on to or were still on the stage of redemptive history when their story was told. In Isaiah the picture is more complex. On the one hand, the servant is identified as the nation of Israel, set apart by God to be a light to the nations by mediating his glorious presence through their faithfulness to Yahweh. Yet Israel has failed miserably as Yahweh's servant. Instead of being a light to the nations, they themselves are blind. Instead of being his messenger, they are deaf. Instead of distinguishing themselves by faithful and exclusive devotion to Yahweh, they are characterized by the idolatry of the nations around them. The Lord's revealed purpose of working through Israel as his servant to realize his creational and redemptive purposes appears to be in serious jeopardy.

So in response to Israel's failure as the servant of the Lord, Yahweh raises up a new servant. This new servant is an individual who will restore Israel and be a light to the nations of Yahweh's salvation (49:1–12). This individual servant will obey where Israel failed, trusting in the Lord for vindication in the midst of suffering (50:4–9). Through the vicarious suffering of this servant for the sins of the people, Yahweh accomplishes the redemption he promised (52:13 – 53:12). The saving work of this individual servant inaugurates the new covenant and creates servants who reflect God's glory to the ends of the earth (54:1–17). Through this servant God will fulfil his original purpose for creation and fulfil his covenant promises to Abraham and David. As a prophet this servant will announce the word of the Lord to the ends of the earth. As a priest this servant will offer his own life as a sacrifice for the sins of his people (Jew and Gentile alike). As a king the servant will rule over his people and establish a kingdom that will transform creation itself.[60] Thus, this individual Isaianic servant seems to be a culmination of previous servants, embodying elements of the previous servants and anticipating their fulfilment in a singular individual who will transcend all who came before him.

But when Isaiah penned these words, such a servant was nowhere to be found. He could only inspire God's people to eagerly anticipate the day when this individual servant would finally come to announce the good news that the kingdom of God was at hand, offer his own life as a sacrifice for sin, and rise from the dead as the rightful king of creation.

60 Given the threefold nature of the servant's identity and work, it is not surprising that scholars have seen the Isaianic servant as a new Moses, a Davidic figure, or even in priestly terms; for a helpful summary see Hugenberger 1995: 111–119.

7
Jesus: the servant par excellence

> For I tell you that Christ became a servant to the circumcised to show God's truthfulness, in order to confirm the promises given to the patriarchs, and in order that the Gentiles might glorify God for his mercy. As it is written,
>
> 'Therefore I will praise you among the Gentiles,
> and sing to your name.'
>
> (Rom. 15:8–9)

When it comes to Jesus' identity as the servant of the Lord, there is no shortage of scholarship.[1] The overwhelming focus of scholarly attention has been fixated on the extent to which the New Testament authors describe the identity and work of Jesus with language borrowed from the servant figure of Isaiah 40 – 55, and there is a broad consensus that these chapters played an important role in shaping the early church's proclamation of Jesus, likely originating with Jesus himself.[2] As a result there are numerous passages in the Gospels, Acts and the epistles that use language from the Isaianic servant passages to explain the identity and work of Jesus. Indeed, the sheer number of places where servant language is

---

[1] For a helpful bibliography of works until 2003, see Janowski and Stuhlmacher 2004: 462–492.

[2] While this conclusion is widely embraced with varying nuances, a notable exception is Morna Hooker (Hooker 1959; 1998: 88–103), who contends that there is no evidence that Jesus interpreted his mission in the light of Isa. 53; instead, it was Paul who first made such a connection. Given his well-known work on detecting OT allusions and echoes, it is surprising that Richard Hays concludes there is 'very little evidence' that the Isaianic servant shaped Mark's presentation of Jesus (Hays 2016: 86–87). He reaches a similar conclusion regarding Matthew ('lack of strong intertextual references to Isaiah's portrayal of the Suffering Servant', 160), though he sees more evidence in both Luke and John. By contrast, as we will see below, there is ample evidence in both Mark and Matthew for the influence of the Isaianic servant on their respective presentations of Jesus.

applied to Jesus makes it impossible to treat every possible passage, though this chapter will seek to address a large number of those texts. But in this fascination with Jesus as the suffering servant of Isaiah, what has too often been overlooked is that the New Testament presents Jesus as the fulfilment of previous servants such as Adam, Moses and David. Through his life, ministry, death, resurrection and ascension, Jesus fulfils the roles of each of these key servants while simultaneously avoiding their failures.

So while the main focus of this chapter will be the numerous places where the New Testament portrays Jesus as the Isaianic servant, we will also briefly explore how the New Testament presents Jesus as the fulfilment of previous servants, marking him off as the servant of the Lord par excellence.

Servant language applied to Jesus

The New Testament writers apply servant language to various aspects of Jesus' life, ministry, death and resurrection. But before we look at the numerous examples of these, we must first look at two passages that appear to frame the entirety of Jesus' life, ministry, death and resurrection against the backdrop of the Isaianic servant.

The first is the famous Christ-hymn in Philippians 2:5–11,[3] where Paul writes:

> Have this mind among yourselves, which is yours in Christ Jesus,
> who, though he was in the form of God,
> did not count equality with God a thing to be grasped,
> but emptied himself,
> by taking the form of a servant,
> being born in the likeness of men.
> And being found in human form,
> he humbled himself
> by becoming obedient to the point of death,
> even death on a cross.
> Therefore God has highly exalted him

[3] I am using the term 'hymn' as a convenient way of referring to this passage without claiming it was an actual song used in early Christian worship. Many argue that it was in fact an early Christian worship song; see discussion in Martin 1997: 1–41. Others argue that this passage is simply exalted prose; see e.g. Fee 1992: 29–46. A decision either way does not affect the argument here.

and bestowed on him the name
that is above every name,
so that at the name of Jesus
every knee should bow,
in heaven and on earth and under the earth,
and every tongue confess that
Jesus Christ is Lord,
to the glory of God the Father.

Although a number of Old Testament motifs and backgrounds are likely present in this hymn, the Isaianic servant seems to have pride of place.[4] The various allusions and echoes can be summarized as in Table 5.[5]

Table 5 Isaianic allusions and echoes in the Christ-hymn

Verse	*Word/phrase in Philippians 2:5–11*	*Passage from Isaiah*
2:7	Emptied himself	Isaiah 53:12
2:7	Form of a servant	Isaiah 52:13–14; 53:11
2:7	Form of a servant	Isaiah 49:7 or 53:11 (LXX = *douleuonta*)
2:7	Likeness of men	Isaiah 52:14; 53:2
2:8	Found in appearance as a man	Isaiah 52:14; 53:2–3
2:8	Humbled himself	Isaiah 53:3–4, 7–8
2:8	Obedient to the point of death	Isaiah 53:7–8, 12
2:8	Death on a cross	Isaiah 52:14; 53:3–8
2:9	God highly exalted him	Isaiah 52:13; 53:12
2:10	Every knee will bow	Isaiah 45:23
2:11	Every tongue confess	Isaiah 45:23
2:11	To the glory of God	Isaiah 45:24–25

Admittedly, some of the proposed allusions and echoes are stronger than others. But considered together their cumulative weight indicates that

[4] In addition to the Isaianic servant, Paul likely draws on the creation (Gen. 1:26–27; Ps. 8:5) and fall (Gen. 3) of Adam, the Son of Man from Dan. 7 and the exaltation of David's Lord from Ps. 110:1; for a summary see Harmon 2015: 59–66.

[5] Taken from ibid. 202–203. Others who prioritize the Isaianic background include Hofius (1991) and Stuhlmacher (2018: 325–326).

Paul presents the person and work of Jesus against the backdrop of the Isaianic servant.[6] Beyond these verbal connections there are a number of conceptual parallels between the Isaianic servant and the description of Christ here in Philippians 2:5–11. First, Isaiah 52:13 – 53:12 places strong emphasis on the humanity of the servant (52:14; 53:2–3) with a focus on his lowliness and ordinary appearance; in a similar fashion Philippians 2:6–8 describes Christ's entrance into the world as a lowly slave/servant who gave every appearance of being an ordinary human being. Second, Isaiah 52:13 – 53:12 emphasizes the obedience of the servant even in the face of brutal suffering (53:4–8): Philippians 2:6–8 emphasizes Christ's obedience even to the point of death. Third, the servant is marked by his humility and meekness (53:7), which is also a distinctive attribute of Christ in Philippians 2:6–8. Fourth, just as the Isaianic servant ultimately lays down his life as a sacrifice for sin (52:13 – 53:12), Jesus obeys to the point of death on a cross (2:8). Fifth, the Isaianic servant experiences exaltation/vindication after his death (53:11–12); so too Christ after his death is highly exalted and given the name above every name (2:9–11). Sixth, Paul clearly quotes from Isaiah 45:23 in Philippians 2:10, showing that the larger context of Isaiah may be in view. Finally, there is a similar progression in both Isaiah 52:13 – 53:12 and Philippians 2:5–11 in which a figure moves from a state of exaltation to a state of humiliation and then is exalted to an even higher state of exaltation. Based on this evidence, it is reasonable to conclude that Paul is drawing upon the imagery and language of the suffering servant of Isaiah 52:13 – 53:12 to describe the work of Christ.

The second passage to consider is Luke 4:16–30, which is widely recognized as programmatic for the entirety of Luke's Gospel.[7] While attending his home-town synagogue of Nazareth, Jesus reads from Isaiah 61:1–2 (with a line from Isa. 58:6 inserted):

> The Spirit of the Lord is upon me,
> because he has anointed me
> to proclaim good news to the poor.

[6] Scholars continue to debate whether Paul wrote the hymn himself or is borrowing it from someone else. But even if Paul is borrowing it from someone, his use of it indicates that he embraces its content and intent.

[7] For a straightforward summary of the importance of this passage within Luke, see Green 1992: 24–32.

He has sent me to proclaim liberty to the captives
and recovering of sight to the blind,
to set at liberty those who are oppressed,
to proclaim the year of the Lord's favour.
(Luke 4:18–19)[8]

He then announces that this passage has been fulfilled in the hearing of those gathered. Jesus is initially well received, but when he begins to highlight God's work among Gentiles during Old Testament days the crowd turns on him and attempts to throw him over the brow of the hill.

From the remainder of Luke's Gospel it becomes clear that this citation of Isaiah 61:1–2 serves as a sort of mission statement that explains what the reader is about to see Jesus do, and the nature of that mission has an Isaianic hue. As David Pao notes: 'the significance of the Isaianic quotation in Luke 4:16–30 lies in the introduction of the Isaianic New Exodus with the claim that Christians are now the legitimate heirs of the ancient Israelite tradition'.[9] It is true that Isaiah 61:1–2 is not one of the traditionally identified servant songs, nor does its immediate context indicate that the servant is in view. However, numerous scholars have noted the parallels between the description of the unidentified figure of Isaiah 61:1–4 and the servant of Isaiah 40 – 55; indeed, W. A. M. Beuken has gone so far as to argue that Isaiah 61 is an interpretation of the servant's work described in Isa. 40 – 55.[10] So while we cannot be certain that Luke sees the figure of Isaiah 61 as the servant, the nature of the mission described by Isaiah 61 bears a number of striking similarities to that of the Isaianic servant.

Also worth noting in connection with this Isaianic framing of Jesus' ministry is the possibility that Luke has framed the narrative of Acts as the fulfilment of the servant's mission to restore Israel and be a light of salvation to the Gentiles (Isa. 49:6).[11] While holding the Christ child in his arms. Simeon alludes to Isaiah 49:6 when he describes Jesus as:

---

[8] Luke has omitted the line 'to heal the brokenhearted' from Isa. 61:1 and replaced it with 'to set at liberty those who are oppressed' from Isa. 58:6. For discussion of the textual details, see Pao 2002: 72–74.

[9] Ibid. 77.

[10] Beuken 1989: 411–442. Like the servant of Yahweh, the figure of Isa. 61:1–4 (1) has the Spirit of Yahweh upon him (cf. 42:1); (2) is sent by Yahweh (cf. 48:16); (3) announces good news (cf. 52:7); (4) releases prisoners from captivity (cf. 42:7); and (5) comes at a time of Yahweh's favour (cf. 49:8). Pao (2002: 77) is thus correct in stating: 'It is therefore justifiable to conclude that the figure in 61:1 is modeled upon (if not identical with) the servant figure in Isa. 40–55.'

[11] In what follows I am largely following Pao (2002: 84–109).

> a light for revelation to the Gentiles,
> and for glory to your people Israel.
> (Luke 2:32)

Jesus' summary of the message of the Old Testament in Luke 24:44–49 alludes to Isaiah 49:6 when it portrays the gospel going to the ends of the earth. Acts 1:8 also alludes to Isaiah 49:6 when Jesus announces that the disciples will be his witnesses to the ends of the earth. Paul and Barnabas explain their mission to the Gentiles by citing Isaiah 49:6 in Acts 13:47. In Paul's summary of the gospel message before Agrippa, Paul alludes to Isaiah 49:6 and 53:11 (Acts 26:23). Luke's use of Isaiah 49:6 at key points throughout the narrative of Luke–Acts suggests the importance of Jesus' identity as the servant for understanding his life, ministry, death, resurrection, ascension and commissioning of his people as witnesses of the good news.

Birth and early childhood

There is no passage that unambiguously applies servant language to Jesus in connection with his birth or early childhood. Several scholars, however, have suggested possible allusions to servant texts such as Isaiah 42:6; 49:6; and/or 53:2 in Matthew 2:23.[12] Upon returning from Egypt Jesus' parents settled in Nazareth so that 'what was spoken by the prophets might be fulfilled: "He shall be called a Nazarene."' Unlike previous uses of the fulfilment formula in the first two chapters of Matthew, there is no obvious Old Testament text that Matthew is citing.[13] The reference to 'prophets' plural suggests multiple texts are in view,[14] and there are good reasons to think Matthew draws on texts that speak of a 'branch' (Hebr. *nēṣer*) accomplishing God's purposes. Thus, in Isaiah 42:6 Yahweh says to the servant 'I have called you in righteousness', using the same verb for 'called' (Gr. *kaleō*) as here in Matthew 2:23. He also promises to 'keep' (Hebr. *nāṣar*) the servant, using a verb from the same root as the noun for 'branch'. Similarly, in Isaiah 49:6 the servant is sent to bring back 'the preserved of Israel', which in the MT comes from either the qal passive

---

12 For Isa. 42:6 and 49:6, see Davies and Allison 2004: 1.279; for Isa. 53:2, see France 1985: 93–94 and now more recently France 2007: 93–95 as well as Wilkins 2012: 116–119.

13 For a helpful summary of the issues involved, see Davies and Allison 2004: 1.276–283.

14 Suggestions include Gen. 49:26; Judg. 13:5–7; Isa. 4:2–3; 11:1; Jer. 31:6–7.

participle of the Hebrew verb *nāṣar* or the Hebrew adjective *nṣyr*.[15] Either way, it forms a verbal link to the branch concept. Isaiah 53:2 may further this connection. France argues that in calling Jesus a Nazarene, Matthew is tapping into a line of Old Testament expectation of a messiah who would largely be unrecognized and not be taken seriously by his people (Zech. 9 – 14).[16] Isaiah 53:1–3 emphasizes the unimpressive appearance of the servant and the people's rejection of him as one who is despised and considered of no account. Thus, the statement about the servant that 'he grew up before him like a young plant, / and like a root out of dry ground' (Isa. 53:2) stresses his unexpected origins. As a result, calling Jesus a Nazarene 'represent[s] the prophetic expectation that the Messiah would appear from nowhere and would as a result meet with incomprehension and rejection'.[17]

Given the difficulty of the passage and the number of possible Old Testament texts Matthew could be drawing upon, however, it seems best to regard the possible use of servant language here as tentative. The number of explicit citations and strong allusions to servant passages elsewhere in Matthew adds greater weight to this possibility, but stops well short of making it certain.[18]

Baptism

The baptism of Jesus by John the Baptist also appears to have been shaped in part by servant language. When Jesus asks John to baptize him, John initially refuses (Matt. 3:14). Jesus replies, 'Let it be so now, for thus it is fitting for us to fulfil all righteousness' (Matt. 3:15). Michael J. Wilkins has proposed that the expression 'fulfil all righteousness' echoes the description of the suffering servant, who is 'the righteous one' who 'make[s] many to be accounted righteous' (Isa. 53:11).[19] By identifying with his people in baptism, Jesus is acting as the servant of Yahweh, set apart to bear their sins (Matt. 8:17) and eventually give his life as a ransom (Matt. 20:28); in

[15] For a concise discussion of the text-critical issue, see Goldingay and Payne 2006: 2.165–166. As Davies and Allison (2004: 1.279) note, if the proper reading is the adjective, it could be understood as 'a patronymic, "Nazarene". In this case the verse could be referred to Jesus: "and a Nazarene to restore Israel"'.

[16] France 2007: 94.

[17] Ibid. 95.

[18] See further Hill (1979: 2–16), who situates his proposal that Isa. 42:6 and 49:6 may be in view here within the larger use of the servant motif in Matthew.

[19] Wilkins 2012: 119–120.

doing so he fulfils what is necessary for the saving righteousness of Yahweh to be manifested.[20]

When John does finally immerse Jesus in the waters of the Jordan River, the heavens open and the Spirit descends upon Jesus in the form of a dove (Matt. 3:16; Mark 1:10; Luke 3:21).[21] The Father affirms the identity of Jesus, announcing from heaven: 'You are my beloved Son; with you I am well pleased' (Mark 1:11; Luke 3:22; cf. Matt. 3:17).[22] Within this short statement, at least two Old Testament texts are alluded to: Jesus is the beloved Son anticipated in Psalm 2:7 and is the Isaianic servant in whom Yahweh delights (Isa. 42:1).[23] As Craig Blomberg notes, together these two allusions 'reflect the heavenly Father's understanding of Jesus' dual role: one day a kingly messiah, but for now a suffering servant – both appropriate to his unique identity as the divine son'.[24] Jesus' combined identity as the suffering servant and the Davidic king resonates with Matthew's larger typological framework of Jesus as the true Israel who obeys where Israel failed. Within its context in Mark's Gospel this combined allusion presents Jesus as both the true Israel and Israel's messianic servant deliverer who leads his people in the promised new exodus.[25] For Luke, the sonship language borrowed from Psalm 2:7 pushes beyond a reference to David and Israel to Adam himself, who in the genealogy that follows is referred to as 'the son of God' (Luke 3:38). Darrell Bock suggests that, in addition to the clear allusions to Psalm 2:7 and Isaiah 42:1, the language of 'beloved' comes from Isaiah 41:8, where 'the ideas of servant, chosen, and beloved are tied together'; as such it ties together the concepts of

20 France 2007: 119–121.

21 In passing we should note the possibility of an echo of Isa. 11:2, which asserts that the Spirit of the Lord will rest upon the branch from David's line (Isa. 11:1) and that this Spirit-anointed ruler will delight in the fear of Yahweh (Isa. 11:3). This echo seems all the more likely in the light of the combined allusion to Ps. 2:7 and Isa. 42:1 in the Father's announcement from heaven in Matt. 3:17.

22 Both Mark 1:11 and Luke 3:22 describe the voice speaking directly to Jesus (note the second-person pronouns), while in Matt. 3:17 the voice addresses those gathered (note the third-person pronouns). There is no substantial difference in meaning.

23 Gen. 22:2 may also be in the background here: God instructs Abraham to 'Take your son, your only son Isaac, whom you love' (cf. 22:12, 16). Also possible are allusions to Exod. 4:22–23, Isa. 63:7 – 64:12 and Ps. 74:19–20, on which see further Capes 1999: 37–49. If Isa. 63:7 – 64:12 is part of the intertextual matrix, that would highlight the presence of new-exodus motifs, which in Isaiah is accomplished by the suffering servant. Capes further suggests that the dove descending from heaven evokes new-creation motifs based on Gen. 8.

24 Blomberg 2007: 14.

25 Watts 2000: 108–120. While focusing more on the importance of the allusion to Ps. 2:7, Marcus (1992: 48–79) recognizes the contributing role of Isa. 42:1 in Mark's presentation of Jesus' messianic identity.

Messiah, Son, servant and representation of Israel.[26] The servant language borrowed from Isaiah 42:1 (i.e. the Spirit coming upon Jesus and the language of being well-pleased) also anticipates the programmatic description of Jesus' ministry in Luke 4:16–30, which has Isaiah 61:1–2 at its core.[27] Luke thus:

> links the royal messianic status of Jesus with that of the Isaianic Servant of Yahweh as he participates in the unfolding of the eschatological program as indicated in 3:4–6 [which itself is a citation of Isa. 40:3–5]. Moreover, this points forward to Jesus' Nazareth sermon (4:18–19), where the anointment of the Spirit is again explicated by two Isaianic passages (Isa. 58:6; 61:1–2).[28]

While the Gospel according to John does not record Jesus' baptism, it does refer to it indirectly. One day when John the Baptist sees Jesus, he says to the crowds, 'Behold, the Lamb of God, who takes away the sin of the world!' (John 1:29). He goes on to explain this exclamation based on seeing the Spirit descend from heaven on to Jesus in the form of a dove, adding that this identifies him as the Son of God (John 1:30–34). Behind the reference to Jesus as the lamb of God may be an allusion to Isaiah 53:6–10, which describes the servant as a lamb led to the slaughter, a sacrifice for the sins of his people.[29] This possibility is further supported by John's citation of Isaiah 53:1 as an explanation for why people did not believe in Jesus as the Messiah (John 12:37–38). John's presentation of Jesus' death against the backdrop of the sacrifice of the Passover lamb may further suggest that the expression 'the Lamb of God, who takes away the sin of the world' draws on numerous Old Testament

---

26 Bock 2011: 160.

27 On the importance of Isa. 61:1–2 within Luke 4:16–30 and its place within the structure of Luke–Acts, see Pao 2002: 70–84. Pao and Schnabel (2007: 280) note that Luke connects Luke 3:18 and 4:18 (which cites Isa. 61:1) by using the same preposition ('upon'; Gr. *epi*) to describe the Spirit's relationship to Jesus.

28 Pao and Schnabel 2007: 281.

29 See e.g. to varying degrees Carson 1991: 150; Keener 2003: 1:452–454; Köstenberger 2004: 66; Lang 2017: 148–163. Carson (1991: 150) further observes that 'the Aramaic word *ṭalyā* probably spoken by the Baptist can mean either "servant" or "lamb"' before qualifying this observation by noting that 'this presupposes that whoever put this Aramaic expression into Greek somehow avoided a perfectly common and obvious expression, "the servant of the Lord", in order to produce a new and rather strange expression, "the lamb of God"'.

motifs such as the Day of Atonement, the Passover lamb and the suffering servant.[30]

Ministry

As the ministry of Jesus unfolds, the Gospel writers use a combination of explicit citations and subtle allusions to explain specific actions of Jesus in the light of his identity as the servant.

All three Synoptic Gospels record Jesus' healing of Peter's mother-in-law in Capernaum and the subsequent healing of many others at sunset on the same evening (Matt. 8:14–17; Mark 1:29–34; Luke 4:38–41). But only Matthew cites an Old Testament text to explain these actions; according to him: 'This was to fulfil what was spoken by the prophet Isaiah: "He took our illnesses and bore our diseases"' (Matt. 8:17).[31] This direct citation of Isaiah 53:4 portrays Jesus' healing ministry as an act of the Isaianic servant, but in a slightly unexpected manner. Whereas Isaiah 53:4 portrays this act in terms of vicarious suffering, Matthew seems to portray the 'taking' in terms of removing physical ailments from people.[32] This initial dissonance dissipates when one recognizes that the connection between sin and sickness was deeply rooted within Scripture and Jewish tradition;[33] the very presence of sickness in the world is the result of sin entering through Adam's rebellion in the garden. Thus, D. A. Carson is correct when he concludes that:

> Matthew holds that *Jesus' healing ministry is itself a function of his substitutionary death*, by which he lays the foundation for destroying sickness ... Thus the healings during Jesus' ministry can be

30 This conclusion does not demand that John the Baptist himself had all of these associations in mind when he identified Jesus this way. It is entirely possible that like the high priest Caiaphas he spoke better than he realized (John 11:49–52). As Carson (1991: 150) observes, 'It is not that he thought the Baptist wrong; rather, as a post-resurrection Christian John could grasp a fuller picture than was possible for the Baptist. In particular he understood a great deal more about the significance of the Messiah's sacrificial death. It is hard to imagine that he could use an expression such as "Lamb of God" *without* thinking of the atoning sacrifice of his resurrected and ascended Saviour'; emphasis original.

31 Matthew's rendering of Isa. 53:4 does not match the LXX or the Targums, suggesting that he is offering his own translation from the Hebrew.

32 Davies and Allison (2004: 2.38) note two Jewish texts (*T. Jos.* 17:7; *b. Sanh.* 98a–b) that appear to interpret the infirmities of Isa. 53:4 as physical.

33 See e.g. Gen. 19:11; Exod. 4:11; Deut. 28:28–29; 2 Kgs 6:18; Mark 2:1–12; John 9:2; *b. Meg.* 17b; *Ned.* 41a; *Sabb.* 55a.

> understood not only as the foretaste of the kingdom but also as the fruit of Jesus' death.[34]

Understood another way, connecting servant language to Jesus' healing ministry is a demonstration of his meekness and mercy as 'he identifies with humanity in its suffering'.[35]

Several chapters later Matthew again cites a servant passage to explain both what Jesus does and why he does it. After healing a man with a withered hand on the Sabbath, the Pharisees conspire to destroy Jesus (Matt. 12:9–14). Despite withdrawing from the area 'many followed him, and he healed them all and ordered them not to make him known' (Matt. 12:15–16). Matthew states that 'This was to fulfil what was spoken by the prophet Isaiah' (Matt. 12:17), which introduces a citation of Isaiah 42:1–4.[36] As with the citation of Isaiah 53:4 in Matthew 8:17, Jesus' healing ministry is explained in terms of the Isaianic servant. But with the citation of Isaiah 42:1–4 the focus rests more on Jesus' character as the servant. As the Spirit-anointed one in whom Yahweh delights, he will bring justice to the nations. Despite the opposition he will not contend with them by stooping to their level. Rather than exploit the miraculous healings for his own selfish aggrandizement, he heals the most vulnerable with remarkable gentleness and compassion.

The larger context of Matthew 12 provides further insight into the significance of the citation from Isaiah 42:1–4. Three times in this chapter Matthew records Jesus asserting that he is 'greater' than an Old Testament institution or person:

> I tell you, *something greater than the temple* is here.
> (Matt. 12:6)

> For just as Jonah was three days and three nights in the belly of the great fish, so will the Son of Man be three days and three nights in the heart of the earth. The men of Nineveh will rise up at the judgment with this generation and condemn it, for they repented at

[34] Carson 1994: 206; emphasis original.

[35] Davies and Allison 2004: 2.38.

[36] As is often noted, this is the longest OT citation in Matthew's Gospel. Since it matches no known extant form of Isa. 42:1–4, it seems likely that it is Matthew's own translation from the Hebrew; for a concise summary of the textual differences, see Blomberg 2007: 43.

> the preaching of Jonah, and behold, *something greater than Jonah* is here.
> (Matt. 12:40–41)

> The queen of the South will rise up at the judgment with this generation and condemn it, for she came from the ends of the earth to hear the wisdom of Solomon, and behold, *something greater than Solomon* is here.
> (Matt. 12:42)

Considered together, Jesus claims that he is greater than the three foundational institutions of Israel – priesthood, kingship and the prophetic office. Given that the citation of Isaiah 42:1–4 (the longest OT citation in Matthew) sits in the midst of this chapter, it is possible that Matthew is presenting Jesus as the one who transcends each of these institutions individually because as the servant he embodies all three of them as the true Israel who obeys where the nation failed.[37]

Also within Matthew 12 is another potential allusion to an Isaianic servant text. Immediately after the citation of Isaiah 42:1–4, Matthew recounts Jesus' healing/exorcism of a blind and mute man (Matt. 12:22–37). While the crowds wonder if Jesus could be the son of David, the Pharisees accuse him of casting out demons by the power of Beelzebub (Matt. 12:23–24). Jesus responds by asserting that it is the Spirit of God who empowers him to cast out demons, and this is evidence that God's kingdom is present (Matt. 12:28). He then adds: 'Or how can someone enter a strong man's house and plunder his goods, unless he first binds the strong man? Then indeed he may plunder his house' (Matt. 12:29). This language may allude to Isaiah 49:24–25:

> Can the prey be taken from the mighty,
> or the captives of a tyrant be rescued?
> For thus says the LORD:
> 'Even the captives of the mighty shall be taken,
> and the prey of the tyrant be rescued,

[37] Recall that in my discussion of the Isaianic servant I observed how the servant carries out priestly, royal and prophetic roles. Keener (2009: 360–361) goes so far as to claim that in this citation of Isa. 42:1–4 'Matthew here provides a hermeneutical key for his entire Gospel; his interpretation of Isaiah may explain the Israel typology predominant in texts cited in the editorial asides of his infancy narrative.'

for I will contend with those who contend with you,
and I will save your children.'

Isaiah 53:12 may also be in view, where Yahweh says of the servant:

Therefore I will divide him a portion with the many,
and he shall divide the spoil with the strong,
because he poured out his soul to death
and was numbered with the transgressors;
yet he bore the sin of many,
and makes intercession for the transgressors.

Given that Isaiah 49:1–8 announces the individual servant who will obey where the nation of Israel failed, it seems reasonable to conclude that it is through the work of the servant that Yahweh takes the captives of the mighty and rescues the prey of the tyrants. Whereas both Matthew and Mark use the expression 'plunder his house' to describe the work of the strong man, Luke 11:22 uses 'divides his spoil', perhaps in an effort to bring out the potential echo of Isaiah 53:12.[38] In any case, Rikki Watts helpfully summarizes the picture that emerges from combining these two texts from Isaiah: 'On the one hand, Jesus is apparently described in terms used of Yahweh himself (Isa. 49; cf. [Mark] 1:21f) while on the other, the imagery is related to that of the messianic "servant" (Isa. 53; cf. [Mark] 1:11).'[39]

One final event in Jesus' life that picks up servant language is the transfiguration (Matt. 17:1–13 // Mark 9:2–13 // Luke 9:28–36).[40] In the aftermath of Jesus' appearance being changed, Luke 9:31 records that Moses and Elijah 'appeared in glory and spoke of his exodus, which he was about to fulfil in Jerusalem' (AT). Given Luke's use of Isaiah throughout both

[38] See similarly Garrett 1989: 45 and Pao and Schnabel 2007: 323–324. Although both Luke 11:22 (*diadidōmi*) and Isa. 53:12 (*merizō*) use different verbs for the act of dividing or distributing, both do use the same word for spoil (*skylon*). Even with the difference, at least a conceptual parallel is present. Although the language is less explicit in Mark 3:27, Watts (2000: 147–152) nevertheless contends that an allusion to Isa. 53:12 is possible, since it aligns with Mark's larger presentation of an Isaianic new exodus that runs through Mark. If so, the combination of Isa. 49:24–26 and 53:12 present Jesus as both 'the stronger one of the INE [Isaianic New Exodus] who, after binding Satan, the strong one, is spoiling his realm and loosing the captives' (149–150) and the servant through whom the 'NE [New Exodus] is to be effected' (152).

[39] Watts 2000: 152.

[40] The intertextual matrix of OT allusions and echoes that informs this event is both rich and complex; for a concise summary, see Blomberg 2007: 55–56.

his Gospel and Acts, it seems likely that the exodus in view is the new exodus promised in Isaiah, which as we have seen is accomplished by the servant. Jesus will fulfil this exodus through his death and resurrection as the suffering servant. Similarly to Jesus' baptism, God the Father speaks from heaven, saying: 'This is my beloved Son, with whom I am well pleased; listen to him' (Matt. 17:5; cf. Mark 9:7; Luke 9:35).[41] As noted above, this pronouncement combines allusions to Psalm 2:7 and Isaiah 42:1, identifying Jesus as the promised Davidic king and the Isaianic servant.[42] But with the addition of the command 'listen to him' an additional Old Testament allusion appears – Jesus is the prophet greater than Moses to whom God's people must listen (Deut. 18:15–18). The combination of these three different Old Testament figures – the Davidic king, the Isaianic servant and the prophet greater than Moses – portray Jesus as the ultimate fulfilment of these three servant figures.

An additional echo of Isaiah 53 may be present in the discussion between Jesus and his three disciples (Peter, James and John) after the transfiguration. In response to the disciples' question about Elijah's role in God's eschatological plans, Jesus responds: 'Elijah does come first to restore all things. And how is it written of the Son of Man that he should suffer many things and be treated with contempt?' (Mark 9:12). Based on the assertion that the Old Testament ('it is written') testifies about the approaching suffering of the Son of Man, Rikki Watts has argued for an allusion to Isaiah 53.[43] While acknowledging that the reference to the Son of Man stems from Daniel 7, he concludes that 'Isaiah 53 apparently provides the basic quarry for details of the suffering motif which is then filled out and developed by allusions to other texts concerning suffering and vindication.'[44]

---

41 Only Matthew includes the phrase 'with whom I am well-pleased', thus matching the exact wording of the baptismal pronouncement. Within the textual tradition of Mark and Luke it appears some later scribes sought to add the phrase.

42 Bock (2011: 165) suggests that Luke intentionally changes the title 'the beloved' (*ho agapētos*) from the baptismal announcement to 'chosen' (*ho eklelegmenos*) here at the transfiguration to highlight the allusion to Isa. 42:1, which identifies the servant as God's chosen instrument. He further suggests that the perfect participle 'shows that Jesus has already occupied the position of the "chosen one"; enthronement is not the point here'.

43 Watts 2000: 259–269. Building on the work of Moo (1983: 90–91), Watts argues that the expression 'suffer many things and be treated with contempt' is best explained as a summary of the servant's suffering described in Isa. 53:3–7.

44 Watts 2000: 269.

Death/resurrection/ascension

While to this point we have noted a number of places where servant language is used to describe events or actions in Jesus' ministry, without question servant language is most consistently applied to Jesus in connection with his death and resurrection. These servant references range from subtle echoes to explicit citations, and often highlight Jesus' vicarious suffering for his people.

As an example of a more subtle echo, Luke 9:51 records that 'Now it came about when the days of his ascension were being fulfilled he set his face to go into Jerusalem' (AT). This verse marks a turning point in Luke, where Jesus begins his final journey to Jerusalem to culminate his redemptive work. Just as Luke used fulfilment language in the transfiguration account to describe the exodus Jesus was about to fulfil in Jerusalem (9:31), so also here Luke applies fulfilment language to Jesus' 'ascension' (*analēmpsis*).[45] This unexpected reference to the ascension is likely a reference to the totality of Jesus' redemptive work in Jerusalem, including his death and resurrection and culminating in his ascension to heaven.[46] In saying that Jesus 'set his face' to go to Jerusalem, Luke may echo Isaiah 50:7, where in the midst of his suffering the servant says:

> But the Lord God helps me;
>   therefore I have not been disgraced;
> therefore I have set my face like a flint,
>   and I know that I shall not be put to shame.

Such an echo sets the opposition that Jesus is about to face on his journey to Jerusalem within the sufferings experienced by the Isaianic servant.[47]

On his way to the cross Jesus makes a number of predictions of his soon approaching passion, and the Isaianic servant texts provide part of the

---

[45] Bock (1994: 2.967–968) concludes that the ascension/reception into heaven described here in 9:51 is what 9:31 refers to as Jesus' exodus.

[46] While this is the only NT occurrence of the noun *analēmpsis*, Luke uses the cognate verb *analambanō* three times to describe Jesus' ascension to heaven in Acts 1:2, 11, 22 (cf. 1 Tim. 3:16). The only LXX occurrence of the noun (*Pss Sol.* 4.18) refers to a man's death.

[47] Admittedly, the wording is not an exact match between Luke 9:51 and Isa. 50:7 LXX; the former uses the verb *stērizō* while the latter uses *tithēmi*. Craig Evans has argued that this expression should be understood more broadly against its use in OT prophetic texts (esp. Ezek. 21:2–6) to communicate a combined sense of divine commissioning and resolve on the prophet's part; see Evans 1982: 545–548; 1987: 80–84. So even if Luke is not echoing Isa. 50:7, certainly a conceptual parallel is present.

Old Testament textual background for the wording of these predictions. At the simplest level, the repeated use of the verb *paradidōmi* (to hand over, deliver, betray) in both the passion predictions and passion narratives likely derives from Isaiah 53.[48] According to Isaiah 53:6 LXX, the 'Lord handed over [*paradidōmi*]' the servant for our sins. Isaiah 53:12 says of the servant that 'his soul was given over [*paradidōmi*] to death' (NETS) and that 'because of their sins he was given over [*paradidōmi*]' (NETS). As Douglas Moo concludes, 'the strong element of scriptural necessity that pervades the [passion] sayings raises the possibility that it is related to, or derived from, an OT passage'.[49]

By itself the use of this verb is not enough to establish dependence on Isaiah 53, but other echoes of servant language in these passion predictions strengthen the claim. In Mark 10:33–34 Jesus concludes the prediction by stating that the Gentiles 'will mock him and spit on him, and flog him and kill him'. The language of spitting (*emptyō*) and flogging (*mastigoō*) likely stems from Isaiah 50:6 LXX, where the servant gives his back to scourges (*mastigas*) and is spit upon (*emptysma*).[50] The repetition of *emptyō* in Mark 14:65 to describe Jesus' suffering at the hands of the Roman soldiers, along with other language borrowed from Isaiah 50:6 (see below), confirms this allusion.

Based on these stronger allusions, other fainter echoes may take on greater significance. The repeated refrain of 'suffer many things' (Matt. 16:21; Mark 8:31; 9:12; Luke 9:22; 17:25) may be a general reference to 'the various scriptural prefigurements of Jesus' sufferings';[51] yet, when combined with the use of the verb 'be rejected' (*exoudeneō*) in Mark 9:12 an echo of Isaiah 53 may be in view.[52] In addition to borrowing the language of spitting and flogging from Isaiah 50:6, the statement in Mark

48 See especially Moo 1983: 92–97. This verb occurs in the following Passion predictions: Matt. 17:22 // Mark 9:31 // Luke 9:44; Matt. 20:18 // Mark 10:33 // Luke 18:32; Matt. 26:24 // Mark 14:21 // Luke 22:22; Matt. 26:45 // Mark 14:41. In the passion narratives it occurs in Matt. 26:1, 45; Mark 14:21, 41; Luke 20:20; John 19:9.

49 Ibid. 92. As we will see below, *paradidōmi* (as well as close cognates) occurs a number of times in the epistles in reference to the death of Jesus (e.g. Rom. 4:25; 8:32; Gal. 1:4; 2:20; 5:2, 25; 1 Peter 2:23).

50 Ibid. 88–89.

51 Ibid. 91.

52 See Watts (2000: 260–264), who follows Moo (1983: 89–91). While the verb 'be rejected' (*exoudeneō*) may stem from Ps. 118:22 (an OT text used frequently to explain the rejection of Jesus), it does occur in several LXX manuscripts (Symmachus, Aquila, Theodotion) of Isa. 53:3. Based on the evidence from 'OT origins, conceptual and linguistic parallels' Watts (2000: 264) concludes that if any OT text is behind the expression in Mark 9:12b 'it is Isaiah 53'.

10:33 that the Jewish leaders will 'condemn him to death' may echo Isaiah 53:8, where the servant is taken away 'by oppression and judgement' and 'cut off out of the land of the living'.[53]

Similar predictions of Jesus' death can also be found in John's Gospel, though in his own distinctive idiom. On several occasions Jesus refers to his death as being lifted up or exalted (John 3:14; 8:28; 12:32), using the same Greek verb (*hypsoō*) found in Isaiah 52:13 LXX to describe the exaltation of the servant:

> See, my servant shall understand;
> and he shall be exalted [*hypsoō*], and glorified [*doxazō*]
> exceedingly.
> (NETS)

Two additional factors verify the allusion to Isaiah 52:13. First, John also repeatedly uses the verb 'glorify' (*doxazō*) in connection with Jesus' death (7:39; 12:16, 23, 28; 13:31–32; 17:1, 5).[54] Second, shortly after Jesus proclaims that when he is lifted up he will draw all people to himself (12:32), John cites Isaiah 53:1 to explain why so many did not believe in Jesus despite his numerous signs (John 12:37). Thus, John presents the death and resurrection of Jesus as the exaltation and glorification of the Isaianic servant.[55]

Less certain, though still worth noting, are the possible echoes of servant motifs in Jesus' description of himself as the Good Shepherd (John 10:11–18). Ezekiel 34 and 37 are probably the primary Old Testament background. In contrast to the wicked shepherds (i.e. leaders) of God's people in Ezekiel's day (Ezek. 34:1–10), God promises to shepherd his people by setting up 'one shepherd, my servant David' (Ezek. 34:23). When God restores his people by raising them from the dead (Ezek. 37:1–14), he will gather them into a renewed land and 'my servant David shall be king over them, and they shall all have one shepherd' (Ezek. 37:24). Yet neither of those texts describes the shepherd laying down his life for the sheep, as

---

53 Watts 2000: 266. In addition to the conceptual parallels, the LXX uses the noun *krisis* (judgment) and Mark 10:33 uses the cognate verb *katakrinō* (to condemn, judge).

54 On the Isaianic background of these two verbs as used in John's Gospel, see Moo 1983: 97–100.

55 For a concise summary of the matrix of OT backgrounds present here, see Köstenberger 2007: 474–479.

Jesus states three times in this passage (John 10:11, 15, 17). That language may come from Isaiah 53, where the servant lays down his life for his people (53:10–12), who are described as sheep (Isa. 53:6).[56] Perhaps the reference to the shepherd who is also David the servant of Yahweh led to a connection with the suffering servant of Yahweh in Isaiah 53, creating the composite picture of the shepherd who lays down his life for the sheep.

In the final days before Jesus entered Jerusalem, James and John approach their master with a request to sit on his right and left hand in his kingdom (Matt. 20:20–28; Mark 10:35–45). When the other disciples become indignant, Jesus responds by explaining that in his kingdom greatness and leadership work differently from how they do in the world:

> But whoever would be great among you must be your servant, and whoever would be first among you must be slave of all. For even the Son of Man came not to be served but to serve, and to give his life as a ransom for many.
> (Mark 10:43b–45)[57]

There are good reasons for seeing Isaiah 53 as the primary (though certainly not exclusive!) Old Testament background for what Jesus says here.[58] Perhaps the best place to begin is at the end of the passage, where Jesus announces that part of the purpose of his coming as the Son of Man is 'to give his life as a ransom for many'; this phrase likely alludes to Isaiah 53:12, where the servant 'poured out his soul to death' and 'bore the sin of many'.[59] That allusion explains why Jesus frames this act as an act of

---

56 On this possibility, see Moo 1983: 146–147. Another possibility is Zech. 13:7, which speaks of a shepherd who stands next to Yahweh who is struck and as a result his sheep scatter.

57 The parallel in Matt. 20:26b–28 is essentially identical; the only noteworthy difference is that instead of 'slave of all' (Mark 10:44) Matthew has 'your slave' (20:27). Luke does not have a direct parallel, though a similar discussion about greatness occurs in the hours before Jesus is arrested (22:24–27). Jesus responds by noting that a leader must be 'as one who serves' (22:26), and then points to himself as one among them who serves.

58 For a substantive defence of this conclusion, see especially Watts 2000: 269–287.

59 It is also possible that Isa. 43:3–4 may be in view; indeed Grimm (1981: 231–277) goes so far as to argue it is the primary background. However, Watts (2000: 280–281) is likely correct that Isa. 53 is the primary background, with Isa. 43:3–4 playing a secondary role. He poses the question 'Where in the OT is there any such general concept of a "serving" figure, in an eschatological context, who gives his life for "the many"?', before concluding that Isa. 53 is the obvious answer.

serving rather than being served. It is true that the Greek word used here (*diakoneō*) is never used in the Isaianic servant songs. But the nature of this service is further described as being a 'slave' (*doulos*) of all, a term applied to the Isaianic servant in Isaiah 49:3, 5, 7. In addition to the fact that *diakoneō* and *douleuō* (including its related substantive *doulos*) are near synonyms, it is possible that the choice of *diakoneō* was driven in part by the fact that the verb *douleuō* does not form the passive voice.[60] Although the idea of 'ransom' is not explicitly used in Isaiah 53, it does occur repeatedly throughout Isaiah 40 – 55, where Yahweh repeatedly announces his intention to ransom his people (41:14; 43:1, 14, 22–24; 45:13; 51:11; 52:3).[61] He does so through a new exodus accomplished by his servant.[62]

Once Jesus finally arrives in Jerusalem, several events lead up to his death and resurrection that are described with servant language, or at least are consistent with descriptions of the Isaianic servant. Otto Betz has argued that the account of Jesus' anointing at Bethany in preparation for his death and burial draws language from Isaiah 52:14 – 53:1.[63] The silence of Jesus before his accusers (Matt. 26:63; 27:12, 14; Mark 14:61; 15:5; Luke 23:9; John 19:9) may reflect Isaiah 53:7, where in the face of opposition the servant 'opened not his mouth, like a lamb led to the slaughter and a sheep before its shearers'.

Along these lines, the Last Supper is worth particular note. While a number of Old Testament allusions and echoes inform the description of this final Passover meal that Jesus shares with his disciples,[64] Isaiah 53 is

60 Watts 2000: 274; see BDAG s.v. *douleuō*. Watts also raises the possibility that the use of *diakoneō* focuses on service to others, while *doulos* emphasizes service to God; if so, the point would be to portray a 'more nuanced allusion to the "servant" which emphasizes that aspect of his general "service" toward God that results specifically in service towards others as per Isaiah 53:11.'

61 Seven of the eight occurrences of *lytroō* in Isa. 40 – 55 LXX render the Hebrew verb *gā'al* (the one exception is 51:11, where it renders *pādâ*); the one occurrence of the noun *lytron* in Isa. 45:13 translates the Hebrew noun *mĕḥîr*. As ibid. (277) notes, ransom language occurs in connection with the original exodus, return from exile and the new exodus that Yahweh promises.

62 Although the language of ransom is not connected to the servant, Watts is certainly correct that 'the literary structure of Isaiah 52 – 54 strongly suggests that Yahweh's INE redemption of Israel is intimately related to the "death" of his "servant" "for the many"' (278).

63 For discussion of the Matthew passage, see Betz 1998: 78–80; for discussion of the Markan parallel, see Betz 1987: 250–252.

64 For discussion of the Matthean version, see France 1971: 121–123; on the Markan version, see Watts 2000: 349–362; for the Lukan version, see Pao and Schnabel 2007: 381–383.

part of that intertextual matrix. Jesus explains that the cup represents 'the blood of the (new) covenant' that is 'poured out for many' (Matt. 26:28; Mark 14:24; Luke 22:20).[65] Such language echoes the act of the servant 'pouring out his soul/life to death' (Isa. 53:10) and 'bearing the sin of many' (Isa. 53:12). Although the reference to the (new) covenant is often understandably identified as alluding to Jeremiah 31:31–34, it should be noted that both Isaiah 54:10 ('covenant of peace') and 55:3 ('an everlasting covenant, / my steadfast, sure love for David') identify a new covenant resulting from the work of the Isaianic servant. Within the context of Mark's Gospel such an allusion coheres with his larger framework of the Isaianic new exodus accomplished by the servant.[66] Luke confirms that he has Isaiah 53 in mind when just a few verses later (22:37) he records Jesus' quoting Isaiah 53:12 as a Scripture that must be fulfilled: 'For I tell you that this Scripture must be fulfilled in me: "And he was numbered with the transgressors." For what is written about me has its fulfilment.'[67] As Moo notes, Luke sees in this one citation of Isaiah 53:12 a summary of 'the events of the passion as a whole, which picture the sinless Messiah rejected, mocked and crucified by his own people'.[68] As such, Luke invites the reader to view the entirety of the events connected with Jesus' passion at least in part through the lens of the Isaianic servant.

Several aspects of Jesus' suffering also appear to echo Isaianic servant texts. After the Jewish leaders condemn Jesus to death, the guards standing next to Jesus 'began to spit on him and to cover his face and to strike him, saying to him, "Prophesy!" And the guards received him with blows' (Mark 14:65//Matt. 26:67–68; cf. 27:30). As noted above in the discussion of Mark 10:33–34, the specific language used to describe the guards delivering blows (*rhapisma*) and spitting (*emptyō*) stems from Isaiah 50:6, where the servant endures suffering at the hands of his enemies.[69] Being crucified between two convicted criminals (Matt. 27:38; Mark 15:27; Luke

65 There are slight variations between the three synoptic accounts. Only Luke mentions the 'new' covenant, while only Matthew mentions 'the forgiveness of sins'.

66 See Watts 2000: 360–362.

67 It is also worth noting that in between the Last Supper and this citation of Isa. 53:7, Luke records Jesus explaining to his disciples that greatness in the kingdom is rooted in serving others because 'I am among you as the one who serves' (Luke 22:27). This story appears to be the Lukan parallel to Matt. 20:20–28//Mark 10:35–45 discussed above.

68 Moo 1983: 137.

69 See further ibid. (139–144), who notes that *rhapisma* 'occurs only in Isa. 50:6 in the LXX and only in contexts related to the mockery of Christ in the NT' (139).

23:33) coheres well with the description of the servant as being 'numbered with the transgressors' (Isa. 53:12).[70] While hanging on the cross, Jesus prays for the Father to forgive those who are crucifying him (Luke 23:34a),[71] which is analogous to the Isaianic servant who 'makes intercession for the transgressors' (Isa. 53:12).[72] The Jewish leaders' mockery of Jesus while on the cross (Matt. 27:39–43; Mark 15:29–32; Luke 23:35–38) corresponds to Isaiah 53:3–4, which describes the servant as being despised, forsaken and struck by God while he was in fact bearing the sins of his people.[73] Even the detail that Jesus was buried in the tomb of a rich man named Joseph of Arimathea (Matt. 27:57) lines up with the servant being 'with a rich man in his death' (Isa. 53:9).

When the apostles began preaching the good news about Jesus after the Day of Pentecost, they regularly identified him as the Isaianic servant. In the aftermath of healing a man on his way into the temple,[74] Peter preaches to the crowds gathered at Solomon's Portico in the temple complex. He highlights Jesus' identity as the servant:

> The God of Abraham, the God of Isaac, and the God of Jacob, the God of our fathers, glorified his servant Jesus, whom you delivered over and denied in the presence of Pilate, when he had decided to release him.
> (Acts 3:13)

The assertion that God glorified his servant Jesus alludes to Isaiah 52:13 (LXX), which asserts that Yahweh's servant 'shall be exalted and glorified exceedingly' (NETS). The expression 'delivered over' (*paradidōmi*)

---

[70] Surprisingly, Pao and Schnabel (2007: 396) contend there is no connection to Isa. 53:12, since there are no verbal connections. While that is true, the fact that Luke 22:37 cites the line 'he was numbered with the transgressors' from Isa. 53:12 as a way of summarizing the entirety of Jesus' suffering and death surely suggests a strong thematic parallel.

[71] There is some uncertainty as to whether this sentence is original, as it is absent from some of the earliest witnesses (e.g. 𝔓[75] B D* W Q). But as Metzger (2002: 154) notes, although the saying may not be part of the original text, it 'bears self-evident tokens of its dominical origin' and was probably 'incorporated by unknown copyists relatively early in the transmission of the Third Gospel'. For an argument that this line is in fact original, see Garland 2011: 921–923.

[72] Stuhlmacher 2004: 156. For a discussion of the details, see Moo (1983: 151–154), who concludes that while a connection to Isa. 53:12 cannot be excluded, it does not seem likely.

[73] See also Moo 1983: 162.

[74] According to Acts 3:10, the crowds 'were filled with wonder and amazement' in response to this healing. Given the allusion to Isa. 52:13 in Acts 3:13, there may be an additional echo of Isa. 52:14 here in 3:10; see Bock 1987: 188 and Witherington 1998: 179–180.

continues the use of this language from the Gospels, which appropriate the verb from Isaiah 53:6, 12 to describe the handing over of Jesus to be crucified. In the following verse, Peter also refers to Jesus as the 'Righteous One' (Acts 3:14), which echoes the title given to the servant in Isaiah 53:11. But what is perhaps most noteworthy is that God glorifying his servant Jesus is framed as the culmination of his promises to Abraham, Isaac and Jacob. As we saw in the previous chapter, the work of the Isaianic servant brings to fulfilment the promises made to Abraham and David. Thus, Peter may be following cues from Isaiah in identifying Jesus as the servant whom the Father glorifies because he brings God's creational and redemptive purposes to fulfilment.

Echoes of the Isaianic servant continue through the rest of Peter's sermon (Acts 3:17–26). Peter asserts that God foretold through the prophets 'that his Christ would suffer' (3:18); at least part of the Old Testament textual matrix behind that statement is the suffering servant of Isaiah 53.[75] The promise that God will blot out the sins of those who repent may stem in part from Isaiah 43:25, where God promises a new exodus and a new creation (Isa. 43:18–25), which of course in the context of Isaiah 40 – 55 is accomplished by the servant. Peter concludes this sermon by reminding his hearers of God's promise to Abraham that in his offspring all the nations will be blessed (Acts 3:25, citing Gen. 12:3; 18:18). How has God fulfilled this promise? Peter explains: 'God, having raised up his servant, sent him to you first, to bless you by turning every one of you from your wickedness' (Acts 3:26). Peter sees the resurrection of Jesus the servant as the fulfilment of the promise to Abraham, which is exactly what Isaiah 40 – 55 argues. By beginning (Acts 3:13) and ending his message with a reference to God raising his servant Jesus, Peter frames the entirety of what he says against the backdrop of Jesus as the Isaianic servant. One might even say that for Peter, Jesus' identity as the Isaianic servant informs and explains the other scriptural descriptions of his identity.

Jesus is again referred to as the servant in the very next chapter. After Peter and John are released from their hearing before the Jewish leaders (Acts 4:1–22), they gather with their fellow believers to pray (Acts 4:23–31). As part of that prayer they cite Psalm 2:1–2, which was spoken 'through the mouth of our father David, your servant' (Acts 4:25). As we have

[75] See further Marshall 2007: 546.

already seen in chapter 5, God had promised his servant David a descendant who would rule over an eternal kingdom (2 Sam. 7). Reflecting on this promise, David the servant writes Psalm 2, where he depicts humanity's rebellion against Yahweh and his anointed, which is clearly a reference to the promised Davidic descendant. The church sees in this psalm a description of 'your holy servant Jesus, whom you anointed' and his suffering at the hands of both the Jewish and Gentile leaders (Acts 4:27). Identifying themselves as 'your servants' (Acts 4:29),[76] they ask for boldness to continue to proclaim the gospel while God performs signs and wonders 'through the name of your holy servant Jesus' (Acts 4:30). Given the clear echoes of the Isaianic servant in Acts 3:12–26, there appears to be here in Acts 4:23–31 an intentional combination of the Isaianic servant motif with the offspring of David the servant as Yahweh's anointed. As Darrell Bock notes, the two terms 'anointed/ messiah/Christ' and 'servant' 'represent the foundational Christological categories for Luke . . . For Luke, the Servant is the Christ and the portrait of the Servant is predominantly that of Isaiah 40 – 61.'[77] But as with the sermon in Acts 3:12–26, we can perhaps go a step further and conclude that the title of servant seems to function as the overarching category that provides further explanation of Jesus' identity as the anointed one.

These allusions and echoes of the Isaianic servant resound even louder when considered in the light of the citation of Isaiah 53:7–8 in Acts 8:26–40.[78] An Ethiopian eunuch, returning from worshipping in Jerusalem, is reading from Isaiah while riding in his chariot.[79] The Spirit prompts Philip to join him, and the eunuch asks him to explain the passage he is reading. Luke specifies that the passage being read is Isaiah 53:7–8, which he then cites (Acts 8:32–33). When the eunuch asks whether Isaiah is referring to himself or someone else, Philip 'opened his mouth, and beginning with this Scripture he told him the good news about Jesus' (Acts 8:35). Not only does Isaiah 53:7–8 provide the interpretive key for

[76] We will return to this important observation in chapter 9.

[77] Bock 1987: 207.

[78] For a summary of additional OT allusions and echoes in this passage, see Marshall 2007: 573–575. For discussion of the details of the citation, see Bock 1987: 225–230.

[79] As Pao (2002: 140–142) points out, the inclusion of this story about a eunuch (note Isa. 56:3–5) is part of Luke's larger programme of showing that 'outcasts are now included in the restored people of God' that has taken place through the Isaianic new exodus accomplished by Jesus the servant.

the suffering and death of Jesus; it serves as a launching point for Philip to explain the good news about Jesus throughout the rest of the Old Testament.[80]

When we turn to the New Testament epistles, we find a number of texts that explain the significance of Jesus' death and resurrection with servant language. The place to begin is with Peter's citation of portions of Isaiah 53 in 1 Peter 2:21–25:

> For to this you have been called,
> because Christ also suffered for you,
> leaving you an example,
> so that you might follow in his steps.
> He committed no sin [Isa. 53:9],
> neither was deceit found in his mouth [Isa. 53:9].
> When he was reviled, he did not revile in return;
> when he suffered, he did not threaten,
> but continued entrusting himself to him who judges justly.
> He himself bore our sins [Isa. 53:4, 11–12]
> in his body on the tree,
> that we might die to sin
> and live to righteousness.
> By his wounds you have been healed [Isa. 53:5].
> For you were straying like sheep [Isa. 53:6],
> but have now returned to the Shepherd
> and Overseer of your souls.

Perhaps surprisingly, this citation occurs in the context of Peter admonishing servants how to live as God's people in the midst of their service. Peter presents Christ the suffering servant as an example for servants of how they should respond to unjust treatment from their masters. Yet the power of this example is rooted in the substitutionary nature of Christ's suffering for his people. By bearing the sins of his people Christ enables them to 'die to sin and live to righteousness' even in the face of unjust suffering. Peter's use of Isaiah 53 as a framework for understanding the

80 Although the text does not indicate Philip used other OT texts to explain the gospel, that seems likely in the light of the parallel to Luke 24:27, where Jesus explains the necessity of the Christ's suffering 'beginning with Moses and all the Prophets' and continuing on into 'all the Scriptures the things concerning himself'.

life, death and resurrection of Jesus coheres with what we saw in Acts 3:12–26 (see above).[81]

In Paul's letters there are a number of allusions to Christ as the Isaianic servant. Romans 15 provides a good starting point. Paul explains that part of his ministry philosophy is not 'to preach the gospel . . . where Christ has already been named, lest I build on someone else's foundation' (Rom. 15:20). As an explanation for this approach, he cites Isaiah 52:15:

> Those who have never been told of him will see,
> and those who have never heard will understand.
> (Rom. 15:21)

The 'him' referred to in Isaiah 52:15 is the suffering servant, making it clear that Paul sees Jesus as the suffering servant. This conclusion is further confirmed by what Paul writes earlier in the chapter: 'For I tell you that Christ became a servant to the circumcised to show God's truthfulness, in order to confirm the promises given to the patriarchs, and in order that the Gentiles might glorify God for his mercy' (Rom. 15:8–9a). This claim is supported by a series of Old Testament citations (2 Sam. 22:50/Ps. 18:49; Deut. 32:43; Ps. 117:1; and Isa. 11:1). Yet it should also be pointed out that this dual mission of Christ as the servant coheres with the description of the Isaianic servant's mission to 'raise up the tribes of Jacob and to bring back the preserved of Israel' as well as to be 'a light for the nations, / that my salvation may reach to the end of the earth' (Isa. 49:6).

Paul's use of Isaiah 53:1 in Romans 10:16 further confirms these conclusions from Romans 15. In an effort to explain why so many Jews have rejected the gospel, Paul cites Isaiah 53:1: 'Lord, who has believed what he has heard from us?' In Isaiah 53:1 the content of the rejected message is the good news about the suffering servant taking upon himself the sins of his people. So, just as in Romans 15, Paul stops short of identifying Jesus as the suffering servant; instead, he seems so confident

---

[81] Jobes (2005: 192–193) goes so far as to claim that the apostle Peter was the originator of the Christological use of Isa. 53 in the early church. No doubt Peter is an important figure in the church's understanding of Christ as the suffering servant, but this claim fails to appreciate that the identification likely goes back to Jesus himself; see Betz 1998: 70–87 and Stuhlmacher 2004: 147–162.

that the reader will make or already knows the connection that he can leave it unstated.[82]

In addition to these indirect references in contexts where Paul discusses his apostolic ministry, there are direct descriptions of Jesus' identity and work that borrow language from Isaiah 53. To conclude his discussion of Abraham's faith in God's promise (Rom. 4:1–25), Paul writes:[83] 'It [faith] will be counted [as righteousness] to us who believe in him who raised from the dead Jesus our Lord, who was delivered up because of our trespasses and raised for our justification' (Rom. 4:24–25 AT). The phrase 'delivered up because of our trespasses' likely stems from Isaiah 53:12 LXX, which states that the servant 'was delivered up because of our sins' (AT).[84] The claim that Jesus was 'raised for our justification' may echo Isaiah 53:11, where the servant is said to 'justify many' (NIV).[85] Paul appears to return to this echo of Isaiah 53:11 in the very next chapter when he states that through Christ's obedience 'the many will be made righteous'.[86]

An additional allusion to Isaiah 53 may be found in Romans 8:32–34, where in explanation of his claim that God is for his people Paul writes:

> He who did not spare his own Son but gave him up for us all, how will he not also with him graciously give us all things? Who shall bring any charge against God's elect? It is God who justifies. Who is to condemn? Christ Jesus is the one who died – more than that, who was raised – who is at the right hand of God, who indeed is interceding for us.

---

82 Cf. Wagner 2003: 335, who notes that although Paul never identifies Christ as the servant of Isa. 53 in Rom. 10 or 15, that identification 'lingers behind the text as a virtually unavoidable implication of Paul's reading of Isaiah'. The most likely reason Paul leaves the connection unstated is that he is more focused on identifying his own life and ministry with the Isaianic servant, which will be discussed in the next chapter.

83 For discussion of this allusion, see Hofius 2004: 180–182. Based on this proposed allusion and the larger context of Rom. 3 – 4, Otfried Hofius argues that Rom. 4:25 should be translated 'He was handed over [to death] *to atone for* our trespasses, and raised *for* our justification.' Even Morna Hooker, a noted sceptic regarding the influence of Isa. 53 on the early church's understanding of Jesus, sees an echo of Isa. 53 here (Hooker 1998: 101–103).

84 Both texts share the verb *paradidōmi* modified by the preposition *dia* with an accusative plural noun. Whereas Rom. 4:25 has 'trespasses' (*paraptōmata*) Isa. 53:12 LXX has 'sins' (*hamartias*), but this difference is not enough to dismiss the allusion.

85 Rom. 4:25 uses the noun *dikaiōsis* (justification), while Isa. 53:11 LXX uses the verb *dikaioō* (justify). Hofius (2004: 180–182) suggests that this phrase in Rom. 4:25 depends on the MT of Isa. 53:11.

86 See also Hofius 2004: 182–183; Evans 2012: 161.

The claim that God 'gave up' (*paradidōmi*) his Son for his people uses the same verb as Romans 4:25. By itself this may not be significant. But the mention of God as the one who justifies draws a further connection to Romans 4:25, as well as Isaiah 53:11.[87] Additionally, the statement that Christ intercedes for believers certainly coheres with Isaiah 53:12, where the servant 'makes intercession for the transgressors'.

In 1 Corinthians 15:3–5 Paul states a concise summary of the gospel that likely contains allusions to various portions of Isaiah 53:[88]

> For I delivered to you as of first importance what I also received:
> that Christ died for our sins [Isa. 53:4a, 5, 6b, 8b, 11b, 12b–c]
> in accordance with the Scriptures,
> that he was buried [Isa. 53:9a],
> that he was raised on the third day [Isa. 52:13; 53:10b, 11a]
> in accordance with the Scriptures,
> and that he appeared to Cephas [Isa. 52:15b; 53:1],
> then to the twelve.

While it is certainly possible to quibble with some of the proposed allusions to or echoes of Isaiah 53 noted in brackets, it is difficult to deny the strong probability that Isaiah 53 has influenced this creedal statement of the gospel. If, as many suggest, Paul is adapting a 'catechetical summary' already in use within the early church,[89] the numerous points of influence from Isaiah 53 are shown to be present in the earliest years of the Christian movement. In any case, Paul's use of this summary coheres well with his other uses of Isaiah 53 to explain the work of Jesus.

Throughout Paul's letters there are a number of additional texts that use a form of the verb *paradidōmi* or *didōmi* with a reflexive pronoun to describe the death of Christ, language that is likely drawn from Isaiah 53:6, 10–12, where the servant gives his life as an offering for sin:[90]

> *who gave himself* for our sins to deliver us from the present evil age,
> according to the will of our God and Father.
> (Gal. 1:4)

---

87 Similarly, Wagner 2003: 334.
88 In what follows I am following Hofius (2004: 177–180).
89 See e.g. Stuhlmacher 1968: 266–282.
90 On this usage, see Perrin 1970: 204–212; Stuhlmacher 2018: 328–329.

> I have been crucified with Christ. It is no longer I who live, but Christ who lives in me. And the life I now live in the flesh I live by faith in the Son of God, who loved me and *gave himself* for me.
> (Gal. 2:20)

> And walk in love, as Christ loved us and *gave himself* up for us, a fragrant offering and sacrifice to God.
> (Eph. 5:2)

> Husbands, love your wives, as Christ loved the church and *gave himself* up for her.
> (Eph. 5:25)

> who *gave himself* as a ransom for all, which is the testimony given at the proper time.
> (1 Tim. 2:6)

> *who gave himself* for us to redeem us from all lawlessness and to purify for himself a people for his own possession who are zealous for good works.
> (Titus 2:14)

The consistent pattern is that Jesus gives himself for (the sins of) his people, with the preposition *hyper* carrying the sense of 'in the place of'.[91] This substitutionary idea most naturally originates in the substitutionary death of the servant for the sins of his people. The example from 1 Timothy 2:6 adds an additional wrinkle, as it uses the term 'ransom' (*antilytron*) to further describe Jesus' self-giving for his people. As such it is similar to Mark 10:45, where Jesus explains his death as the servant giving his life as a 'ransom' (*lytron*) for many.[92]

In addition to these texts that echo the specific language of the Isaianic servant, there are descriptions of Jesus' identity and work that appear to borrow conceptually from Isaiah 53. In Galatians 3:13–14 Paul describes the work of Jesus as follows:[93]

---

91 For discussion of the use of *hyper* with this soteriological sense, see Hengel 1981: 35–37; Harris 2011: 211–217; Stuhlmacher 2018: 328–329.

92 It is also possible that Isa. 42:6–7 and 49:6–8 lie behind these ransom sayings; see Edwards 2009: 264–266.

93 What follows is a brief summary of what is argued in Harmon 2010: 141–146.

> Christ redeemed us from the curse of the law by becoming a curse for us – for it is written, 'Cursed is everyone who is hanged on a tree' – so that in Christ Jesus the blessing of Abraham might come to the Gentiles, so that we might receive the promised Spirit through faith.

The claim that Christ redeemed his people from the curse of the law shows grammatical and conceptual parallels with Galatians 1:4 and 2:20, both of which describe the death of Jesus in terms of Isaiah 53. Christ becoming a curse for his people coheres well with the description of the suffering servant taking upon himself the covenant curses that his people deserved for their rebellion against God. The application of Deuteronomy 21:23 to Jesus' death on the cross is additional confirmation of that connection.[94] The purpose of Christ's death as a curse for his people – stated in verse 14 – also has Isaianic roots. The parallelism between the blessing of Abraham coming to the Gentiles and the gift of the Spirit likely alludes to Isaiah 44:3–5, where God promises 'I will pour my Spirit upon your offspring, / and my blessing on your descendants' (44:3) and includes Gentiles within the fulfilment of his promises to Israel.[95]

In the very next chapter, Paul again describes the work of Jesus in similar fashion: 'But when the fullness of time had come, God sent forth his Son, born of woman, born under the law, to redeem those who were under the law, so that we might receive adoption as sons' (Gal. 4:4–5). The act of Christ redeeming people under the law runs parallel to the statement in 3:13.[96] In Galatians 4:1–7 Paul portrays the work of Christ as accomplishing the promised new exodus, and in particular the Isaianic new exodus.[97] At the centre of Isaiah's promised new exodus is the work of the servant, who suffers for the sins of his people and through his death and resurrection restores them from exile.

One final allusion to Isaiah 53 should be noted.[98] At the end of a section explaining the high priestly ministry of Jesus, the author of Hebrews

---

94 A connection between Deut. 21:23 and Isa. 53 is found as early as the second century in the writings of Justin Martyr; see Bailey 2004: 324–417.

95 See further Harmon 2010: 146–150.

96 This parallel is further enhanced by Paul's use of the same rare verb for 'redeem' (*exagarazō*) in both texts; outside these two passages the verb occurs only in Eph. 5:16 and Col. 4:5.

97 See discussion in Harmon 2010: 161–167.

98 As noted by Evans 2012: 162–163.

writes that 'Christ, having been offered once to bear the sins of many, will appear a second time, not to deal with sin but to save those who are eagerly waiting for him' (Heb. 9:28). The expression 'bear the sins of many' likely stems from Isaiah 53:12, where the servant bears the sins of many. Also possible is an echo of Isaiah 53:4, where the servant bears the sins of his people. What should be noted here is that servant language is linked to Jesus' role as our high priest, which is consistent with the priestly role that the Isaianic servant fulfils for his people.

Other potential allusions and echoes of servant language describing the work of Jesus have been proposed that cannot be discussed here.[99] Admittedly some of the proposed allusions and echoes may seem rather faint. But the number of clear citations and allusions that present Jesus as the servant lend greater plausibility to some of the fainter echoes discussed. The sheer cumulative force of the evidence is more than sufficient to demonstrate the Isaianic servant is one of the major New Testament paradigms for understanding the identity and work of Jesus

Jesus as the fulfilment of previous servants

To this point we have focused on the numerous places where Isaianic servant language is used to describe the identity and work of Jesus. But the fact that Jesus is described in ways that show he is the fulfilment of previous servants such as Adam, Moses, Joshua and David provides additional evidence that Jesus is not merely the promised Isaianic servant; he is also the servant who fulfils and surpasses previous servants of the Lord.

Adam

Luke 3:1 – 4:13 provides the clearest example in the Gospels of Jesus obeying where Adam before him had failed. The account of Jesus' baptism concludes with the Father announcing 'You are my beloved Son; with you I am well pleased' (Luke 3:22). As noted above, this proclamation identifies Jesus as both the Isaianic servant and the Davidic king. Yet within the context, Luke goes further. The genealogy that follows (Luke 3:23–38) concludes with 'the son of Adam, the son of God'. This

[99] See e.g. 1 Cor. 5:7; 1 Peter 1:11; 1 John 3:5.

identification invites the reader to see Jesus' victory over Satan and his temptations in the wilderness that follows (Luke 4:1–13) against the backdrop of Adam's failure in the garden. But the importance of Adam for understanding Jesus' identity and work in the Gospels goes well beyond Luke's genealogy and temptation narrative. As Brandon Crowe has impressively demonstrated, a careful study of the Gospels reveals a 'pervasive Adam Christology' that portrays Jesus as the one who vicariously obeys for his people where Adam failed.[100]

By contrast, the presence of Adam-Christology in Paul's letters is widely recognized and discussed.[101] Jesus is the one who obeys where Adam failed, bringing the free gift of eternal life and justification to all who are identified with Jesus by faith (Rom. 5:12–21). In contrast to the death brought by Adam, Jesus rose from the dead as the firstfruits of all who trust in him; his resurrection anticipates the day when Christ will exercise the dominion over creation that God commissioned Adam to exercise (1 Cor. 15:20–28). In contrast to Adam's natural body, believers will one day receive a resurrection body that is governed by God's Spirit (1 Cor. 15:42–49). These examples are merely the tip of the iceberg; a number of additional passages likely reveal an underlying Adam Christology.[102]

As the one who obeyed where Adam had failed, the New Testament presents Jesus as the one who fulfils the commission of Adam, the original servant of the Lord.

Moses

The portrayal of Jesus as a new Moses is most prominent in the Gospel of Matthew.[103] The five lengthy teaching blocks (5:1 – 7:29; 9:36 – 10:42; 13:1–52; 17:22 – 18:35; 23:1 – 25:46) may be an intentional parallel to the five books of the Torah, stressing Jesus' identity as a Moses-like figure. Like Moses before him, Jesus goes up on a mountain to provide God's people with an explanation of what it means to live as his covenant people (Matt. 5:1 – 7:29), though in contrast Jesus himself gives rather than mediates the 'law'. Arguably the most obvious example, though, is the

100 Crowe 2017: 16.
101 See e.g. Scroggs 1966; Wright 1992: 18–40; Dunn 1996a: 98–128; Fee 2007: 513–529.
102 See e.g. Rom. 6:6; 8:29; 2 Cor. 3:18; 4:4–6; Eph. 4:17–24; Phil. 2:6–8; Col. 1:15; 3:10.
103 See especially Allison 1993: 137–270; much of what follows here is discussed in great detail by Allison.

transfiguration (Matt. 17:1–8), where Moses actually appears with Elijah. God echoes the words of Deuteronomy 18:15–18 when he exhorts Jesus' disciples to listen to him, thus identifying Jesus as the prophet greater than Moses. When celebrating the Passover – a celebration of Moses leading God's people out of their Egyptian bondage – the night before his death and imbuing it with eschatological significance, Jesus echoes the words of Exodus 24:8, where Moses seals the Sinai covenant with the Israelites (Matt. 26:17–29). Even the Great Commission that concludes Matthew's Gospel may echo Mosaic traditions from the Old Testament and Jewish literature.

Here it is also worth recalling my discussion of Acts 3:12–26, where Peter identifies Jesus as the prophet greater than Moses promised in Deuteronomy 18:15–18. By framing that sermon with references to Jesus as the servant, Peter invites the listener to understand Jesus' identity as the prophet greater than Moses in the light of his identity as the servant.

The pervasive presence of the new exodus motifs in the New Testament also indirectly connects Jesus' identity as a new Moses with the work of the servant. Scholars have demonstrated the presence of this motif in Mark,[104] Luke–Acts,[105] John,[106] and Paul's letters.[107]

As the promised prophet greater than Moses, Jesus fulfils and transcends the role of Moses the servant of the Lord.

Joshua

There is a surprising lack of Joshua typology present in the New Testament; indeed, he is mentioned by name only twice (Acts 7:45; Heb. 4:8).[108] In the latter passage, Joshua is described as not having given God's people rest; therefore, a future sabbath rest remains for the people of God (Heb. 4:8–10). Although the text does not come out and explicitly state the connection, it seems a reasonable inference that Jesus is the greater Joshua who brings his people into the promised eschatological rest. From a

104 Marcus 1992: 12–47; Watts 2000.

105 Pao 2002.

106 Meeks 1967.

107 Scott 1993: 121–186; Wright 1999: 26–35; 2013: 656–680, 718–727, 876–879, 1013–1026, 1068–1073, 1333–1338, 1344–1348.

108 For a robust discussion of possible examples of Joshua typology in the NT, see Ounsworth 2012. There are, however, more examples from the early church fathers; see Farber 2016: 285–364.

typological perspective, one can also see Jesus as the greater Joshua who defeats the enemies of God's people to give them possession of their inheritance, but nowhere does the New Testament explicitly make this connection.

David

Jesus' identity as the son of David is well established in the Gospels, but is most prominent in Matthew.[109] The opening line of Matthew identifies Jesus as the son of David (Matt. 1:1), and the genealogy that follows highlights his descent from David's line (Matt. 1:6, 17). When the angel Gabriel appears to Joseph in a dream, he addresses him as 'son of David' (Matt. 1:20). At various points people cry out to Jesus as the son of David (Matt. 9:27; 15:22; 20:30–31), often in the context of requesting healing; indeed, in response to his healings the crowds wonder if he may in fact be the son of David (Matt. 12:23). When Jesus enters Jerusalem, the crowds hail him as the son of David (Matt. 21:9, 15). Jesus even asks his opponents how the Christ can be the son of David if David calls him Lord in Psalm 110:1 (Matt. 22:41–46).

Jesus' identity as the promised Davidic king is also frequently mentioned in Luke–Acts. In addition to many of the same emphases found in Matthew, Luke has his own distinctive use of this theme. In response to the birth of John the Baptist, his father Zechariah is filled with the Holy Spirit and prophesies:

> Blessed be the Lord God of Israel,
>   for he has visited and redeemed his people
> and has raised up a horn of salvation for us
>   in the house of his servant David.
> (Luke 1:68–69)

John's role is to prepare the way for Jesus, who is here referred to as a 'horn of salvation' coming from the house of David. Yet as part of his interest in highlighting various servants of the Lord, Luke refers to David as Yahweh's servant (i.e. 'his servant David'). As the one from the line of Yahweh's servant David, Jesus will save his people in fulfilment of the

[109] David is mentioned by name 59× in the NT: Matthew (17); Mark (7); Luke (13); John (2); Acts (11); Romans (3); 2 Timothy (1); Hebrews (2); Revelation (3).

promises to Abraham (Luke 1:70–74a). The purpose of that redemption is that his people 'might serve him without fear, / in holiness and righteousness before him all our days' (Luke 1:74b–75). Just as we saw in Isaiah 40 – 54, the work of the servant creates a servant people.

We have already noted the reference to David as Yahweh's servant in Acts 4:25–30 (see above). Two additional passages from Acts deserve brief mention. The first is Paul's sermon in the synagogue in Pisidian Antioch (Acts 13:26–41). He argues that raising Jesus from the dead is the means by which God fulfils his promise in Isaiah 55:3 to give his people the blessings of the Davidic covenant (Acts 13:34).[110] In the larger context of Isaiah 55, those promises come to fulfilment through the work of the suffering servant. The second is Acts 15:13–18, where James cites Amos 9:11–12 to support his conclusion that Gentiles do not need to be circumcised in order to be saved. He asserts that the salvation of the Gentiles is part of God rebuilding the fallen tent of David. David Pao has argued that Luke sets this passage within the larger framework of the Isaianic new exodus in which fulfilling the promises to David plays an important role.[111]

As the son of David, Jesus is the one who reigns over an eternal kingdom and receives what was promised to David the servant of the Lord.[112]

Israel

Jesus as the one who obeys where Israel as a nation failed emerges as a significant theme in Matthew 1 – 4.[113] The Gospel opens by tracing the genealogy of Jesus Christ 'the son of David, the son of Abraham', demonstrating that Jesus is the fulfilment of Israel's hope and history (Matt. 1:1–17). By applying Isaiah 7:14 to the impending birth of Jesus, Matthew indicates that the salvation he brings is at least in part from the sin that led to Israel's exile (Matt. 1:18–25). A similar note is struck by

110 For discussion of this citation, see Bock 1987: 249–254. Note that in the aftermath of this sermon and the opposition from the Jews, Paul announces their turn to focusing on the Gentiles and justifies this with a citation of Isa. 49:6. We will return to this citation in the next chapter.

111 See Pao 2002: 136–138.

112 For an early attempt to explore the relationship between the son of David and servant of Yahweh themes, see Lohmeyer 1953.

113 What follows is adapted from Gladd and Harmon 2016: 23–25 and Harmon 2020: 82–87; see also Beale 2011: 406–423.

the citation of Micah 5:2 to explain to King Herod that the promised Davidic king will be born in Bethlehem (Matt. 2:1–12). When Joseph and Mary return from hiding out in Egypt, Matthew explains that this happened to fulfil Hosea 11:1, 'Out of Egypt I called my son' (Matt. 2:13–15). Just as God's Son Israel was brought out of Egypt, so too his greater Son Jesus is brought out of Egypt. As Beale rightly summarizes:

> Matthew portrays Jesus to be recapitulating the history of Israel because he sums up Israel in himself. Since Israel disobeyed, Jesus has come to do what they should have, so he must retrace Israel's steps up to the point they failed, and then continue to obey and succeed in the mission Israel should have carried out.[114]

The portrait of Jesus obeying where Israel failed continues with his baptism (Matt. 3:1–17). Just as Israel passed through the waters of the Red Sea on their way out of Egypt (Exod. 14:1–31) and through the waters of the Jordan River on their way into the Promised Land (Josh. 3:1–17), so now Jesus goes down into and emerges from the waters of the Jordan to lead the Isaianic new exodus (Isa. 11:15; 42:15; 43:2, 16–17; 44:27–28; 50:2; 51:9–11). Like Israel before him, Jesus is led into the wilderness by God's Spirit; yet unlike Israel, who disobeyed God, Jesus obeys (Matt. 4:1–11).[115] Having passed this test, Jesus enters the Promised Land to establish his rightful rule over it (Matt. 4:12–17). He begins to regather the tribes of Israel around himself by calling twelve disciples (Matt. 4:18–22). Through his ministry of preaching, teaching, healing and casting out demons, Jesus is crushing the serpent's head and gathering together the eschatological people of God (Matt. 4:23–25).

This brief sketch coheres well with the pattern regarding the servant in Isaiah 40 – 54. Israel as a nation was commissioned to be the servant of Yahweh, yet failed in this mission. So God raises up a new individual servant who obeys where Israel failed, restores Israel and acts as a light of salvation to the nations.[116]

---

114 Beale 2012: 710.

115 The portrayal of Jesus recapitulating Israel's experience in the wilderness is highlighted by the citations of Deut. 6:13, 16, 8:3, all of which occur in the context of Moses retelling Israel's failure in the desert.

116 Wilkins (2012: 115–132) goes so far as to argue that Matthew presents each stage of Jesus' ministry in a way that is informed by Isa. 53.

Conclusion

At this point there should be no doubt that the New Testament presents Jesus as the servant of the Lord par excellence. Not only is the totality of Jesus' identity and work presented as fulfilling the role of the Isaianic servant of the Lord, but specific elements of his life, ministry, death, resurrection and ascension are also portrayed as actions of the Isaianic servant. Yet Jesus' identity as the servant of the Lord extends beyond the repeated citations, allusions, echoes and thematic parallels to the Isaianic servant. The New Testament writers also use servant language in connection with identifying Jesus as the fulfilment of each of the servant figures discussed in the previous chapters. Thus, Jesus is the servant who obeys where Adam the servant failed, crushing the serpent and exercising the dominion Adam was commissioned to exercise. He is the servant who is the prophet greater than Moses, authoritatively leading his people in a new exodus from their bondage to sin. Jesus is the servant who gives his people a greater rest than Joshua, bringing them into the eschatological rest of the new creation. He is the servant who is David's greater son, defeating sin, death and the devil through his death and resurrection and ascending to the right hand of the Father to rule over an eternal kingdom. Jesus is the servant who obeys where Israel failed, not only bringing restoration to a remnant of Israel but becoming a light of salvation to the nations. He is indeed the servant of servants, bringing to fulfilment all that God began to do through his previous servants. And like every servant before him, Jesus the servant creates a servant people, a theme we will explore in the next two chapters.

8
The apostles: servants of Christ

> For am I now seeking the approval of man, or of God? Or am I trying to please man? If I were still trying to please man, I would not be a servant of Christ.
> (Gal. 1:10)

Even though the line of individual servants climaxes in the person of Jesus Christ, that is not the end of the servant theme in Scripture. Throughout our study we have seen the consistent pattern that God uses an individual servant to create a servant people. Therefore, we should expect that the work of Jesus the servant par excellence would produce servants. That is exactly what we see in the New Testament. Through the work of Jesus the servant, a servant people has come into existence.

We will explore this development from two angles. In this chapter we will look at God's use of the apostles and their ministry co-workers as his servants to advance his redemptive purposes in the world. In the following chapter we will see how the church as a whole is a servant people that God uses to bring to fruition both his creational and redemptive purposes. Although Paul by far gives the most attention to his identity as a servant of Christ, other individuals such as Peter, James, Jude and Paul's ministry co-workers also use this designation as an important aspect of their identity.

Paul the servant of Christ

There are several places in Paul's letters where he uses language borrowed from Isaianic servant texts to describe his identity and commission as an apostle to the Gentiles. Outside his letters, we find important confirmation from a key text in Acts.

Galatians

Galatians is likely the earliest extant Pauline letter. Written as early as AD 48, Paul is responding to opponents who are attempting to persuade the Gentile believers in Galatia that they must observe the Mosaic law in order to be justified before God. As part of their attack against Paul, they appear to have questioned his status as an apostle on the same level as Peter, James and John, the so-called pillars of the Jerusalem church (Gal. 2:9). As part of his response, Paul recounts his conversion and commission as an apostle to the Gentiles to demonstrate that he received the gospel and his apostolic status directly from Jesus Christ himself. He sets the stage for this lengthy defence (1:11 – 2:21) with a programmatic statement: 'For am I now seeking the approval of man, or of God? Or am I trying to please man? If I were still trying to please man, I would not be a servant of Christ' (Gal. 1:10). When calling himself a 'servant of Christ' Paul uses the noun *doulos*, which can refer to a slave. As such, Paul's point could be claiming that he is under the ownership and complete authority of Christ. But Paul could also be using this expression to identify himself as a servant of the Lord, part of the long line of individual servants we have been exploring. While it is possible both senses are in view, the fact that Paul will allude to and echo portions of Isaiah 49 in the passage that follows suggest the latter is in view.

Paul first alludes to Isaiah 49 in 1:15–16, where he recounts his encounter with the risen Christ:[1]

> But when God, who from my birth set me apart and called me by His grace, was pleased to reveal His Son in me, so that I could preach Him among the Gentiles, I did not immediately consult with anyone.
> (CSB)

The combination of the phrase 'from my mother's womb' and the verb 'called' comes from Isaiah 49:1, where the servant claims he has been called from his mother's womb. The expression 'reveal His Son in me' may stem

[1] What follows is a summary of what is argued at length in Harmon 2010: 78–86. While there is similar language in other prophetic call narratives (esp. Jer. 1:5), the number of additional echoes of Isa. 49 in the context of Gal. 1 – 2 indicate that Paul has Isaiah in mind here.

from Isaiah 49:3, where God states he will be glorified in the servant.[2] The use of the verb *euangelizō* (preach) also has Isaianic roots, where the content of that good news is the redemption of God's people (composed of Jew and Gentile) through the work of the servant.[3] The call to preach the gospel 'among the Gentiles' likely echoes similar expressions in Isaiah 42:6, 8; 49:6; 52:5, 7 and 66:19 that explain the mission of the servant to the nations. The cumulative effect of these allusions and echoes indicates that Paul sees his conversion/commission as apostle to the Gentiles prefigured in God's commissioning of the servant in Isaiah 49.[4]

This conclusion is confirmed by the residual echoes of Isaiah 49 within the remainder of Galatians 1 – 2. At the conclusion of describing his ministry activities in Syria and Cilicia (Gal. 1:21), Paul insists that he was known to the churches in Judea only by reputation (1:22–23). As a result of hearing about Paul's transformation from persecutor to preacher of the gospel, Paul states: 'And they glorified God in me' (Gal. 1:24 AT).[5] Paul repeats the prepositional phrase 'in me' (*en emoi*) from 1:16, where God revealed his Son 'in me' (*en emoi*). God's purpose of revealing his Son 'in' Paul (Gal. 1:16) was now coming to fruition as the Judean churches saw Christ at work in Paul (Gal. 1:24) through his radical transformation and preaching of the gospel.

---

[2] In Isa. 49:3 LXX Yahweh, using the verb *doxazō*, says to the servant, 'in you I will be glorified', whereas Gal. 1:16 has the expression 'to reveal his Son in me', using the verb *apokalyptō*. But as Carey Newman has shown, the aorist passive of *doxazō* often describes the visible manifestation of God's presence (e.g. Isa. 24:21–23; Ezek. 28:22; 39:13; Hag. 1:8; 2 Thess. 1:10), suggesting that these two verbs 'bear the same semantic cargo' when referring to 'God's eschatological self-manifestation' (Newman 1992: 206). It is also possible that the use of *apokalyptō* echoes Isa. 52:10 and/or Isa. 53:1, where Yahweh reveals his arm in the presence of all the nations (52:10); that revelation of Yahweh's arm is specifically tied to the work of the servant in Isa. 53:1. While most English versions translate 'to reveal his Son *to me*', the CSB more accurately has 'in me'. In the eight other occurrences of the construction *apokalyptō* + the preposition *en* in the LXX/NT, not once does *en* indicate the recipient of revelation. Instead, it marks (1) the time when something is revealed (Num. 24:4, 16; Dan. 2:19; 1 Peter 1:5); (2) the sphere/location of a revelation (Judg. 5:2; 1 Sam. 2:27; Prov. 11:13); or (3) the actions or being by which something is revealed (Ezek. 16:36; 22:10). The most likely reason for this unusual expression is an echo of Isa. 49:3, for, as we will see below in the discussion of Gal. 1:24, Paul will return to this expression.

[3] See discussion in Harmon 2010: 67–70.

[4] In addition to ibid. 103–106, see also Ciampa 1998: 125.

[5] Most English translations render this 'they glorified God *because of* me'. While this translation is preferred by BDAG s.v. *en* 8, translating the phrase 'in me' is preferable for the following reasons: (1) the parallel to Gal. 1:16 suggests Paul intends the phrase to be understood in a similar fashion; (2) there are several more common ways to express the idea 'because of me' (e.g. *dia* + accusative, *apo* + genitive, *ek* + genitive, *epi* + genitive or dative); (3) the parallels in John 13:31–32, 17:10 where this phrase is also used with the verb *doxazō* clearly have the sense of 'in me'. See further Ciampa 1998: 124–125.

When Paul moves forward in Galatians 2:1–10 to describe a visit to Jerusalem, an echo of Isaiah 49 once again appears. In response to divine revelation, Paul went to Jerusalem to set before the leaders of the church his gospel message 'in order to make sure I was not running or had not run in vain' (Gal. 2:2). Although faint, this concern about running 'in vain' is likely an echo of Isaiah 49:4, where the servant expresses concern that he has 'laboured in vain'.[6] An echo of Isaiah 49:4 is even clearer in Galatians 4:11, where Paul worries that he has 'laboured over you in vain'.[7] Paul also refers three times to his ministry to the Gentiles (2:2, 8–9), which likely picks up the echoes of the Isaianic servant's mission to the nations mentioned in my discussion of 1:16.

Paul's presentation of his calling as the servant of Isaiah 49 culminates in Galatians 2:20, where he climactically states:

> I have been crucified with Christ. It is no longer I who live, but Christ who lives in me. And the life I now live in the flesh I live by faith in the Son of God, who loved me and gave himself for me.

This important verse brings together two threads that on the surface may seem to be in tension. We noted in the previous chapter that Paul presents Jesus as the suffering servant of Isaiah 53, using its language to describe the death of Jesus in both Galatians 1:4 and 2:20. Yet I have also been arguing in this chapter that Paul sees his commission as the apostle to the Gentiles as the fulfilment of the servant's mission described in Isaiah 49. Galatians 2:20 brings these two themes together. Paul again echoes Isaiah 49:3 with the phrase 'in me' yet also describes the death of Jesus in the language of Isaiah 53 ('gave himself for me'). The bridge that connects them is Paul's participation in Christ's crucifixion and Christ's subsequent indwelling of Paul, which is so complete that he can claim that in one sense he no longer lives. As I have summarized elsewhere:

> *In other words, Jesus Christ the suffering Servant of Isa. 53, who gave himself for Paul, now lives in Paul to carry out the mission of the*

---

[6] Isa. 49:4 LXX uses the adverb *kenōs*, while Gal. 2:2 has the prepositional phrase *eis kenon*. Paul uses this same expression in 2 Cor. 6:1 (where it is immediately followed by a citation of Isa. 49:8), Phil. 2:16 (2×) and 1 Thess. 3:5 to express his concern that his apostolic ministry may prove to be in vain.

[7] Here Paul uses the same verb (*kopiaō*) found in Isa. 49:4, along with the same prepositional phrase (*eis kenon*) found in Gal. 2:2.

Servant portrayed in Isa. 49 to be a light to the nations. Because of this truth, Paul can refer to his own apostolic mission as the fulfilment of the Servant's commission in Isa. 49 to be a light to the nations, since it is ultimately Christ who fulfils that mission through him. As a result, God's intention of revealing his Son 'in' Paul (Gal. 1:16) reaches its intended goal of God being glorified 'in' Paul (Gal. 1:24), because Christ lives 'in' Paul (Gal. 2:20) to fulfil the Servant's commission to be a light to the nations.[8]

2 Corinthians 5:11 – 6:10

Paul's identity and status as an apostle is a central concern of 2 Corinthians, and in 2:14 – 7:4 he provides a lengthy discussion of its nature. For our purposes we are most interested in 5:11 – 6:10, where Paul draws on multiple Isaianic texts to describe 'the essence and exercise' of his apostolic ministry.[9] The motivation for Paul's service to the Lord is the love of Christ shown in his death and resurrection for his people (2 Cor. 5:11–15). Truly understanding who Christ is means no longer regarding him from a worldly perspective (2 Cor. 5:16). What follows is a succinct summary of the radical transformation the gospel of Christ produces: 'Therefore, if anyone is in Christ, he is a new creation. The old has passed away; behold, the new has come' (2 Cor. 5:17). Paul draws his language here from two different texts in Isaiah.[10] The first is Isaiah 43:18–19:

> Remember not the former things,
> nor consider the things of old.
> Behold, I am doing a new thing;
> now it springs forth, do you not perceive it?
> I will make a way in the wilderness
> and rivers in the desert.

In Isaiah the contrast between the former things and the new thing is a contrast between Israel's pitiful state of exile because of their sinful rebellion and the new exodus that Yahweh is about to perform to redeem them. This new exodus will result in the transformation of creation, which

[8] Harmon 2010: 119; emphasis original.
[9] I have borrowed this phrase from Harris (2005: 411).
[10] In what follows I am largely following Beale (1994: 219–232).

although hinted at here in Isaiah 43:18–21 is even more clearly expressed in the second text Paul draws upon, Isaiah 65:17:

> For behold, I create new heavens
>   and a new earth,
> and the former things shall not be remembered
>   or come into mind.

These two texts are part of the larger Isaianic narrative of God's restoring his people from exile through a new exodus that results in a new creation accomplished by his individual servant. As Beale rightly argues, the restoration described in Isaiah 40 – 66 sets the backdrop for Paul's discussion of reconciliation in 2 Corinthians 5:18–21.[11] This Isaianic background may further be evident if one recognizes a possible echo of Isaiah 53 in the summary statement of the gospel found in 2 Corinthians 5:21: 'For our sake he made him to be sin who knew no sin, so that in him we might become the righteousness of God.' Although not a direct citation of Isaiah 53, the conceptual overlap is significant,[12] and further confirms that Paul is describing his ministry of reconciliation as an ambassador of Christ within an Isaianic framework.

In the light of what God has done for his people through this Isaianic gospel, Paul urges the Corinthians 'not to receive the grace of God in vain' (2 Cor. 6:1). This final phrase likely echoes the concern of the servant in Isaiah 49:4 about the possibility of labouring in vain, a text I discussed above in Galatians. This echo of Isaiah 49:4 is confirmed by the fact that Paul grounds this concern by citing Isaiah 49:8: 'For he says, "In a favourable time I listened to you, and in a day of salvation I have helped you." Behold, now is the favourable time; behold, now is the day of salvation' (2 Cor. 6:2). The day of salvation referred to in Isaiah 49:8 is the

---

11 'Simply put, Paul understands both "new creation" in Christ as well as "reconciliation" in Christ (2 Cor. 5:18–20) as the fulfilment of Isaiah's promise of a new creation in which Israel would be restored to a peaceful relationship with Yahweh. And Israel's exile in Isaiah is seen as representative of humanity's alienation from God, since Paul is applying Isaiah's message for Israel to the Gentiles' (ibid. 225).

12 See similarly Hofius 2004: 183. He identifies the following points of contact: (1) 'him who knew no sin' (2 Cor. 5:21) = 'he did no sin' (Isa. 53:9 LXX); (2) 'he made him to be sin [for us]' (2 Cor. 5:21) = 'the Lord delivered him over for our sins' (Isa. 53:6 LXX); (3) 'so that we might become the righteousness of God in/by him' (2 Cor. 5:21) = 'The righteous one, my servant, will make many righteous' (Isa. 53:11 MT). For his extended argument that 2 Cor. 5:18–21 is based on Isa. 52 – 53, see Hofius 1989: 1–14.

work of the servant restoring a remnant of Israel to Yahweh and being a light of salvation for the Gentiles to the ends of the earth. By echoing Isaiah 49:4 and citing Isaiah 49:8 Paul equates the good news of God's reconciling the world to himself with this Isaianic day of salvation. Paul and his ministry co-workers (note that he says 'we') are 'working together' with God to bring the ministry of reconciliation to the world. He then further explains the nature of their ministry: 'We put no obstacle in anyone's way, so that no fault may be found with our ministry, but as *servants* of God we commend ourselves in every way' (2 Cor. 6:3–4a). Considered in isolation, referring to himself and his ministry co-workers as servants could easily be understood as a general reference to their submission to God. But given that Paul has been drawing language from Isaiah 49, their identity as servants takes on a specifically Isaianic hue. Paul sees his ministry of reconciliation as a fulfilment of the servant's mission.[13] It is this conviction that empowers him and his ministry co-workers to endure the various forms of suffering that come from taking the message of reconciliation to the ends of the earth (2 Cor. 6:4b–10).

Romans

We have already noted Paul's use of servant language to describe the work of Jesus in Romans. But even more prominent is his use of Isaianic servant language to describe his own identity and ministry.[14] The place to begin is Romans 15:14–21. In the previous paragraph Paul portrayed Jesus as the servant to both Jews and Gentiles (Rom. 15:8–13). From that starting point Paul moves on to explain his apostolic ministry. His boldness in writing to the Romans is grounded in the grace that God has given him (Rom. 15:14–15), which he then further explains in verse 16 as 'to be a servant [*leitourgos*] of Christ Jesus to the Gentiles, serving as a priest [*hierourgeō*] of the gospel of God, so that the offering of the Gentiles may be acceptable, sanctified by the Holy Spirit' (AT). Though rendered 'minister' in most

---

[13] Unlike in Galatians, Paul does not explain how he puts together Christ as the servant of Isa. 53 with his own identity as the servant of Isa. 49. Beale (1994: 230–231) suggests that it is 'corporate representation which allows Paul in his own mind to understand how the very context of the Isaiah 49 Servant could apply to himself without distorting the way in which he thought it may have been intended originally. Furthermore, in that he was continuing the mission of Jesus, the Servant, he could easily apply the Servant prophecy to himself.' But in the light of what Paul says in Galatians, it seems more likely that Paul made this connection because of his conviction that Christ dwelled in him to fulfil the mission of the servant.

[14] On this theme in Romans, see especially Wagner 1998: 193–222; 2003.

English translations, the noun *leitourgos* in this context refers to someone who serves as a priest.[15] The priestly nature of this service is confirmed by Paul's use of the verb *hierourgeō* (serving as a priest), which always refers to acting 'in some cultic or sacred capacity'.[16] As a priestly servant, Paul ministers the gospel to the Gentiles. The purpose of this priestly ministry can be understood in two different ways. Paul may be saying that he offers the Gentiles to the Lord as a sacrifice that is pleasing because they are set apart by the Holy Spirit.[17] Alternatively, Paul could be saying that through his priestly service the Gentiles offer themselves to the Lord as those set apart by the Holy Spirit.[18] What tips the scales in favour of the first view is the likelihood that Paul has Isaiah 66:18–20 in view here. That text envisions those who have been redeemed by Yahweh going out to the nations to proclaim the glory of the Lord, and those who respond to this message are described as an offering to Yahweh.

Later in this same paragraph Paul draws on another Isaianic text to explain his ministry. As an explanation for his ambition to preach the gospel where Christ had not already been proclaimed, Paul cites Isaiah 52:15:

> Those who have never been told of him will see,
> and those who have never heard will understand.
> (Rom. 15:21, citing Isa. 52:15)

In its original context, Isaiah 52:15 describes the response of the nations and their kings to the message about the servant. Paul sees in this text a prefiguration of his apostolic ministry to the Gentiles. Wagner is certainly correct that 'Paul has found his own ministry inextricably linked with the mysterious outworking of God's redemptive purpose for Israel as well as for the Gentiles.'[19]

This explanation in Romans 15 coheres with what Paul already presented in Romans 10:14–17. In a series of questions, the apostle explains the

---

15 Although this noun can be used in a general sense to refer to an assistant or servant (see BDAG s.v. *leitourgos*), it can also have the specific sense of one who serves as a priest (see e.g. Heb. 8:2, where it refers to Christ as our high priest). This noun and its cognates are used frequently in the LXX with reference to priestly service 'because it was public, fixed, and regulated by law, and the welfare of the people of God depended on it' (Silva 2014a: 3.104).

16 BDAG s.v. *hierourgeō*.

17 See e.g. Moo 2018: 906–907; Schreiner 2018: 740–741.

18 See e.g. Peterson 2017: 517–518.

19 Wagner 2003: 336.

process by which the gospel advances. In response to the question 'And how are they to preach unless they are sent?' Paul cites Isaiah 52:7: 'How beautiful are the feet of those who preach the good news!' (Rom. 10:15, citing Isa. 52:7). The good news announced in Isaiah 52:7 is the proclamation that Yahweh is establishing his reign by baring his holy arm in the sight of all the nations. The heralds announcing this good news are those redeemed by Yahweh, and the means by which Yahweh bares his arm is through the work of the suffering servant. What follows in Romans 10:16 confirms that Paul makes this connection; as an explanation for the fact that not all people obey the gospel, Paul cites Isaiah 53:1: 'Lord, who has believed what he has heard from us?' (Rom. 10:16, citing Isa. 53:1). In Isaiah 53:1 the message not being believed is the astonishing work of the suffering servant, who is taking upon himself the sins of his people (both Jew and Gentile alike). Paul not only identifies his gospel message about Jesus Christ with the good news about the suffering servant in Isaiah 53, but:

> he also uncovers in Isaiah 52–53 a prophecy of his own crucial role in God's redemptive plan. He is one of those depicted in Isaiah 52:7, a herald sent to broadcast the good news that God reigns, that Jesus is Lord. Through his apostolic ministry, people are able to hear, believe, and call upon the Lord.[20]

Colossians 1:24–29

Paul's identity as a servant of Christ also comes to the fore in Colossians. He concludes a section describing the Colossians' reconciliation with God through the work of Christ by identifying himself as a 'servant' (*diakonos*) of the gospel (Col. 1:23). In the paragraph that follows (Col. 1:24–29), Paul expands on his identity as a servant:

> Now I rejoice in my sufferings for you, and I am completing in my flesh what is lacking in Christ's afflictions for his body, that is, the church. I have become its servant [*diakonos*], according to God's commission that was given to me for you, to make the word of God fully known, the mystery hidden for ages and generations but now revealed to his saints. God wanted to make known among the

[20] Ibid. 180.

> Gentiles the glorious wealth of this mystery, which is Christ in you, the hope of glory. We proclaim him, warning and teaching everyone with all wisdom, so that we may present everyone mature in Christ. I labour for this, striving with his strength that works powerfully in me.
> (Col. 1:24–29 CSB)

Scholars have debated what Paul means when he claims that his sufferings complete 'what is lacking in Christ's afflictions for his body' (Col. 1:24 CSB).[21] The larger scope of Colossians as well as the rest of Paul's writings make it clear that he is not indicating that Christ's suffering was somehow insufficient for the redemption of his people.[22] Instead, Paul likely has in view the 'Messianic woes' that Jewish apocalyptic writers anticipated would come in connection with the arrival of the end times; as such there was a specific amount of suffering that must take place before the consummation (cf. Rev. 6:9–11).[23] Although there is clearly a sense in which all believers experience these sufferings, the immediate context of Colossians 1:24–29 suggests that Paul has in view affliction that is specific to him in his role as an apostle.[24] He suffers these afflictions 'for the sake of the church' (Col. 1:24); as such he uniquely experiences 'imitative sufferings of Christ in fulfilling the prophecy of Israelite and Gentile salvation'.[25] Paul's claim to suffer for the sake of the church is rooted at least in part in his conviction that through his life and ministry the mission of the Isaianic servant is fulfilled.[26] Whereas in other texts we have seen Paul focus on fulfilling the mission of the Isaianic servant to be a light of salvation for the Gentiles, here he indicates that his suffering fulfils the servant's mission. White summarizes the parallels between Paul's sufferings and those of the Isaianic servant as follows:

> For instance, the Servant is portrayed as having a marred visage that caused people to be taken aback (Isa. 52:14). Paul recounts that

21 For a careful discussion of each word in Col. 1:24, see Clark 2015: 51–71.

22 See e.g. Col. 1:19–20; 2:15. It is also worth noting that the term 'affliction' (*thlipsis*) is never used in the NT with reference to Christ's redemptive suffering.

23 See e.g. Bauckham 1975: 168–170; Allison 1985: 63–64; Pao 2012: 125–126.

24 For a helpful discussion of the issues, see Beale 2019: 137–141.

25 Ibid. 141.

26 See e.g. Bruce 1984: 82–83; Dunn 1996b: 116; Moo 2008: 152; and especially White 2016: 181–198. Beale (2019: 159–160) argues that also in view is the Son of Man figure from Dan. 7, who as a Messianic figure suffers tribulation for and with his people Israel.

> the Corinthians and the Galatians had similar reactions to his appearance (2 Cor. 11:10; Gal. 4:14). The Servant was 'despised and rejected by men' (Isa. 53:3). Paul's peristasis catalogs (1 Cor. 4:9–14; 2 Cor. 4:8–9; 6:4–10; 11:23b–27) give ample testimony to the fact that he was similarly treated. The Servant was stricken and afflicted by God (Isa. 53:4). Likewise, Paul was no stranger to bodily afflictions (2 Cor. 12:7; Gal. 4:13). The Servant bore 'stripes' (Isa. 53:5). Paul, too, had been flogged with rods and whips (2 Cor. 11:24–25). Paul must have noticed these convergences between the Servant's fate at the hands of his people and his own, and it is hardly likely that he thought they were merely coincidental. Here, too, he had a role to play: participating in – indeed completing – the Servant's prefigured hardships as he fulfilled the Servant's task of bringing his gospel to the Gentiles (Rom. 15:19).[27]

Thus, in suffering as the Isaianic servant Paul acts as a servant (*diakonos*) of the church (Col. 1:25). More precisely, Paul lives out his commission as the Isaianic servant by being a servant to the church through both his suffering and efforts 'to make the word of God fully known' among the Gentiles (Col. 1:25–28; cf. Isa. 49:6).[28] Paul 'labours' (*kopiaō*) to do this, just as the Isaianic servant 'labours' (*kopiaō*) in his mission (Isa. 49:4). Paul insists this labour is empowered by Christ powerfully working 'in me' (*en emoi*), an expression that as we saw in Galatians is rooted in God's promise to the Isaianic servant 'in whom I will be glorified' (Isa. 49:3; Gal. 1:15–16, 24).

Philippians 2:16

I discussed the Christ-hymn of 2:6–11 in the previous chapter, noting that it portrays Christ as the Isaianic servant. Immediately following this hymn, Paul exhorts the Philippians to work out their salvation with fear and trembling, since God is the one working in them (Phil. 2:12–13). Paul further unpacks this command in 2:14–16a, where he calls believers to live

---

[27] White 2016: 197; see similarly Beale 2019: 142.

[28] Compare the conclusion of White (2016: 197): 'because Paul believed that he had been called to fulfill what was still lacking with regard to the Servant's commission in the second servant song (Isa. 49:1–13), it is not surprising that he was equally convinced of his calling to take on part of the sufferings that were prophesied for the Servant in the fourth servant song (Isa. 52:13–53:12)'.

as 'blameless and innocent, children of God' who are 'lights in the world'.[29] The reason behind Paul's exhortation is 'so that in the day of Christ I may be proud that I did not run in vain or labour in vain'. The expression 'labour in vain' echoes the concern of the servant in Isaiah 49:4, as noted above. Two additional factors reinforce the presence of the echo. First, the extensive echoes of the Isaianic servant texts in the Christ-hymn make an additional echo of Isaiah 49:4 plausible. Second, referring to believers as 'lights in the world' (Phil. 2:15) may be an echo of Isaiah 49:6, where the servant is described as a light of salvation for the Gentiles.[30]

Ephesians 3:1–13

In writing to the Ephesians, Paul gives a window into his self-understanding and how his role as the apostle to the Gentiles fits within the larger scope of God's redemptive plan (Eph. 3:1–13). He calls his ministry 'the stewardship of God's grace that was given to me' and a 'mystery . . . made known to me by revelation' (Eph. 3:2–3). Paul uses a word for 'stewardship' (*oikonomia*) that refers to the activities and responsibilities related to running a household, which in the ancient world were often (though not always) delegated to servants and/or slaves.[31] As used in Paul's letters, the term 'mystery' (*mystērion*) generally has the sense of something that was hidden in the Old Testament that has now been revealed with the coming of Christ and his gospel.[32] The content of this mystery is that 'the Gentiles are fellow heirs, members of the same body, and partakers of the promise in Christ Jesus through the gospel' (Eph. 3:6). Paul continues:

> I was made a *servant* [*diakonos*] of this gospel by the gift of God's grace that was given to me by the working of his power. This grace was given to me – the least of all the saints – to proclaim to the Gentiles the incalculable riches of Christ, and to shed light for all about the administration of the mystery hidden for ages in God who created all things. This is so that God's multi-faceted wisdom

29 There are a number of OT allusions and echoes in this passage; see discussion in Harmon 2015: 237–271.

30 We will return to this possibility in the next chapter.

31 See Silva 2014b: 2.465–469.

32 On this important term, see Carson 2001: 393–436 and especially Beale and Gladd 2014.

> may now be made known through the church to the rulers and authorities in the heavens.
> (Eph. 3:7–10 CSB)

Paul's description of his apostolic commission corresponds with his account in Galatians. He identifies himself as a servant (cf. Gal. 1:10) who has been called to proclaim the gospel to the Gentiles (cf. Gal. 1:16).[33] In both passages Paul attributes his status as an apostle to God's grace given to him (Gal. 1:15; Eph. 3:7–8). While here in Ephesians 3:7–10 Paul explicitly ties his apostolic ministry to the advancement of God's redemptive plan formulated before creation, in Galatians 1:15–16 such a concept is only able to be inferred by recognition of the allusion to Isaiah 49 and its original context. Finally, the claim that his apostolic ministry was carried out 'by the working of his power' (Eph. 3:7) is at least consistent with Paul's identification of Christ's living in him to carry out the mission of the servant (Gal. 2:20).[34]

Although Paul does not appear to allude to Isaiah 49 here in Ephesians 3:1–13 as he does in Galatians 1:15–16, there are some strong conceptual parallels. The mention of light in connection with the message of the gospel going to the Gentiles lines up with the mission of the servant to be a light of salvation to the Gentiles (Isa. 49:6). As part of their explanation of the nature of the 'mystery' here in Ephesians 3, Beale and Gladd argue for the importance of Isaiah, concluding that the work of an individual servant who embodies Israel in himself (Isa. 49:3) and dies for the nation (Isa. 53) produces servants – both Jews and Gentiles – who are identified with the Messiah (Isa. 54:17).[35] If this proposed background for the 'mystery' is correct, yet another connection between Paul's apostolic ministry and the mission of the servant is established.

Also worth noting is the conflated citation of Isaiah 52:7 and 57:19 found in Ephesians 2:17. Paul sees in these two texts the grounds for his claim that Jesus himself is our peace and is thereby able to establish peace

---

[33] It is true that Paul uses *doulos* in Gal. 1:10 and *diakonos* here in Eph. 3:7. But as I have noted, sharp distinctions between these terms do not stand up to scrutiny of how the biblical authors use the various terms for 'servant'; see the discussion in chapter 1.

[34] Within the context of Ephesians, God's power is linked to the resurrection of Christ and his authority over creation (1:19–23), which lines up well with Paul's assertion in Gal. 2:19–20 that the risen Christ lives inside him.

[35] Beale and Gladd 2014: 169–170. We will return to this passage in the next chapter.

between Jews and Gentiles through his death on the cross (Eph. 2:14–16).[36] The use of Isaiah 52:7 and 57:19 in connection with his understanding of Jesus' identity and work leads into the discussion of his identity as a servant of the gospel (3:1–13).

Acts 13:46–47

Paul's own testimony gleaned from his letters is more than sufficient to demonstrate that his self-understanding as an apostle was decisively shaped by Isaiah 49. But we also have confirmation from Acts, where Paul also frames his ministry in the light of the Isaianic servant.

The relevant passage comes in the aftermath of Paul's sermon in the synagogue at Pisidian Antioch (Acts 13:13–41). Because the sermon was so well received, Paul and his ministry partner Barnabas were asked to return the following week (Acts 13:42–43). This time, however, some of the local Jews push back, contradicting what he said and reviling him (Acts 13:44–45). In response, Paul says:

> It was necessary that the word of God be spoken first to you. Since you thrust it aside and judge yourselves unworthy of eternal life, behold, we are turning to the Gentiles. For so the Lord has commanded us, saying,
>
> 'I have made you a light for the Gentiles,
> that you may bring salvation to the ends of the earth.'
>
> (Acts 13:46–47)

Paul defends his turn to focus on preaching the gospel among the Gentiles with a citation of Isaiah 49:6. He introduces this citation as a direct command from the Lord, which further supports my conclusion that Paul understood his conversion and commission described in Galatians 1:15–16 in terms of the servant in Isaiah 49. The ministry pattern of the word going to the Jews first and then the Gentiles corresponds with the description of the servant both restoring Israel and being a light of salvation to the Gentiles (Isa. 49:5–6). By 'rejoicing and glorifying the word of the Lord' and believing in the good news of salvation through Jesus (Acts 13:48), the mission of the servant to be a light of salvation to the ends of the earth is coming to fruition.

36 For a robust discussion of this combined citation, see Moritz 1996: 23–55.

Luke's use of Isaiah 49:6 elsewhere also confirms my conclusion from Galatians that Paul sees himself as the servant of Isaiah because Jesus the servant dwells in him to fulfil the mission to be a light of salvation to the nations. As we have already seen, in Luke 2:32 Simeon applies Isaiah 49:6 to Jesus, identifying him as the light of salvation to the Gentiles. We have also noted the possible echoes of Isaiah 49:6 in the summary statement of the Old Testament in Luke 24:44–49 and the commissioning of Jesus' followers to be witnesses in Acts 1:8. Luke does not come out and explain this progression, but it seems reasonable that a similar logic is at work in Luke–Acts: Christ the servant dwells in Paul to fulfil the mission of the servant to be a light to the nations.

Conclusion

The number of texts where Paul describes his conversion and apostolic commission in language borrowed from Isaiah (and in particular Isaiah 49) makes it clear that central to Paul's self-understanding is his identity as a servant of Christ.[37] Through him the risen Christ was fulfilling the mission of the Isaianic servant to be a light of salvation to the nations. Christ the suffering servant accomplishes this mission by dwelling inside Paul to such a degree that the entirety of Paul's life is the sphere in which God's transforming and glorious grace is put on display.

Paul's ministry co-workers

Despite the clear evidence that Paul understood his apostolic ministry as a fulfilment of the Isaianic servant sent to be a light of salvation to the Gentiles, he does not appear to have understood this identity in a strictly exclusive manner. We have already seen a hint of this in Acts 13:47, where Luke records him applying the language of Isaiah 49:6 both to himself and Barnabas. The same is true of 2 Corinthians 5:16 – 6:2, where Paul uses the plural pronoun 'we' to refer to himself and his ministry co-workers as ambassadors for Christ, proclaiming the ministry of reconciliation in fulfilment of the Isaianic servant's mission to be a light to the nations. That pattern continues in Paul's letters, where he applies servant language to his ministry co-workers.

---

[37] For a similar conclusion, see Ciampa 1998: 125; Wilk 1998: 367–369.

The clearest example is Timothy. In what is likely the final letter written before his death, Paul uses a variety of metaphors to portray the nature of gospel ministry, such as soldier, farmer, worker and vessel (2 Tim. 2:3–6, 15, 20–21). This series of metaphors culminates with Paul's referring to Timothy as a servant of the Lord:

> And the Lord's servant must not be quarrelsome but kind to everyone, able to teach, patiently enduring evil, correcting his opponents with gentleness. God may perhaps grant them repentance leading to a knowledge of the truth, and they may come to their senses and escape from the snare of the devil, after being captured by him to do his will.
> (2 Tim. 2:24–26)

Since the defining characteristics of the Lord's servant revolve around teaching, Paul clearly has in view Timothy's role as a leader in the church rather than a general description of what must be true of all believers. At least a few of these characteristics show similarities to descriptions of the Isaianic servant (see Table 6 on p. 195).[38]

While it is true that there are no direct verbal parallels in 2 Timothy 2:24–26, there are clearly conceptual parallels between the description of the Lord's servant and the Isaianic servant. Paul uses this language to paint a picture of the kind of ministry leader that Timothy is called to be. There are similarities to the qualifications listed for elders/overseers elsewhere in the pastoral epistles (1 Tim. 3:1–7; Titus 1:5–9), with the key similarity being the emphasis on the ability to teach and correct opponents; the unique nature of Timothy's role as Paul's delegate, however, should caution against too quickly seeing the title 'servant of the Lord' as extended to elders/overseers in general. In a similar vein Paul refers to Timothy as 'a good servant of Christ Jesus' if he follows Paul's instructions (1 Tim. 4:6). Apparently, the apostle had no qualms about referring to one of his closest ministry co-workers as a 'servant of the Lord' or 'servant of Christ' in a way that highlighted Timothy's leadership role within the church.[39]

---

[38] The similarities have been noted (mostly in passing) by several scholars: Lock 1924: 101; Kelly 1963: 190; Marshall and Towner 2004: 765; Towner 2006: 546, 665–666.

[39] Note also the opening line of Phil. 1:1, 'Paul and Timothy, servants of Christ Jesus'.

Table 6 Isaianic parallels in 2 Timothy 2:24–26

The Lord's servant (2 Timothy)	*Isaianic servant of the Lord*
Not be quarrelsome (2:24)	He will not cry aloud or lift up his voice, or make it heard in the street (42:2)
Kind (2:24)	A bruised reed he will not break, and a faintly burning wick he will not quench (42:3)
Patiently enduring evil (2:24)	I gave my back to those who strike, and my cheeks to those who pull out the beard; I hid not my face from disgrace and spitting. But the Lord God helps me; therefore I have not been disgraced; therefore I have set my face like a flint, and I know that I shall not be put to shame. (50:6–7) He was oppressed, and he was afflicted, yet he opened not his mouth; like a lamb that is led to the slaughter, and like a sheep that before its shearers is silent, so he opened not his mouth. (Isa. 53:7)
Gentleness (2:25)	A bruised reed he will not break, and a faintly burning wick he will not quench (42:3)
God may perhaps grant them repentance leading to a knowledge of the truth, and they may come to their senses and escape from the snare of the devil, after being captured by him to do his will (2:25–26)	I will give you as a covenant for the people, a light for the nations, to open the eyes that are blind, to bring out the prisoners from the dungeon, from the prison those who sit in darkness (42:6–7).

Although this example from 2 Timothy 2:24–26 is the clearest, there are other places where Paul describes his ministry co-workers as servants by using the term *doulos*. He refers to Apollos, Cephas and himself as servants of Christ (1 Cor. 3:5; 4:1). As I observed in my discussion of 2 Corinthians 5:11 – 6:10, Paul uses the plural 'we' when describing his apostolic ministry. Similarly, in 2 Corinthians 4:5 Paul writes that he and his ministry co-workers are 'your servants for Jesus' sake'. Epaphras is described as 'our beloved fellow servant' (Col. 1:7) and 'a servant of Christ Jesus' (Col. 4:12) in a letter sent from Paul and Timothy (Col. 1:1). Tychicus is similarly described as a 'fellow servant in the Lord' (Col. 4:7). The term *diakonos* is also applied to a number of Paul's ministry co-workers such as Apollos (1 Cor. 3:5), Archippus (Col. 4:17), Epaphras (Col. 1:7), Erastus (Acts 19:22), Fortunatus (1 Cor. 16:15–18), Phoebe (Rom. 16:1), Timothy (2 Cor. 3:6; 6:4; 1 Thess. 3:2) and Tychicus (Eph. 6:21; Col. 4:7).[40]

The overlap and fluidity of such terminology clearly indicates that these were far from fixed titles, and it is impossible to distinguish specific activities that characterize one term from another. It is also worth noting that with the exception of 2 Timothy 2:24–26 these terms are consistently used without any explicit Old Testament background.

Peter the servant of Christ

Unlike his first epistle, where he identifies himself as 'an apostle of Jesus Christ' (1 Peter 1:1), Peter introduces himself as 'Simeon Peter, a servant and apostle of Jesus Christ' (2 Peter 1:1). He uses the term *doulos*, so it is certainly possible that the emphasis falls on Christ's complete ownership of him as his slave. Yet the use of this designation may also/instead signal that Peter understands himself as part of the line of servants of the Lord who have been set apart with a specific role in the advancement of God's redemptive purposes. After his brief survey of various servants of God in both the Old Testament and the New Testament, Jerome Neyrey summarizes that these servants are:

> trusted members of the circle that surrounds the sheik, the pharaoh, the king, or God. As officials in the household of God they have an honorable and proper role and status in regard to other members of that household . . . As officials in the household of God they have specific rights and duties.[41]

---

40 Data for this list is taken from Ellis 1993: 184. If one includes places where a co-worker is mentioned as engaging in *diakonia* (ministry, service), the list also includes people such as Achaicus (1 Cor. 16:15–18) and Mark (2 Tim. 4:11).

41 Neyrey 1993: 144; see similarly Davids 2006: 161.

So it is certainly plausible that Peter uses the term 'servant' because he sees himself as part of the line of the Lord's servants, though he does not in any way develop this idea in the letter.[42]

James the servant of God and of the Lord Jesus Christ

The straightforward nature of James's opening line fits the character of the entire letter: 'James, a servant of God and of the Lord Jesus Christ' (Jas 1:1). Rather than highlight that he is the half-brother of Jesus, James prefers the designation 'servant'. The use of the noun *doulos* could certainly stress James's total submission to the authority of Jesus. But given his position of leadership within the early church in Jerusalem (Acts 15:12–19), it is also reasonable to think that James saw himself within the line of individual servants God raised up to lead his people during key moments in redemptive history.[43] The specific form of this title is unique, as James is the only person in the New Testament to describe himself as a servant of God and of the Lord Jesus Christ.[44] Nowhere does James present Jesus as the servant of Yahweh, but it is hard to believe he was unfamiliar with such a designation if Acts 3 – 4 is an accurate reflection of the earliest beliefs and preaching of the early church. So perhaps James uses the unusual expression here in James 1:1 because he sees himself as a servant of God's servant, the Lord Jesus Christ. But at best this must remain a possible inference.

Jude the servant of Christ

Despite being the half-brother of Jesus, Jude opens his letter by identifying himself simply as 'a servant of Jesus Christ and brother of James' (Jude 1). By using the term *doulos* to describe his relationship to Jesus, Jude emphasizes his complete and total surrender to the authority of Jesus over his life. But he also may be drawing on the long list of servants before him who had a key role in the advancement of God's redemptive

---

42 Here it should be noted that 1 Peter 2:18–25 discusses Jesus' identity as the suffering servant (see the previous chapter) and holds him up as a model for believers, whom he also identifies as servants/slaves of God in 2:16 (see the following chapter).

43 Moo 2000: 48–49.

44 Ibid. 49.

purposes.[45] As such the title 'contains a claim to authority . . . based on his call to serve the Lord rather than on his family relationship with the Lord'.[46] While we cannot be certain about the specifics, it is apparent from the preservation of this letter along with the evidence from the early church that Jude had some kind of leadership role within the early Christian movement.[47] Although Jude does not expand on his self-understanding as a servant of Jesus Christ, it should be pointed out that the three descriptions of believers that follow ('called, beloved in God the Father and kept for Jesus Christ') may be drawn from the Isaianic servant songs.[48] If so, this may increase the possibility that Jude sees himself in some sense as a servant of the Lord in this more specialized sense.

John the servant of Christ

In the opening lines of Revelation, John describes what follows as:

> The revelation of Jesus Christ, which God gave him to show to his servants [*douloi*] the things that must soon take place. He made it known by sending his angel to his servant [*doulos*] John, who bore witness to the word of God and to the testimony of Jesus Christ, even to all that he saw.
> (Rev. 1:1–2)

I will return to the designation of all believers as servants in the next chapter; what interests me here is John's describing himself as a servant of Jesus Christ. Given his status as an apostle,[49] it is certainly possible that he sees himself in the line of individual servants raised up by God to advance his redemptive purposes. Yet the fact that in the previous sentence all believers are identified as servants warrants caution in making a definitive conclusion.

---

45 See also Bauckham 1983: 23; Schreiner 2003: 427–428.

46 Bauckham 1983: 23.

47 For a helpful summary of the possible ways Jude engaged in ministry, see Bateman 2017: 19–26. The two main possibilities seem to be serving as an elder in the Jerusalem church or as an itinerant missionary.

48 Bauckham 1983: 25.

49 While disputed, I am persuaded that the author of Revelation is the apostle John, who also authored the fourth Gospel account and the three NT letters. For a helpful discussion of various views and a defence of the traditional view of authorship, see Beale 1999: 34–36 and Osborne 2002: 2–5.

Conclusion

Although the line of individual servants culminates in Jesus, it does not terminate with him. As Isaiah 40 – 54 anticipated, the work of the suffering servant has created servants. Several key leaders within the early church describe themselves or are described as a servant of Christ, servant of God or servant of the Lord. By far the apostle Paul makes the most use of servant language. In fact, Paul's conviction that his life and ministry were prefigured in the description of the servant in Isaiah 49 is a central feature of his self-understanding. By dwelling in Paul, Christ the suffering servant was fulfilling the mission of the servant to be a light of salvation to the Gentiles. Servant terminology is also applied to several of Paul's ministry co-workers, but with the exception of Timothy in 2 Timothy 2:24–26 none of those descriptions borrow language from Old Testament servant passages. The exception to this general observation is that in both Acts 13:46–47 and 2 Corinthians 5:11 – 6:2 Paul uses the plural 'we' to describe his ministry in language borrowed from Isaiah 49, suggesting that he viewed his ministry co-workers as participating in the servant's mission. Peter, James, Jude and John also open their respective writings by referring to themselves as servants of Christ, raising the possibility that they too saw themselves in the long line of individual servants God uses to advance his creational and redemptive purposes, but giving no clear indication that such is the case.

But the servant theme does not end with these key ministry leaders within the early church. As we will see in the next chapter, God is not finished until he has formed a servant people.

9
The church: a servant people

> No longer will there be anything accursed, but the throne of God and of the Lamb will be in it, and his servants will worship him. (Rev. 22:3)

To this point the focus of our study has been individual servants of the Lord whom God has raised up to advance his creational and redemptive purposes. Along the way, however, we have noted that God uses the work of an individual servant to produce a servant people. That was clearly the case with Adam, who through being fruitful and multiplying would produce offspring who would share in and carry forward his servant role. There is also a sense in which the work of Moses the servant leads to Israel as a nation being formed into a servant people. Yet in Isaiah 40 – 55 we discovered that Israel's failure to carry out their mission as the servant of the Lord led to the promise that God would raise up a new individual servant, one who would obey where Israel failed, redeem Israel and the nations from their slavery to sin, and create a servant people.[1]

In the light of this Old Testament expectation, it is reasonable to expect that the work of Jesus the servant par excellence would produce a servant people. In the previous chapter we have seen how key individuals such as Paul (and even his ministry co-workers), James, Peter, John and Jude are identified as servants of God or servants of Christ. But does the role of the servant extend beyond these key individuals to believers in general and/or the body of Christ as a whole? The answer is a resounding yes. As we will see, the New Testament applies servant language/imagery to believers and describes them carrying out the servant's mission.

[1] Harris (2001: 133) suggests that based on the use of *doulos* in the LXX, it is 'antecedently probable that in the New Testament the figurative and titular use of *doulos* would not be restricted to leaders of God's people, the actual texts confirm this and indicate that being a slave of God or of Christ is a privileged role open to all believers'.

Gospels and Acts

There are several texts in both the Gospels and Acts that directly or indirectly apply servant language and or imagery to believers in general.

Mark 10:43–45

I have already discussed Jesus using servant language to refer to himself in Mark 10:43–45. In contrast to what constitutes greatness among the Gentiles, Jesus states:

> But it shall not be so among you. But whoever would be great among you must be your servant, and whoever would be first among you must be slave of all. For even the Son of Man came not to be served but to serve, and to give his life as a ransom for many.
> (Mark 10:43–45)

With so much focus on Jesus identifying himself as the Isaianic servant, the point of his doing so is often neglected. Jesus presents his self-sacrificial death as a pattern of life that his followers should emulate. In the immediate context Jesus' words are directed to the twelve apostles, but there is no substantive reason to restrict their application to them. In addition to presenting a compelling picture of Jesus, Mark also writes his Gospel as a discipleship manual. The path to greatness in God's kingdom is not in acquiring certain positions of power but in emulating the self-sacrificial love of Jesus through tangible acts of service to others. The Isaianic pattern of the individual servant creating a servant people through his suffering, death and vindication comes to fruition in the work of Jesus' creating a servant people.

Luke–Acts

We have already noted the prominence of servant language in Luke–Acts, highlighting its application to both Jesus and Paul. But Luke also applies servant language to both individuals and believers in general.

Servant language is especially prominent in Luke 1 – 2, where it is applied both individually and corporately. The first person identified as a servant of the Lord is Mary. In response to the angel Gabriel announcing to her that she will bear the promised descendant of David despite being a virgin (Luke 1:26–38), Mary responds, 'Behold, I am the servant [*doulē*] of the Lord, let it be to me according to your word' (Luke 1:38). She uses the same term in Luke 1:48, when in her song of praise she proclaims that God her Saviour 'has looked on the humble estate of his servant [*doulē*]'. At one level Mary could simply be expressing her humility and submission to the Lord. Yet given her special role within redemptive history, one should not rule out the possibility that Mary sees herself as part of the line of individual servants raised up by God for a particular purpose.[2] As David Garland notes, 'As a "slave of the Lord" she has an exalted status as one close to the Lord and willing to perform the humblest service out of loyalty and love.'[3] After noting the application of this term to Joshua, David and Israel, Garland concludes, 'The compliant and faithful Mary represents what God called Israel to become.'[4]

Garland's observation leads naturally into the next occurrence of servant language in Luke 1:54. Near the conclusion of her song of praise, Mary exclaims:

> He has helped his servant Israel,
>   in remembrance of his mercy,
> as he spoke to our fathers,
>   to Abraham and to his offspring for ever.
> (Luke 1:54–55)

Mary's language echoes Isaiah 41:8–10, where Israel is described as Yahweh's servant and Abraham's offspring.[5] It is because Israel is Yahweh's servant that he promises to strengthen, help and uphold Israel with his right hand. Mary understands that the son she bears as the servant of the Lord will be used by God to reverse the fortunes of Israel the servant of the Lord. Although Mary does not make the connection in her song, the stage seems to be set for seeing Jesus as the servant of the Lord who embodies what Israel failed to be.

---

[2] The fact that Mary's statement in Luke 1:48 echoes the words of Hannah (mother of Samuel) in 1 Sam. 1:11 further suggests she likely understood her special role as a servant of the Lord.

[3] Garland 2011: 83.

[4] Ibid.

[5] There are also echoes of Ps. 98:3 (97:3 LXX) and Mic. 7:20 in these two verses: the former contributes the reference 'in remembrance of his mercy' while the latter combines the ideas of mercy and fulfilling the promise to Abraham and his offspring; see the summary in Pao and Schnabel 2007: 262.

Several months later when John the Baptist is born, Luke records another song of praise, this time from John's father, Zechariah (Luke 1:68–79). The first half of this song is especially relevant for our study:

> Blessed be the Lord God of Israel,
> for he has visited and redeemed his people
> and has raised up a horn of salvation for us
> in the house of his servant [*paidos*] David,
> as he spoke by the mouth of his holy prophets from of old,
> that we should be saved from our enemies
> and from the hand of all who hate us;
> to show the mercy promised to our fathers
> and to remember his holy covenant,
> the oath that he swore to our father Abraham, to grant us
> that we, being delivered from the hand of our enemies,
> might serve [*latreuein*] him without fear,
> in holiness and righteousness before him all our days.
> (Luke 1:68–75)

Connecting the soon approaching redemption of God's people with David the servant of the Lord recalls restoration texts such as Ezekiel 34:23–24 and 37:24–27. As we saw in chapter 5, those texts announce a day when a descendant of Yahweh's servant David will shepherd his people in the land and God's presence will be with them. That eschatological promise is rooted in the covenant that God made with David in 2 Samuel 7, which as we saw was an extension of God's covenant with Abraham. Isaiah 40 – 55 also brings together the fulfilment of both the Abrahamic (Isa. 51:1–3; 54:1–3) and Davidic promises (Isa. 55:3–4) in the work of the suffering servant.

While there are many elements to the promise that God swore to Abraham, Zechariah highlights one central feature: the gift of serving the Lord 'without fear, / in holiness and righteousness before him all our days' (Luke 1:74–75).[6] The nature of this service has a priestly hue, as shown by the use of the verb *latreuō*, which 'refers to the total service one gives

[6] Syntactically the infinitive 'to give' (*dounai*) could either express the purpose of God swearing the oath to Abraham or the content of that oath (thus making it epexegetical). While a decision is difficult, the sense of the expression remains essentially the same either way. The content of that gift is expressed by the infinitive *latreuein* (to serve) making it the direct object.

to God, not just to the worship or sacrificial service that a faithful Jew would render in the temple or synagogue'.[7] As such it echoes texts in Exodus that state the purpose of Yahweh redeeming his people is so that they may serve him (Exod. 3:12; 4:23; 7:16; 8:1; 9:1, 13; 10:3, 7–8, 11, 24, 26; 12:31), as well as Joshua's charge to Israel to serve Yahweh (Josh. 24:14–24).[8] Such fearless service is carried out in holiness and righteousness in the presence of the Lord, further accentuating its priestly nature.[9] Once again, the work of an individual servant (in this case the descendant of Yahweh's servant David) produces a servant people.

In the very next chapter we are introduced to another self-proclaimed servant. While Mary and Joseph are presenting Jesus in the temple, a 'righteous and devout' man named Simeon approaches the parents (Luke 2:22–35). Because the Holy Spirit had revealed to him that this was 'the Lord's Christ' Simeon takes the child in his arms and prays:

> Lord, now you are letting your servant [*doulos*] depart in peace,
> according to your word.
> (Luke 2:29)

Noteworthy is the fact that in the lines that follow Simeon applies the language of Isaiah 49:6 to the Christ child, identifying him as 'a light for revelation to the Gentiles, / and for glory to your people Israel' (Luke 2:32). As a result, it seems most likely that Simeon does not see himself as part of the line of key individual servants, though. However, by alluding to Isaiah 49:6 Luke may be foreshadowing the transferral of Jesus the servant's mission to the apostles and his people. If so, Simeon as a servant of the Lord serves as a witness to Jesus the servant of the Lord, a role that God's people as individuals and as a body are given in Acts (see discussion below).

---

7 Bock 1994: 1.186.

8 In all of these texts, the LXX uses *latreuō* to describe the nature of the service.

9 There is a fascinating parallel in Wisdom 9.1–8. As an expansion of 1 Kgs 3:6–9, Solomon prays for God to grant him wisdom. He acknowledges that God made all things by his wisdom, and formed man to 'rule the world in holiness and righteousness' (Wis. 9.3 AT), the same terms used here in Luke 1:74. Solomon goes on to pray that God will not reject him 'from among your servants [*paidōn*]' (9.4 AT). He needs such wisdom to rule as a king of Israel and build a temple that is 'a copy of the holy tent that you prepared beforehand from the beginning' (9.8 NETS). While we cannot know if Luke was familiar with this text from Wisdom of Solomon, the parallels are striking.

For the remainder of Luke's Gospel, servant language focuses on Jesus. Yet in the concluding chapter there are indications that in some sense the mission of Jesus the servant is transferred to the apostles and ultimately the entirety of his people. While appearing to his gathered disciples on the evening of resurrection Sunday (Luke 24:36–49), Jesus reminds them that 'everything written about me in the Law of Moses and the Prophets and the Psalms must be fulfilled' (Luke 24:44). After opening their minds to understand the Scriptures (Luke 24:45), Jesus says this:

> Thus it is written, that the Christ should suffer and on the third day rise from the dead, and that repentance for the forgiveness of sins should be proclaimed in his name to all nations, beginning from Jerusalem. You are witnesses of these things. And behold, I am sending the promise of my Father upon you. But stay in the city until you are clothed with power from on high.
> (Luke 24:46–49)

Normally when the biblical authors use an expression such as 'thus it is written' an explicit citation of a specific Old Testament text follows. But here the phrase introduces Jesus' summary of the message of the Old Testament. That summary centres on three verbs: suffer, rise and be proclaimed.[10] The first two actions are performed by Jesus, and both are rooted in previous Old Testament allusions earlier in Luke and later in Acts.[11] The third action of the gospel being proclaimed is where the disciples come in: they are the ones who will announce repentance and forgiveness of sins in Jesus' name to all the nations. Indeed, they are 'witnesses of these things' (Luke 24:48). As Holly Beers points out, there are several connections to Isaianic servant language in verses 47–48.[12] The proclamation of forgiveness (Gr. *aphesis*) recalls Jesus' combined citation of Isaiah 58:6 and 61:1 in the synagogue at Nazareth (Luke 4:18–19). Just as Israel the servant is described as a witness (Gr. *martys*; Isa. 43:10, 12; 44:8),

---

[10] In Greek each of these verbs is an infinitive; grammatically they are either epexegetical to the adverb *houtōs* (thus) or markers of indirect discourse. Either way they indicate the content of what is written in Scripture.

[11] Pao and Schnabel (2007: 401) note the following examples: Ps. 118:22 (Luke 20:17; Acts 4:11); Isa. 53:12 (Luke 22:37); Ps. 31:5 (Luke 23:46); Pss 22:7, 18; 69:21 (Luke 23:34–36); Ps. 2:1–2 (Acts 4:25–26); Isa. 53:7–8 (Acts 8:32–33); Ps. 16:8–11 (Acts 2:25–28; 13:35); and Isa. 55:3 (Acts 13:34).

[12] Beers 2016: 124–125.

so now the disciples are given this title (Luke 24:47). The proclamation extending to 'all nations' recalls the mission of the Isaianic servant to be a light of salvation to the ends of the earth (Isa. 49:6, applied to Jesus in Luke 2:32).

This last observation finds further confirmation in Acts 1:8. Shortly before Jesus ascends to heaven, he tells his disciples: 'But you will receive power when the Holy Spirit has come upon you, and you will be my witnesses in Jerusalem and in all Judea and Samaria, and to the end of the earth' (Acts 1:8). As David Pao points out, there are several points of connection between this text and Luke 24:47–49.[13] Each of them addresses Jesus' followers as witnesses who must wait in Jerusalem for power to come upon them so they can go from Jerusalem to the nations/ends of the earth. Like the Isaianic servant (Isa. 42:1; 61:1), the disciples will have the Spirit of the Lord 'upon' (*epi*) them to carry out their mission.[14] Of further interest is that the phrase 'to the end of the earth' that concludes Acts 1:8 is an echo of Isaiah 49:6, where the mission of the servant extends 'to the end of the earth'.[15] The parallels between Luke 24:47–49 and Acts 1:8 make it likely that Isaiah 49:6 also informs Luke 24:47–49.

Considered together, then, Luke 24:46–49 and Acts 1:8 present Jesus the servant transferring his mission to his servant people.[16] In the previous chapter we saw that Paul uses servant language from Isaiah 49:6 in Acts 13:47 to justify his mission to the Gentiles. Here we may note that when Paul appears before Agrippa in Acts 26:1–29, he brings together several elements found in Luke 24:46–47.[17] As part of his defence Paul says:

> To this day I have had the help that comes from God, and so I stand here testifying both to small and great, saying nothing but what the prophets and Moses said would come to pass: that the Christ must

13 Pao 2002: 84–86.

14 Helpfully noted by Beers (2016: 131–132).

15 See Pao 2002: 85–86. He notes that the Greek phrase *heōs eschatou tēs gēs* (to the ends of the earth) occurs five times in the LXX, four of which are in Isaiah (8:9; 48:20; 49:6; 62:11). Of these texts, Isa. 49:6 and its context has the clearest connections. The echo is confirmed by the citation of Isa. 49:6 in Acts 13:47, where Paul cites this same text to describe his mission to the Gentiles.

16 It is true that based on the larger context Acts 1:8 appears to be spoken only to the apostles. But in Luke 24:36–49 it is clear that more than just the apostles were gathered together (see vv. 33–35). As we will see, the rest of Acts shows the servant's mission being carried out by more than just the apostles.

17 Pao 2002: 86.

> suffer and that, by being the first to rise from the dead, he would proclaim light both to our people and to the Gentiles.
> (Acts 26:22–23)

Just as in Luke 24:46–47, Paul mentions (1) the fulfilment of Scripture in Christ; (2) the suffering of Christ; (3) his resurrection; and (4) the mission to the Gentiles. The description of his mission as proclaiming light to both the Jews and the Gentiles echoes the mission of the servant in Isaiah 49:5–6, who not only restores the remnant of Israel but is a light of salvation for the nations.

That the mission of Jesus the servant is passed on to his people as a whole and not merely the apostles is most explicitly seen in Acts 4:23–31. We have already noted in a previous chapter how this passage refers to both David (v. 25) and Jesus (vv. 27, 30) as servants of the Lord. But as part of their prayer in response to Peter and John being released from custody, they also identify themselves as servants of the Lord:

> And now, Lord, look upon their threats and grant to your servants to continue to speak your word with all boldness, while you stretch out your hand to heal, and signs and wonders are performed through the name of your holy servant Jesus.
> (Acts 4:29–30)

The people praying this prayer are not merely the apostles; verse 23 states that Peter and John return 'to their friends'. The logic of the passage seems rather clear – Jesus the holy servant continues his work through his servants. The bold preaching and miraculous signs they perform are done 'through the name of your holy servant Jesus' (Acts 4:30).

The servant identity of God's people is shown not only by referring to them as such; as Holly Beers has argued, it is also shown by portraying God's people carrying out the mission of the Isaianic servant.[18] The suffering/persecution of believers, their non-violent response and their ultimate vindication are part of a larger servant motif that is applied to both Jesus and his people in Acts.[19] Like Jesus the servant before them,

[18] What follows is drawn from Beers (2016: 126–175).

[19] Beers (ibid. 177) is careful to note that Luke preserves the uniqueness of the atoning nature of Jesus' suffering in distinction from the suffering of his people. Yet as Beers points out, within Isaiah itself the suffering of the servant is broader in nature than vicarious atonement for his people.

Peter and John (Acts 4:1–31), the apostles (Acts 5:12–42) and Stephen (Acts 7:1–60) suffer for carrying out the mission of the servant to proclaim the good news, respond non-violently in the face of injustice and are vindicated in some fashion.[20] Through his proclamation of the good news Philip carries out the servant's mission (Acts 8:26–40), as does Ananias in his healing and commissioning of Saul (Acts 9:10–19). Even the language describing Cornelius and the Gentiles who believe in response to Peter's preaching may signal not only that they are participating in the Isaianic new exodus, but are included within the servant vocation (Acts 10:1–48).[21]

Even if some of Beers's proposed connections to servant language and motifs are debatable, the cumulative effect of her argument is persuasive: Luke portrays the followers of Jesus the servant as a servant people, carrying out the Isaianic servant's mission.

Paul's letters

Given the extent to which Paul uses Isaianic servant language and imagery to describe his conversion and apostolic commission, we might suspect that he would be reticent to use similar language for believers in general. But that is not the case. There are at least two texts where he borrows language from Isaianic servant texts to describe believers.

Romans 8:33–34

We have already seen that Paul uses Isaianic servant language to describe the death and resurrection of Jesus as well as his own apostolic ministry. So it should perhaps come as little surprise that he appears also to apply servant language to all believers in Romans 8:33–34. After affirming God's unshakable commitment to his people (Rom. 8:31), Paul argues from the greater to the lesser: 'He who did not spare his own Son but gave him up for us all, how will he not also with him graciously give us all things?'

[20] In Acts 3 – 5, vindication for Peter, John and the rest of the apostles takes the form of being released from custody by the Jewish authorities. For Stephen, however, his vindication is seen in the description of his face as 'the face of an angel' (Acts 6:15) as well as his vision of the Son of Man standing at the right hand of God (Acts 7:55–56). If Jesus' request for God not to hold the sin of his executioners against them in Luke 23:34 is original, Stephen's similar request here in Acts 7:60 provides a further parallel between himself and Jesus the servant. So even though Acts never refers to Stephen as a/the servant, 'a complex series of allusions and echoes contribute to the likelihood that both Stephen and Jesus carry out facets of the same servant mission' (ibid. 140).

[21] See the argument in ibid. 151–154.

(Rom. 8:32). The language of God not sparing his son likely echoes Genesis 22, while the expression 'gave him up for us all' probably derives from God delivering up the servant for the sins of the people in Isaiah 53.[22] In verses 33–34 Paul asks and answers a series of questions to demonstrate the security that believers have by virtue of being in Christ. Wilk has persuasively argued that in doing so Paul borrows from Isaiah 50:7–8 (LXX).[23] He notes three points of contact, summarized in Table 7.[24]

Table 7 Isaianic allusions and echoes in Romans 8:33–34

Romans 8:33–34	*Isaiah 50:7–9 LXX (NETS)*
Who shall bring any charge against [*tis enkalesei kata*] God's elect? It is God who justifies [*ho dikaiōn*]. Who is to condemn [*tis ho katakrinōn*]? Christ Jesus is the one who died – more than that, who was raised – who is at the right hand of God, who indeed is interceding for us.	And the Lord became my helper; therefore I was not disgraced, but I have set my face like solid rock, and I realized that I would not be put to shame, because he who justified [*ho dikaiōsas*] me draws near. Who is the one who contends [*tis ho krinomenos*] with me? Let him confront me at once. Yes, who is the one who contends with me? Let him draw near me. Look, the Lord helps me; who will harm [*tis ho kakēsei*] me? Look, all of you will become old like a garment, and as it were a moth will devour you.

Isaiah 50:4–9 is the third of the servant songs, focusing on the servant's obedience even in the face of intense persecution and suffering. The servant expresses his confidence that God who justifies him is near (Isa. 50:8; cf. Rom. 8:33), which is immediately followed by the question 'who

22 See also Seifrid 2007: 634.

23 See Wilk 1998: 280–284.

24 The connections are more evident in the Greek text, which I have supplied in brackets where relevant.

is the one who contends with me' (Isa. 50:8; cf. Rom. 8:34). Because the Lord helps the servant, he rhetorically asks 'who will harm me' (Isa. 50:9; cf. Rom. 8:34). Although the sequence in Romans 8:33–34 is slightly different, the conceptual and verbal similarities are sufficient to indicate that Paul is borrowing language from Isaiah 50:7–9.

Thus, Paul takes language describing the Isaianic servant and applies it to all believers. The vindication in the midst of persecution and suffering experienced by Christ the servant will also be experienced by his people. Because Christ has died, risen and now intercedes for his people, they cannot be separated 'from the love of God in Christ Jesus our Lord' (Rom. 8:39). By virtue of their union with Christ the servant, believers are a servant people who will be vindicated on the last day.

Galatians 5:13

Paul argues at length in Galatians 3:1 – 5:1 that believers are justified by faith in Christ and no longer under the authority of the Mosaic law. That argument culminates in his statement that 'For freedom Christ has set us free; stand firm therefore, and do not submit again to a yoke of slavery' (Gal. 5:1). But given the possibility that his readers will misunderstand the nature of the freedom he has in view, Paul writes: 'For you were called to freedom, brothers. Only do not use your freedom as an opportunity for the flesh, but through love serve one another' (Gal. 5:13). Whereas before their conversion believers are enslaved (*douloō*) to the elements of this world (Gal. 4:3), believers are now called to serve (*douleuō*) one another in love.[25] The gospel produces a freedom that empowers God's people to live a life of ongoing service to others, and in particular fellow believers. This life of service to others is done not out of grim-faced duty, but rather 'through love'. Because Christ loved us and gave himself for us (2:20), believers are able to serve others through love, which itself is an outworking of genuine faith in Christ (5:6). By following this exhortation to serve one another through love, believers fulfil the intention of the Mosaic law (Gal. 5:14, citing Lev. 19:18). Believers are not left to their own resources to fulfil the command to serve one another through love: they have the Holy Spirit empowering them (Gal. 5:16–26) as they seek to fulfil the law of Christ (Gal. 6:1–10).

[25] That there is no difference between the use of *douloō* and *douleuō* is confirmed by the use of *douleuō* in Gal. 4:8–9 in a way that is clearly synonymous with *douloō* in Gal. 4:3.

By using 'serve' language Paul is likely linking his exhortation here with his conviction that Christ is the Isaianic servant of the LORD who has set his people free from their slavery to sin/elementals/law through his sacrificial death and resurrection (see 1:4; 2:20; 3:13; 4:1–7; 4:21 – 5:1).[26] After describing the freedom that those redeemed by the servant will experience, Isaiah 54:17 states:

> This is the heritage of the servants of the LORD
> and their vindication from me, declares the LORD.[27]

Just as Isaiah 40 – 54 has anticipated, the work of Jesus the suffering servant produces servants who are empowered by the same self-sacrificial love to serve others.[28]

Philippians 2:15

In the well-known Christ-hymn of Philippians 2:5–11, Paul draws on imagery from Isaianic servant texts to describe the work of Christ. Based on what Christ the suffering servant has done for his people, believers are called to work out their salvation with fear trembling, knowing that God himself is at work in them (Phil. 2:12–13). As a specific expression of working out their salvation, Paul commands the Philippians:

> Do all things without grumbling or disputing, that you may be blameless and innocent, children of God without blemish in the midst of a crooked and twisted generation, among whom you shine as lights in the world, holding fast to the word of life, so that in the day of Christ I may be proud that I did not run in vain or labour in vain.
> (Phil. 2:14–16)

Grumbling recalls the Israelite's failure in the wilderness (e.g. Exod. 16:1 – 17:17; Num. 14:1–38; 16:1 – 17:13), suggesting that Paul is calling the

---

[26] See further Harmon 2010: 205–209. What follows is a brief summary of the larger argument provided there. This connection is also noted by Oakes (2015: 170).

[27] In Isa. 54:17 the word rendered 'heritage' (*naḥălâ*) from the MT is translated in the LXX as 'inheritance' (*klēronomia*) to describe this reality, suggesting a further link to Paul's argument in Galatians. So too does the use of 'righteousness' language (which the ESVUK renders 'vindication'), which plays a prominent role here in Galatians.

[28] There may also be parallels to the original exodus, in which God's people were freed from their Egyptian bondage to serve Yahweh (Exod. 4:23; 19:4–6; 20:1–6; Lev. 25:42); see Wilson 2004: 565–568.

Philippians to avoid Israel's mistakes. That conclusion is confirmed by recognizing that Paul's reference to a 'crooked and twisted generation' echoes Deuteronomy 32:5 (LXX), where Moses describes Israel's wilderness generation with the same language. By contrast, believers are said to 'shine like stars in the world' (Phil. 2:15 CSB). This language is borrowed from Daniel 12:3, which says: 'And those who are wise shall shine like the brightness of the sky above; and those who turn many to righteousness, like the stars for ever and ever' (Dan. 12:3). Paul's point in borrowing this language from Daniel 12:3 is to assert that by virtue of their union with Christ believers have already been raised from the dead spiritually and as a result of their transformed lives stand out in the midst of a world still under the curse.

But one should not overlook an additional intertextual echo within Daniel 12:3 itself. The description of God's resurrected people as 'those who turn many to righteousness' echoes the description of the Isaianic suffering servant, who through his own death and resurrection makes 'many to be accounted righteous' (Isa. 53:11).[29] Such a connection suggests that Daniel 12:3 is an interpretation or extension of Isaiah 53 in which all of God's people share in the resurrection of the suffering servant.

The possibility that Daniel 12:3 is an interpretation of Isaiah 53:11 may further indicate that the language of believers shining as stars in the world also draws upon Isaiah 49:6, where the servant is described as 'a light for the nations, / that my salvation may reach to the end of the earth'. Additional evidence suggesting an echo of Isaiah 49:6 comes in Philippians 2:16, where Paul grounds his exhortations in his goal that on the day of Christ he will be able to say that he 'did not run in vain or labour in vain'. As noted in the previous chapter, such language comes from Isaiah 49:4, where the servant expresses his concern about labouring in vain.

In the light of this network of Old Testament allusions and echoes, it seems reasonable that Paul sees believers as a corporate servant figure, indwelled by the risen Christ through the Holy Spirit to carry out the servant's mission of being a light of salvation to the nations. In contrast to the nation of Israel, who failed in their calling to be an obedient servant of the Lord, believers fulfil that mission because Christ the obedient servant of the Lord indwells and empowers them.

---

[29] In both the LXX and DSS of Isa. 53:11 the suffering servant is said to see light; if such a reading is original it would establish a further link between Dan. 12:3 and Isa. 53:11.

Catholic epistles

Although the theme of Christ the servant creating a servant people is not as prominent in the catholic epistles, there is at least one passage where such a conclusion is implied.

1 Peter 2:13–25

Peter writes his first letter to instruct believers how to live as 'sojourners and exiles' in this fallen world, doing so in a way that glorifies God in anticipation of Christ's return (1 Peter 2:11–12). Part of how they do so is to submit themselves to the various authority structures as a means of silencing the ignorant people who criticize them (1 Peter 2:13–15). At the heart of his exhortations lies this fundamental principle: 'Live as people who are free, not using your freedom as a cover-up for evil, but living as servants [*douloi*] of God' (1 Peter 2:16). The slave–free binary was one of the fundamental ways of conceptualizing first-century society (cf. Gal. 3:28), so at first glance referring to believers as 'servants/slaves of God' could easily be a way of highlighting their complete submission to God. But the larger context suggests something more.

In the paragraph that follows (1 Peter 2:18–25), Peter applies this general principle to one specific category of believers: 'Servants [*oiketai*], be subject to your masters with all respect, not only to the good and gentle but also to the unjust' (1 Peter 2:18). The term *oiketēs* refers to a household slave, and the verses that follow show that Peter has this specific situation in view. The switch to *oiketai* in 2:18 indicates that *douloi* in 2:16 is a general reference to all believers, not merely a reference to Christians who are slaves to a human master.

But what is especially noteworthy is that in the course of his instruction to household servants (*oiketai*), Peter draws extensively on Isaiah 53 to describe how 'Christ also suffered for you, leaving you an example, so that you might follow in his steps' (1 Peter 2:21). While the specific instruction in view is directed towards household servants, there is no reason to conclude that Christ's example as the suffering servant applies only to them. Peter sees in the patient endurance of Christ the suffering servant a pattern that he applies to household servants, but also applies more broadly to all believers.

The combination of referring to all believers as 'servants/slaves [*douloi*] of God' and pointing to Christ the suffering servant as an example for believers who are household servants suggests the possibility that Peter sees a connection between Christ the servant and believers as a servant people. Whereas Paul roots that connection in Christ dwelling in believers, Peter draws attention to the pattern of life established by Christ as an example for believers to emulate. These two perspectives should be seen as complementary rather than contradictory or mutually exclusive.

Revelation

The significance of believers as servants/slaves of God or Christ occurs in the opening verse of the book, where John indicates that God gave this revelation to John 'to show to his servants the things that must soon take place' (Rev. 1:1a). God made this revelation through an angel 'to his servant John' (Rev. 1:1b). Based on this interchange, it is difficult to determine whether John views himself as having a place in the line of individual servants God raised up throughout redemptive history, or whether he is simply a servant in the sense that all believers are called servants. Complicating the decision is the fact that 'servant' (*doulos*) is applied to believers in general, key individuals in God's redemptive plan, and even the angel who reveals these things to John (Rev. 19:10; 22:9).

Key individuals as servants/slaves

Between the sixth and seventh trumpet John sees an angel descending from heaven with a small scroll in his hand (Rev. 10:1–2). This angel cries out in a loud voice, and in response the seven thunders sound (Rev. 10:3). After prohibiting John from writing what the seven thunders said (Rev. 10:4–6), the angel swears that 'in the days of the trumpet call to be sounded by the seventh angel, the mystery of God would be fulfilled, just as he announced to his servants [*douloi*] the prophets'. When the seventh trumpet is finally sounded (Rev. 11:15–19), the twenty-four elders fall down before the Lord and say:

> We give you thanks, Lord God, the Almighty,
> who is and who was,
> because you have taken your great power
> and have begun to reign.
> The nations were angry,
> but your wrath has come.

The time has come
for the dead to be judged
and to give the reward
to your servants [*doulois*] the prophets,
to the saints, and to those who fear your name,
both small and great,
and the time has come to destroy
those who destroy the earth.
(Rev. 11:17–18 CSB)

As Osborne notes, there are five different terms used for those who receive a reward (God's servants, prophets, saints, those who fear God's name, and the small and the great); the question is the nature of the relationship between these different groups of people.[30] A decision is difficult, but on the whole it seems most likely that there is some distinction in view between the prophets and saints,[31] especially in the light of Rev. 18:20 where saints, apostles and prophets are distinguished. Yet the very ambiguity of the text highlights the fluid use of the term 'servant/slave' for key individuals in redemptive history as well as a term applied to God's people in general.

Far less ambiguous is the designation of Moses as the servant of God in Revelation 15. After introducing the seven angels with the seven plagues that culminate God's wrath (Rev. 15:1), the scene shifts to God's heavenly throne room, where those who conquered the beast and his image are worshipping (Rev. 15:2). John notes 'And they sing the song of Moses, the servant [*doulou*] of God, and the song of the Lamb' (Rev. 15:3a), which is then recounted (Rev. 15:3b–4). The content of the song draws from a number of Old Testament passages,[32] reinforcing the larger point that

30 See Osborne 2002: 446–447. He summarizes three main views: (1) slaves/servants includes all the other terms, but under that general category there are two subgroups of prophets and saints; (2) slaves/servants includes all the other terms, but under that general category there are three subgroups of prophets, saints and those who fear God (i.e. God-fearing Gentiles); and (3) all these terms together describe the church.

31 See similarly ibid. This conclusion holds whether 'prophets' refers just to the prophets mentioned in the immediate context of Rev. 10 – 11, prophets as a distinct group within the early church, or more likely (in my view) the totality of all God's prophets throughout redemptive history in the light of the strong OT allusions to Ps. 2:1 and Jer. 51:25 (28:25 LXX) in Rev. 11:18.

32 See Beale 2007: 133–134 for a summary; for extended discussion, see Bauckham 1993: 296–307 and Beale 1999: 792–800.

Jesus has led his people in the long-promised new exodus – a new exodus that involves an even greater triumph over an even greater enemy than the original exodus from Egypt.

General references to believers as servants/slaves

In addition to Revelation 1:1a, there are a number of places where believers in general are referred to as servants/slaves. In his message to the church in Thyatira, the risen Jesus commends their service (*diakonia*), but rebukes them for tolerating the teaching of the prophetess Jezebel, who is 'teaching and seducing my servants [*douloi*] to practise sexual immorality and to eat food sacrificed to idols' (Rev. 2:20). There is nothing in the context to suggest that the servants in view are a special class within the church.

When the fifth seal is opened and the souls of those martyred for the faith emerge to call for justice on their oppressors, they are given a white robe and 'told to rest a little longer, until the number of their fellow servants [*douloi*] and their brothers should be complete, who were to be killed as they themselves had been' (Rev. 6:11). While it could be possible to see servants referring exclusively to martyrs, the fact that they are also called 'brothers' (another term applied to all believers) suggests that the term 'servants' is not limited to those who die for the faith. All martyrs are servants, but not all servants end up as martyrs.

Revelation 7:1–17 contains two interconnected visions. In verses 1–8 the four angels with the power to harm the earth and the sea are warned not to cause any destruction 'until we have sealed the servants [*douloi*] of our God on their foreheads' (Rev. 7:3). The total number of those sealed is 144,000, with 12,000 coming from each of the tribes of Israel. In verses 9–17 John sees an innumerable multitude 'from every nation, from all tribes and peoples and languages' (Rev. 7:9) worshipping the Lamb on the throne. They are further identified as those who come out of the great tribulation (Rev. 7:14). They are further described as follows:

> Therefore they are before the throne of God,
>   and serve him day and night in his temple;
>   and he who sits on the throne will shelter them with his presence.
> They shall hunger no more, neither thirst any more;
>   the sun shall not strike them,
>   nor any scorching heat.

For the Lamb in the midst of the throne will be their shepherd,
   and he will guide them to springs of living water,
and God will wipe away every tear from their eyes.
(Rev. 7:15–18)

This great multitude of believers is portrayed as priests who serve (*latreuō*) God day and night in his heavenly temple. The absence of hunger, thirst or scorching heat in the presence of the Lamb foreshadows the description of the new Eden in Revelation 22:1–5, while the claim that God will wipe away every tear anticipates the description of the new heavens and new earth in Revelation 21:3–4. Based on these parallels it seems clear that the term 'servant' is applied here to believers in general, with a view to their priestly identity.

In Revelation 18:1 – 19:5 John sees the climactic judgment on Babylon the great harlot, enemy of God's people throughout the ages. In response to the judgment meted out on Babylon, a great multitude in heaven cries out:

Hallelujah! Salvation and glory and power belong to our God,
   for his judgments are true and just;
for he has judged the great prostitute
   who corrupted the earth with her immorality,
and has avenged on her the blood of his servants [*doulōn*].
(Rev. 19:1–2)

A voice from the throne joins the chorus of the multitude and the praises of the twenty-four elders and the four living creatures, saying:

Praise our God,
   all you his servants [*douloi*],
you who fear him,
   small and great.
(Rev. 19:5)

The language of God avenging the blood of his servants recalls Revelation 6:9, where the souls of those martyred ask God for this very thing. Revelation 19:5 hearkens back to 11:18, which also uses the term 'servants' and further explains it with the expressions 'those who fear your name' and 'small and great'. These further clarifications make it clear that 'servants' refers to all of God's people.

The final reference to God's people as servants comes in Revelation 22:6, which acts as a bookend that corresponds to Revelation 1:1. The angel revealing these visions to John insists again that God's purpose is 'to show his servants what must soon take place' (Rev. 22:6). From first to last, in Revelation God's people are a servant people.

Revelation 22:1–5

Because of its importance for our study, Revelation 22:1–5 warrants special attention. The culminating vision of the new creation is presented as a renewed Garden of Eden. But this is no mere return to humanity's original state before sin and death entered through Adam and Eve's rebellion and idolatry: it is the full realization of God's original purposes for creation:

> Then the angel showed me the river of the water of life, bright as crystal, flowing from the throne of God and of the Lamb through the middle of the street of the city; also, on either side of the river, the tree of life with its twelve kinds of fruit, yielding its fruit each month. The leaves of the tree were for the healing of the nations. No longer will there be anything accursed, but the throne of God and of the Lamb will be in it, and his servants [*douloi*] will worship [*latreusousin*] him. They will see his face, and his name will be on their foreheads. And night will be no more. They will need no light of lamp or sun, for the Lord God will be their light, and they will reign for ever and ever. (Rev. 22:1–5)

Like the original Eden, there is a river flowing out to provide life (Gen. 2:10). The fact that it flows from 'the throne of God and of the Lamb' confirms that Eden was God's original earthly temple sanctuary. Whereas because of Adam and Eve's rebellion humanity was cut off from accessing the tree of life (Gen. 3:22–23), in the new Eden humanity freely eats from its leaves for healing. The curse that fell on creation for Adam and Eve's rebellion (Gen. 3:14–19) is now completely removed, and as a result it is a fit sanctuary for the holiness of God and the Lamb.

Most significantly for our study is the fact that John chooses the title 'servants' to refer to God's redeemed eschatological people. Choosing this designation in the culminating vision of Revelation suggests that for John the title 'servants' is fundamental to his understanding of God's people. The glorified people of God are first a servant people.

Additionally, referring to God's people as 'servants' confirms that, as argued in chapter 2, Adam is the first servant of the Lord. As the initial servant, his role was to produce additional servants by being fruitful, multiplying and filling the earth (Gen. 1:28). Based on the larger context of Genesis 1 – 2 we argued that this servant role was embedded within the concept of humanity being created in God's image. As part of living out this servant role, Adam had both a royal and a priestly role. As a king under the authority of Yahweh the great king, Adam was to rule over and subdue creation, acting as an extension of the Lord's rule over the universe. That is precisely what God's glorified servant people are doing in the new Eden when John says 'they will reign for ever and ever' (Rev. 22:5). As a priest, Adam was called to mediate God's presence to the world and protect the purity of Yahweh's earthly sanctuary. John signals by using the verb *latreuō* (translated in the ESVUK as 'worship') that God's glorified servants exercise a priestly function in the new Eden. This verb consistently has priestly overtones, often referring to serving the Lord within the context of the cultic structures of the priesthood and tabernacle/temple.[33] At last in the new Eden God's servant people are fulfilling their commission to reflect the image of God by ruling over creation as kings and mediating God's presence as priests. No wonder there is no need for the sun or the moon! The radiant light of God's glory illuminates all of creation and is seen most clearly in his glorified servant people.

Conclusion

The work of Jesus the servant has created a servant people.[34] The New Testament demonstrates the servant identity of God's people in three

[33] Cf. BDAG, which claims that in the LXX and NT it refers only to 'the carrying out of religious duties, esp[ecially] of a cultic nature, by human beings' (s.v. *latreuō*). See similarly Strathmann 1976: 4.60, who concludes that the type of service described by *latreuō* 'has sacral significance . . . [it] means more precisely to serve or worship cultically, especially by sacrifice'.

[34] In the light of this evidence, the conclusion of Harris (2001: 133) that 'the church, considered corporately, [is never] spoken of as the slave of God or Christ, although in the LXX Israel as a nation is depicted as Yahweh's *doulos* (Ps. 79:5, Heb. *'am*) or *douloi* (Deut. 32:36; Neh. 1:6)' should be re-evaluated. He does note that 'In the *Shepherd of Hermas* (?c. AD 150), *doulos theou* is a synonym for 'Christian' (e.g. 38:6; 46:1: 48:2, 4)' (ibid. 133, n. 16).

primary ways: (1) directly calling them servants; (2) using servant language to describe them; and (3) showing them carrying out the mission of the servant. The mission of Jesus the servant has in some sense been transferred to his people. Such a transfer in no way undermines the uniqueness of what Jesus the servant accomplishes, since it is the risen Jesus himself who indwells his people by his Spirit to complete the elements of the servant's mission that remain. Only Jesus vicariously suffers for the sins of his people. Only Jesus is the perfect image of God who fulfils Adam's servant commission as a prophet, priest and king. Only Jesus is the prophet greater than Moses, the conqueror greater than Joshua and the king greater than David. Yet he now works in and through the church his servant people to bring to full realization every aspect that remains of the servant's mission.

The nature of the church's role as the servant takes two distinct forms in the New Testament. The first and most frequent is an Isaianic shape. As God's people suffer and endure it without violent response, they follow in the footsteps of Jesus the servant (Rom. 8:33–34; 1 Peter 2:18–25) even as they await their final vindication from the Lord (Rev. 6:9–11). As God's people proclaim the good news of what Jesus the servant has accomplished through his death and resurrection, they are the means by which God restores Israel and shines the light of salvation to the ends of the earth (Acts 1:8; Phil. 2:15). Even the nature of their common life together is guided by the principle of using the freedom Christ purchased for us as a means to serve one another self-sacrificially in love (Gal. 5:13).

The second form of God's people as the servant is Adamic in nature. When at last God consummates all of his promises in a new Eden, humanity will perfectly reflect the image of God. As God's servants, redeemed humanity will exercise the dominion over creation that God commissioned Adam to exercise. They will worship him as priests in his glorious presence. By virtue of their union with Christ the servant God's people will at last fully realize their destiny as image-bearing servants.

10
Conclusion

> Reign thou in Hell thy Kingdom, let mee serve
> In Heav'n God ever blessed, and his Divine
> Behests obey, worthiest to be obey'd.
> (Milton, *Paradise Lost*, Book VI, lines 183–85)

> So you also, when you have done all that you were commanded, say, 'We are unworthy servants; we have only done what was our duty.'
> (Luke 17:10)

> His master said to him, 'Well done, good and faithful servant. You have been faithful over a little; I will set you over much. Enter into the joy of your master.'
> (Matt. 25:21)

Satan's assertion that it is better to reign in hell than serve in heaven is not the final word in Milton's *Paradise Lost*. In Book VI, the angel Abdiel (whose name in Hebrew means 'servant of God') responds by noting that the true nature of 'servitude' (by which he means what we would call slavery) is to submit and surrender oneself to someone who is unworthy. By contrast, to embrace one's identity as a servant of the Lord is to experience the blessings of the one who is most worthy of service.

What we have seen in our study of the servant of the Lord theme is that God uses key individual servants to advance his purposes for both creation and redemption. He began with Adam, commissioning him to exercise royal, priestly and prophetic roles. Through him fulfilling his role as an image-bearing servant of Yahweh, God intended to produce a servant people. But when Adam rebelled, his ability to fulfil his role as servant was radically diminished. Yet even within God's announcement of judgment, he holds out the promise of a future servant who will defeat the serpent through his suffering. From that point forward God begins to raise up a series of individual servants who (to various degrees) exercised these royal, priestly and prophetic roles, albeit not perfectly and not without failure. Through these individual servants God works to create a servant people, while at the same time pointing forward to the ultimate servant who will fulfil these royal, priestly and prophetic roles. This Old Testament eschatological hope begins to take on further clarity as God promises to raise up a servant who will obey where God's people failed, suffer for their sins, be vindicated, establish a new covenant and create a servant people.

Jesus is that servant – the servant par excellence – who fulfils these Old Testament expectations. He embodies everything these previous servants were called to be and do, obeying where they failed. He is the new Adam, the prophet greater than Moses, the conqueror greater than Joshua, the king greater than David, and the suffering servant who bears the sins of his people and is vindicated. Through his life, ministry, death, resurrection and ascension Jesus fulfils the missions of the previous servants.

Yet while the work of Jesus the servant is fulfilled, it is not yet consummated. Through his work Jesus the servant of the Lord has created a servant people whom he indwells and empowers to continue his mission as the servant. He does this not only through key leaders (such as Paul and his ministry co-workers, James, John and Jude) but also his body the church. Believers as individuals and the church as a body live out the mission of Jesus the risen servant by being a light of salvation to the ends of the earth.

Implications

Since biblical theology is not merely a descriptive approach to Scripture, there are a number of implications we can draw from this important biblical theme.

Identity

God has made us to be image-bearing servants. As our Creator, he alone is the one who determines our identity. Like our forefather Adam, human beings are constantly remaking themselves into their own self-chosen image and rejecting their true identity as divine image-bearers created to serve the one true God. That biblical truth is in sharp contrast to our contemporary Western culture, which insists that each of us as individual human beings has the right to determine our own identity, even if that identity flatly contradicts reality. People who are biologically one gender choose to 'self-identify' as another. People of one ethnicity choose to self-identify as a different ethnicity. Celebrities constantly 'remake' themselves, changing their self-created 'brand' as an expression of self-fulfilment. An entire industry of self-help books, podcasts, seminars and products offers the promise that using their product will enable you to take control of your life and live it to the fullest (as defined by you, of course!). But the Bible helps us to see that this is a false gospel that leads people into slavery. Indeed, those who believe they are free to determine their own identity are in fact enslaved to their own whims and desires.

In contrast, the Bible offers the good news that through the work of Jesus we can experience true freedom – not merely freedom from the tyranny of sin, self and Satan, but also the freedom to live out our God-given identity as his servants. True biblical freedom is found in surrendering oneself to the authority of the Lord Jesus Christ. Rather than carry the burden of defining and redefining ourselves, followers of Jesus experience the joy of living for the approval of their heavenly Master rather than the approval of others. We do so not in an effort to earn his favour, but to experience a foretaste of the joy now that will be ours in its fullness on the last day when we hear our Master say, 'Well done, good and faithful servant. You have been faithful over a little; I will set you over much. Enter into the joy of your master' (Matt. 25:21).

Corporate life

The corporate life of the church is servant shaped. The night of his betrayal Jesus set aside his outer garments, picked up a towel and a basin of water and washed the feet of his disciples (John 13:1–20). Afterwards Jesus tells his disciples that he has done this to provide an example of the kind of self-sacrificial service that should characterize their lives as his followers. Paul can think of no better way to call believers to a certain pattern of life (Phil. 2:1–4) than to point them to Jesus the servant of the Lord (Phil. 2:5–11). The mindset of Jesus the servant demonstrated through his life, death, resurrection and exaltation establishes the paradigm for a shared mindset that humbly considers others as more important and looks out for their well-being even when it involves self-sacrifice. Because Christ has broken the chains of our slavery to sin, self and Satan we are free to serve one another through love (Gal. 5:13). Instead of being a collection of individual Christians, as believers we are called to bear each other's burdens just as Jesus the suffering servant bore our greatest burden – the weight of our sin and guilt before a holy God. As we re-enact this kind of self-sacrificial burden bearing we fulfil the law of Christ (Gal. 6:2). Such a corporate life will stand out in a self-driven and self-focused culture that hesitates to surrender any measure of autonomy to love and serve others. And just as happened in the early church, we may find unbelievers strangely drawn to this alternative form of community shaped by self-sacrificial Christlike love.

Mission

While the work of Jesus the servant to atone for our sins is entirely finished, the proclamation of that good news has yet to reach every corner of this planet. It is through his people the church that Jesus continues the servant's mission of being a light of salvation to the nations. As a body of believers the church should make reaching the nations with the gospel the centrepiece of their ministry. We are called to be witnesses through whom Jesus the servant calls sinners to repentance. Such a mission is not merely for those whom the church sends to the far reaches of the earth, as the nations live among us. They are in our neighborhoods, our schools, our workplaces. While the form of such outreach can and should take many different forms, the overarching goal should be the same: proclaiming the good news of what Jesus the servant of the Lord has done though his life, ministry, death, resurrection and ascension.

In addition to this Isaianic-shaped servant mission, the church also participates in the Adamic-shaped mission of Jesus. Christ dwells in his people to empower them to exercise servant-shaped dominion and stewardship not only over creation, but in every area of responsibility that God gives to his people. As the church we are a body of priests, called to mediate God's presence to a world trapped in the darkness of sin and the curse. Through his people Jesus speaks a prophetic word to the dying world around us, testifying not only of their sinful ways but also of the hope that can be found in him alone.

Leadership

The idea of servant leadership has extended well beyond Christian circles, becoming such a common concept that even secular leadership books widely use the expression. Indeed, the expression has become so popular that it is in danger of losing its distinctive biblical meaning. Those who are called to lead in the body of Christ are first called to embody and model Christlike character. At a minimum such character includes a humility that recognizes the nature of the role of a servant. Jesus portrays this humility in Luke 17:10, where he says to his disciples, 'So you also, when you have done all that you were commanded, say, "We are unworthy servants; we have only done what was our duty."' For the Christian leader there is no place for an arrogance that draws attention to oneself. Nor is there room for the sort of self-pity that wallows in how difficult service to the Lord can sometimes be. We serve a crucified and risen servant king, who calls his people to take up their cross and follow him. We do so knowing that all who surrender earthly goods in doing so are promised a hundredfold return and eternal life as well (Matt. 19:29). The defining mark of the Christlike character that Christian leaders are called to embody is self-sacrificial love. As the suffering servant Jesus pointed his disciples to his own example as the paradigm for leadership. Instead of using political manoeuvering and personal charisma to accomplish one's own agenda, the Christian leader seeks to advance God's purposes through self-sacrificially using all available resources. The result is a beautiful and compelling picture of Jesus the servant, who loved us and gave himself for us.

Bibliography

Abernethy, A. T. (2016), *The Book of Isaiah and God's Kingdom: A Thematic Theological Approach*, NSBT 40, Nottingham: Apollos; Downers Grove: InterVarsity Press.

Aldrete, G. S. (2004), *Daily Life in the Roman City: Rome, Pompeii, and Ostia*, Westport, Conn.: Greenwood.

Alexander, T. D. (1997), 'Further Observations on the Term "Seed" in Genesis', *TynB* 48: 363–367.

Allen, D. L. (2012), 'Substitutionary Atonement and Cultic Terminology in Isaiah 53', in D. L. Bock and M. Glaser (eds.), *The Gospel According to Isaiah 53: Encountering the Suffering Servant in Jewish and Christian Theology*, Grand Rapids: Kregel, 171–189.

Allen, L. (1997), '*ṣāḥaq*', in *NIDOTTE* 3: 797.

Allis, O. T. (1950), *The Unity of Isaiah: A Study in Prophecy*, Philadelphia: Presbyterian & Reformed.

Allison, D. C. (1985), *The End of the Ages Has Come: An Early Interpretation of the Passion and Resurrection of Jesus*, Philadelphia: Fortress.

—— (1993), *The New Moses: A Matthean Typology*, Minneapolis: Fortress.

Ashley, T. R. (1993), *The Book of Numbers*, NICOT, Grand Rapids: Eerdmans.

Austel, H. (1980), 'šārat', in *TWOT* 958.

Averbeck, R. E. (2018), 'Slavery in the World of the Bible', in J. S. Greer, J. W. Hilber and J. H. Walton (eds.), *Behind the Scenes of the Old Testament: Cultural, Social, and Historical Contexts*, Grand Rapids: Baker Academic, 423–430.

Bailey, D. P. (1998), 'Concepts of *Stellvertretung* in the Interpretation of Isaiah 53', in W. H. Bellinger and W. R. Farmer (eds.), *Jesus and the Suffering Servant: Isaiah 53 and Christian Origins*, Harrisburg, Pa.: Trinity, 223–250.

—— (2004), '"Our Suffering and Crucified Messiah" (*Dial*, 111.2): Justin Martyr's Allusions to Isaiah 53 in His *Dialogue with Trypho* with Special Reference to the New Edition of M. Markovich', in B. Janowski and P. Stuhlmacher (eds.), *The Suffering Servant: Isaiah 53 in Jewish and Christian Sources*, Grand Rapids: Eerdmans, 324–417.

Barker, M. (1991), *The Gate of Heaven: The History and Symbolism of the Temple in Jerusalem*, London: SPCK.

Barthélemy, D. (1982), *Critique Textuelle De L'ancien Testament*, Orbis biblicus et orientalis 50.2, Göttingen: Vandenhoeck & Ruprecht.

Bateman, H. W. I. (2017), *Jude*, Bellingham, Wash.: Lexham.

Battenfield, J. R. (1982), 'Isaiah 53:10: Taking an "If" out of the Sacrifice of the Servant', *VT* 32.4: 485.

Bauckham, R. F. (1975), 'Colossians 1:24 Again: The Apocalyptic Motif', *EvQ* 47: 168–170.

—— (1983), *Jude, 2 Peter*, WBC 50, Waco, Tex.: Word.

—— (1993), *The Climax of Prophecy: Studies on the Book of Revelation*, Edinburgh: T&T Clark.

Beale, G. K. (1991), 'Isaiah 6:9–13: A Retributive Taunt Against Idolatry', *VT* 41: 257–278.

—— (1994), 'The Old Testament Background of Reconciliation in 2 Corinthians 5–7 and Its Bearing on the Literary Problem of 2 Corinthians 6:14–7:1', in G. K. Beale (ed.), *Right Doctrine from the Wrong Texts? Essays on the Use of the Old Testament in the New*, Grand Rapids: Baker, 217–247.

—— (1999), *The Book of Revelation: A Commentary on the Greek Text*, NIGTC, Grand Rapids: Eerdmans.

—— (2004), *The Temple and the Church's Mission: A Biblical Theology of the Dwelling Place of God*, NSBT 17, Leicester: Apollos; Downers Grove: InterVarsity Press.

—— (2007), 'Revelation', in G. K. Beale and D. A. Carson (eds.), *Commentary on the New Testament Use of the Old Testament*, Grand Rapids: Baker, 1081–1161.

—— (2008), *The Erosion of Inerrancy in Evangelicalism: Responding to New Challenges to Biblical Authority*, Wheaton: Crossway.

—— (2011), *A New Testament Biblical Theology: The Unfolding of the Old Testament in the New*, Grand Rapids: Baker.

—— (2012), 'The Use of Hosea 11:1 in Matthew 2:15: One More Time', *JETS* 55: 697–715.

—— (2019), *Colossians and Philemon*, BECNT, Grand Rapids: Baker Academic.

Beale, G. K., and D. A. Carson (2007), *Commentary on the New Testament Use of the Old Testament*, Grand Rapids: Baker.
Beale, G. K., and B. L. Gladd (2014), *Hidden but Now Revealed: A Biblical Theology of Mystery*, Downers Grove: IVP Academic.
Beers, H. (2016), *The Followers of Jesus as the Servant: Luke's Model from Isaiah for the Disciples in Luke–Acts*, LNTS 535, London: Bloomsbury T&T Clark.
Bergen, R. D. (1996), *1, 2 Samuel*, NAC 7, Nashville: Broadman & Holman.
Berlin, A., and L. V. Knorina (2008), *The Dynamics of Biblical Parallelism*, rev. and expanded edn, Grand Rapids: Eerdmans.
Betz, O. (1987), *Jesus, Der Messias Israels: Aufsätze zur Biblischen Theologie*, WUNT 42, Tübingen: Mohr.
—— (1998), 'Jesus and Isaiah 53', in W. H. Bellinger and W. R. Farmer (eds.), *Jesus and the Suffering Servant: Isaiah 53 and Christian Origins*, Harrisburg, Pa.: Trinity, 70–87.
Beuken, W. A. (1989), 'Servant and Herald of Good Tidings: Isaiah 61 as an Interpretation of Isaiah 40–55', in J. Vermeylen (ed.), *Le Livre d'Isaïe: les oracles et leurs relectures unité et complexité de l'ouvrage*, BETL 81, Leuven: Leuven University Press, 411–442.
Blenkinsopp, J. (2002), *Isaiah 40–55: A New Translation with Introduction and Commentary*, AB 19, New York: Doubleday.
Blomberg, C. (2007), 'Matthew', in G. K. Beale and D. A. Carson (eds.), *Commentary on the New Testament Use of the Old Testament*, Grand Rapids: Baker, 1–110.
Bock, D. L. (1987), *Proclamation from Prophecy and Pattern: Lucan Old Testament Christology*, JSNTSup 12, Sheffield: JSOT.
—— (1994), *Luke*, 2 vols., BECNT 3, Grand Rapids: Baker.
—— (2011), *A Theology of Luke and Acts: Biblical Theology of the New Testament*, Grand Rapids: Zondervan.
Boda, M. J. (2017), *The Heartbeat of Old Testament Theology: Three Creedal Expressions*, Grand Rapids: Baker.
Bray, G. L. (2015), *Augustine on the Christian Life: Transformed by the Power of God*, Wheaton: Crossway.
Bruce, F. F. (1984), *The Epistles to the Colossians, to Philemon, and to the Ephesians*, NICNT, Grand Rapids: Eerdmans.
Capes, D. B. (1999), 'Intertextual Echoes in the Matthean Baptismal Narrative', *BBR* 9: 37–49.

Carson, D. A. (1991), *The Gospel According to John*, PNTC, Grand Rapids: Eerdmans.

—— (1994), 'Matthew', in EBC, 1–492.

—— (2001), 'Mystery and Fulfillment: Toward a More Comprehensive Paradigm of Paul's Understanding of the Old and the New', in D. A. Carson, P. T. O'Brien and M. A. Seifrid (eds.), *Justification and Variegated Nomism: The Paradoxes of Paul*, vol. 2, Grand Rapids: Baker, 393–436.

—— (2018), 'Genesis 1–3: Not Maximalist, Not Minimalist, but Seminal', *TrinJ* 39.2: 143–163.

Ceresko, A. R. (1994), 'The Rhetorical Strategy of the Fourth Servant Song (Isaiah 52:13 – 53:12): Poetry and the Exodus–New Exodus', *CBQ* 56: 42–55.

Charlesworth, J. H. (2010), *The Old Testament Pseudepigrapha*, vols. 1–2, Peabody: Hendrickson.

Childs, B. S. (2001), *Isaiah*, OTL, Louisville: Westminster John Knox.

Ciampa, R. E. (1998), *The Presence and Function of Scripture in Galatians 1 and 2*, WUNT 102, Tübingen: Mohr Siebeck.

Clark, B. T. (2015), *Completing Christ's Afflictions: Christ, Paul, and the Reconciliation of All Things*, WUNT 2.383, Tübingen: Mohr Siebeck.

Clark, W. M. (1969), 'Legal Background to the Yahwist's Use of "Good and Evil" in Genesis 2–3', *JBL* 88: 266–278.

Clements, R. E. (1998), 'Isaiah 53 and the Restoration of Israel', in W. H. Bellinger and W. R. Farmer (eds.), *Jesus and the Suffering Servant: Isaiah 53 and Christian Origins*, Harrisburg, Pa.: Trinity, 39–54.

Clifford, R. J. (1994), *Creation Accounts in the Ancient Near East and in the Bible*, CBQMS 26, Washington, D.C.: Catholic Biblical Association.

Clines, D. J. A. (1968), 'The Image of God in Man', *TynB* 19: 53–103.

Cogan, M. (1974), *Imperialism and Religion: Assyria, Judah, and Israel in the Eighth and Seventh Centuries B.C.E*, SBLMS 19, Missoula, Mont.: Society of Biblical Literature.

Cole, R. D. (2000), *Numbers*, NAC 3B, Nashville: Broadman & Holman.

Cole, R. L. (2013), *Psalms 1–2: Gateway to the Psalter*, HBM 37, Sheffield: Sheffield Phoenix.

Combes, I. A. H. (1998), *The Metaphor of Slavery in the Writings of the Early Church: From the New Testament to the Beginning of the Fifth Century*, JSNTSup 156, Sheffield: Sheffield Academic Press.

Crouch, C. L. (2016), 'Made in the Image of God: The Creation of אדם the Commissioning of the King and the Chaoskampf of Yhwh', *JANER* 16: 1–21.

Crowe, B. D. (2017), *The Last Adam: A Theology of the Obedient Life of Jesus in the Gospels*, Grand Rapids: Baker.

Currid, J. D. (2013), *Against the Gods: The Polemical Theology of the Old Testament*, Wheaton: Crossway.

Curtis, E. M. (1987), 'Man as the Image of God in Genesis in the Light of Ancient Near Eastern Parallels', Ph.D. diss., University of Pennsylvania.

Dahood, M. (1960), 'Textual Problems in Isaiah', *CBQ* 22: 400–409.

—— (1982), 'Isaiah 53,8–12 and Masoretic Misconstructions', *Bib* 63: 566–570.

Davids, P. H. (2006), *The Letters of 2 Peter and Jude*, PNTC, Grand Rapids: Eerdmans.

Davies, W. D., and D. C. Allison (2004), *A Critical and Exegetical Commentary on the Gospel According to Saint Matthew*, 3 vols., ICC, New York: T&T Clark International.

Duhm, B. (1875), *Die Theologie der Propheten als Grundlage für die Innere Entwicklungsgeschichte der Israelitischen Religion*, Bonn: Marcus.

—— (1892), *Das Buch Jesaia*, GHAT, Göttingen: Vandenhoeck & Ruprecht.

Dunn, J. D. G. (1996a), *Christology in the Making: A New Testament Inquiry into the Origins of the Doctrine of the Incarnation*, Grand Rapids: Eerdmans.

—— (1996b), *The Epistles to the Colossians and to Philemon: A Commentary on the Greek Text*, NIGTC, Grand Rapids: Eerdmans.

Edwards, J. C. (2009), 'Reading the Ransom Logion in 1 Tim 2,6 and Titus 2,14 with Isa 42,6–7; 49,6–8', *Bib* 90: 264–266.

Ekblad, E. R. (1999), *Isaiah's Servant Poems According to the Septuagint: An Exegetical and Theological Study*, CBET 23, Leuven: Peeters.

Ellis, E. (1993), 'Coworkers, Paul and His', in *DPL* 184.

Emerton, J. A. (1982), 'The Translation and Interpretation of Isaiah Vi. 13', in E. I. J. Rosenthal, J. A. Emerton and S. C. Reif (eds.), *Interpreting the Hebrew Bible: Essays in Honour of E. I. J. Rosenthal*, Cambridge: Cambridge University Press, 85–118.

Evans, C. A. (1982), '"He Set His Face": A Note on Luke 9:51', *Bib* 63: 545–548.

—— (1987), '"He Set His Face": Luke 9:51 Once Again', *Bib* 68: 80–84.

—— (2012), 'Isaiah 53 in the Letters of Peter, Paul, Hebrews, and John', in D. L. Bock and M. Glaser (eds.), *The Gospel According to Isaiah 53: Encountering the Suffering Servant in Jewish and Christian Theology*, Grand Rapids: Kregel, 145–170.

Farber, Z. (2016), *Images of Joshua in the Bible and Their Reception*, BZAW 457, Berlin: de Gruyter.

Fee, G. D. (1992), 'Philippians 2:5–11: Hymn or Exalted Pauline Prose?', *BBR* 2: 29–46.

—— (2007), *Pauline Christology: An Exegetical-Theological Study*, Peabody, Mass.: Hendrickson.

Foh, S. T. (1974/1975), 'What Is the Woman's Desire', *WTJ* 37: 376–383.

France, R. T. (1971), *Jesus and the Old Testament: His Application of Old Testament Passages to Himself and His Mission*, Downers Grove: InterVarsity Press.

—— (1985), *The Gospel According to Matthew: An Introduction and Commentary*, TNTC, Leicester: Inter-Varsity Press.

—— (2007), *The Gospel of Matthew*, NICNT, Grand Rapids: Eerdmans.

Fretheim, T. (1997), 'šārat', in *NIDOTTE* 4: 256.

Garland, D. E. (2011), *Luke*, ZECNT 3, Grand Rapids: Zondervan.

Garr, W. R. (2000), '"Image" and "Likeness" in the Inscription from Tell Fakhariyeh', *IEJ* 50: 227–234.

Garrett, S. R. (1989), *The Demise of the Devil: Magic and the Demonic in Luke's Writings*, Minneapolis: Fortress.

Gentry, P. J., and S. J. Wellum (2012), *Kingdom Through Covenant: A Biblical-Theological Understanding of the Covenants*, Wheaton: Crossway.

Gesenius, W. (2006), *Gesenius' Hebrew Grammar*, ed. E. Kautzsch and A. E. Cowley, Dover edn, Mineola, N.Y.: Dover.

Gladd, B. L., and M. S. Harmon (2016), *Making All Things New: Inaugurated Eschatology for the Life of the Church*, Grand Rapids: Baker.

Goldberg, L. (1980), '*śākal*', in *TWOT* 877.

Goldingay, J. (1994), '"You Are Abraham's Offspring, My Friend": Abraham in Isaiah 41', in R. S. Hess, P. E. Satterthwaite and

G. J. Wenham (eds.), *He Swore an Oath: Biblical Themes from Genesis 12–50*, Grand Rapids: Baker, 29–54.
—— (2006), *Psalms*. 3 vols., Grand Rapids: Baker Academic.
Goldingay, J., and D. F. Payne (2006), *A Critical and Exegetical Commentary on Isaiah 40–55*, ICC, New York: T&T Clark.
Goshen-Gottstein, M. H. (1987), 'Abraham – Lover or Beloved of God', in M. H. Pope, J. H. Marks and R. M. Good (eds.), *Love and Death in the Ancient near East: Essays in Honor of Marvin H. Pope*, Guilford, Conn.: Four Quarters, 101–104.
Green, J. B. (1992), 'Proclaiming Repentance and Forgiveness of Sins to All Nations: A Biblical Perspective on the Church's Mission', in A. G. Padgett (ed.), *The Mission of the Church in Methodist Perspective: The World Is My Parish*, SHM 10, Lewiston: E. Mellen, 24–32.
Grimm, W. (1981), *Die Verkundigung Jesu und Deuterojesaja*, 2 edn, ANTJ 1, Frankfurt am Main: Peter Lang.
Grisanti, M. (1997), '*pāga*ʿ', in *NIDOTTE* 3: 575.
Haag, H. (1985), *Der Gottesknecht bei Deuterojesaja*, Darmstadt: Wissenschaftliche Buchgesellschaft.
Hamilton, V. (1980), '*dĕmût*', in *TWOT* 192.
Harmon, M. S. (2010), *She Must and Shall Go Free: Paul's Isaianic Gospel in Galatians*, BZNW 168, Berlin: de Gruyter.
—— (2015), *Philippians*, Mentor Commentary, Fearn, Ross-shire, Scotland: Christian Focus.
—— (2020), *Rebels and Exiles: A Biblical Theology of Sin and Restoration*, ESBT, Downers Grove: InterVarsity Press.
Harris, M. J. (2001), *Slave of Christ: A New Testament Metaphor for Total Devotion to Christ*, NSBT 8, Leicester: Apollos.
—— (2005), *The Second Epistle to the Corinthians: A Commentary on the Greek Text*, NIGTC, Grand Rapids: Eerdmans.
—— (2011), *Prepositions and Theology in the Greek New Testament*, Grand Rapids: Zondervan.
Hartley, J. (1980), '*ṣābā*ʾ', in *TWOT* 750.
Hays, R. B. (2016), *Echoes of Scripture in the Gospels*, Waco: Baylor University Press.
Hengel, M. (1981), *The Atonement: The Origins of the Doctrine in the New Testament*, Philadelphia: Fortress.
Hess, R. S. (1996), *Joshua: An Introduction and Commentary*, TOTC 6, Leicester: Inter-Varsity Press; Downers Grove: InterVarsity Press.

Hill, D. (1979), 'Son and Servant: An Essay on Matthean Christology', *JSNT* 2: 2–16.
Höffken, P. (2000), 'Abraham und Gott, Oder: Wer Liebt Hier Wen? Anmerkungen zu Jes 41,8', *BN* 103: 17–22.
Hofius, O. (1989), 'Erwägungen zur Gestalt und Herkunft des Paulinischen Versöhnungsgedankens', in O. Hofius (ed.), *Paulusstudien*, Tübingen: Mohr Siebeck, 1–14.
—— (1991), *Der Christushymnus Philipper 2,6–11: Untersuchungen zu Gestalt und Aussage eines urchristlichen Psalms*, WUNT 17, Tübingen: Mohr.
—— (2004), 'The Fourth Servant Song in the New Testament Letters', in B. Janowski and P. Stuhlmacher (eds.), *The Suffering Servant: Isaiah 53 in Jewish and Christian Sources*, Grand Rapids: Eerdmans, 163–188.
Hooker, M. D. (1959), *Jesus and the Servant: The Influence of the Servant Concept of Deutero-Isaiah in the New Testament*, London: SPCK.
—— (1998), 'Did the Use of Isaiah 53 to Interpret His Mission Begin with Jesus?', in W. H. Bellinger and W. R. Farmer (eds.), *Jesus and the Suffering Servant: Isaiah 53 and Christian Origins*, Harrisburg, Pa.: Trinity, 88–103.
Howard, D. M. (1998), *Joshua*, NAC 5, Nashville: Broadman & Holman.
Hugenberger, G. P. (1995), 'The Servant of the Lord in the "Servant Songs" of Isaiah: A Second Moses Figure', in P. E. Satterthwaite, R. S. Hess and G. J. Wenham (eds.), *The Lord's Anointed: Interpretation of Old Testament Messianic Texts*, Grand Rapids: Baker, 105–139.
Janowski, B., and P. Stuhlmacher (eds.) (2004), *The Suffering Servant: Isaiah 53 in Jewish and Christian Sources*. Grand Rapids: Eerdmans.
Jobes, K. H. (2005), *1 Peter*, BECNT, Grand Rapids: Baker.
Joüon, P., and T. Muraoka (2006), *A Grammar of Biblical Hebrew*, SubBi 27, Rome: Pontifical Biblical Institute.
Kaiser, W. C. (1974), 'The Blessing of David: The Charter for Humanity', in J. H. Skilton, M. C. Fisher and L. W. Sloat (eds.), *The Law and the Prophets: Old Testament Studies Prepared in Honor of Oswald Thompson Allis*, Nutley, N.J.: Presbyterian & Reformed, 298–318.
Keener, C. S. (2003), *The Gospel of John: A Commentary*, 2 vols., Peabody, Mass.: Hendrickson.
—— (2009), *The Gospel of Matthew: A Socio-Rhetorical Commentary*, Grand Rapids: Eerdmans.

Kelly, J. N. D. (1963), *A Commentary on the Pastoral Epistles: I Timothy, II Timothy, Titus*, BNTC, London: A. & C. Black.

Kidner, D. (2008), *Psalms 1–72: An Introduction and Commentary*, TOTC 15, Downers Grove: InterVarsity Press.

Kline, M. G. (1980), *Images of the Spirit*, Eugene: Wipf & Stock.

—— (2000), *Kingdom Prologue: Genesis Foundations for a Covenantal Worldview*, Overland Park, KS: Two Age.

Knight, G. A. F. (1984), *Servant Theology: A Commentary on the Book of Isaiah 40–55*, Grand Rapids: Eerdmans.

Koole, J. L. (1998), *Isaiah III*, 2 vols., Leuven: Peeters.

Köstenberger, A. J. (2004), *John*, BECNT, Grand Rapids: Baker.

—— (2007), 'John', in G. K. Beale and D. A. Carson (eds.), *Commentary on the New Testament Use of the Old Testament*, Grand Rapids: Baker, 415–512.

Kruse, C. G. (1978), 'The Servant Songs: Interpretive Trends Since C. R. North', *SBT* 8: 3–27.

Kselman, J. S. (1976), 'A Note on Numbers Xii 6–8', *VT* 26. doi: 10.2307/1517018.

Lang, M. H. (2017), 'John 1.29, 36: The Meaning of Ἀμνὸς Τοῦ Θεοῦ and John's Soteriology', *BT* 68: 148–163.

Lindsey, F. D. (1985), *The Servant Songs: A Study in Isaiah*, Chicago: Moody.

Lock, W. (1924), *A Critical and Exegetical Commentary on the Pastoral Epistles (I & II Timothy and Titus)*, ICC, Edinburgh: T&T Clark.

Lohmeyer, E. (1953), *Gottesknecht und Davidsohn*, 2nd edn (unchanged), FRLANT 43, Göttingen: Vandenhoeck & Ruprecht.

McKnight, S. (2017), *The Letter to Philemon*, NICNT, Grand Rapids: Eerdmans.

Marcus, J. (1992), *The Way of the Lord: Christological Exegesis of the Old Testament in the Gospel of Mark*, Louisville: Westminster/John Knox.

Margulies, R. (1964), *The Indivisible Isaiah: Evidence for the Single Authorship of the Prophetic Book*, New York: Sura Institute for Research.

Marshall, I. H. (2007), 'Acts', in G. K. Beale and D. A. Carson (eds.), *Commentary on the New Testament Use of the Old Testament*, Grand Rapids: Baker, 513–606.

Marshall, I. H., and P. H. Towner (2004), *A Critical and Exegetical Commentary on the Pastoral Epistles*, ICC, New York: T&T Clark International.

Martin, D. B. (1990), *Slavery as Salvation: The Metaphor of Slavery in Pauline Christianity*, New Haven: Yale University Press.

Martin, O. R. (2015), *Bound for the Promised Land: The Land Promise in God's Redemptive Plan*, NSBT 34, Downers Grove: InterVarsity Press.

Martin, R. P. (1997), *A Hymn of Christ: Philippians 2:5–11 in Recent Interpretation and in the Setting of Early Christian Worship*, Downers Grove: InterVarsity Press.

Matthews, V. H., and D. C. Benjamin (1993), *Social World of Ancient Israel, 1250–587 BCE*, Peabody, Mass.: Hendrickson.

Meeks, W. A. (1967), *The Prophet-King: Moses Traditions and the Johannine Christology*, NovTSup 14, Leiden: Brill.

Melugin, R. F. (1976), *The Formation of Isaiah 40–55*, BZAW 141, Berlin: de Gruyter.

Metzger, B. M. (2002), *A Textual Commentary on the Greek New Testament*, 2nd edn, Stuttgart: Deutsche Bibelgesellschaft.

Middleton, J. R. (2005), *The Liberating Image: The Imago Dei in Genesis 1*, Grand Rapids: Brazos.

Millard, A. R., and P. Bordreuil (1982), 'A Statue from Syria with Assyrian and Aramaic Inscriptions', *BA* 45: 135–141.

Moberly, R. (1997), 'ʾāman', in *NIDOTTE* 1: 431.

Moo, D. J. (1983), *The Old Testament in the Gospel Passion Narratives*, Sheffield: Almond.

—— (2000), *The Letter of James*, PNTC, Grand Rapids: Eerdmans.

—— (2008), *The Letters to the Colossians and to Philemon*, PNTC, Grand Rapids: Eerdmans.

—— (2018), *The Letter to the Romans*, 2nd edn, NICNT, Grand Rapids: Eerdmans.

Moritz, T. (1996), *A Profound Mystery: The Use of the Old Testament in Ephesians*, NovTSup 85, New York: Brill.

Motyer, J. A. (1993), *The Prophecy of Isaiah: An Introduction and Commentary*, Downers Grove: InterVarsity Press.

Newman, C. C. (1992), *Paul's Glory-Christology: Tradition and Rhetoric*, NovTSup 69, Leiden: Brill.

Neyrey, J. H. (1993), *2 Peter, Jude: A New Translation with Introduction and Commentary*, AB 37C, New York: Doubleday.

North, C. R. (1956), *The Suffering Servant in Deutero-Isaiah: An Historical and Critical Study*, London: Oxford University Press.

Oakes, P. (2015), *Galatians*, Paideia, Grand Rapids: Baker.

Ollrog, W.-H. (1979), *Paulus und Seine Mitarbeiter: Untersuchungen zur Theorie und Praxis der Paulinischen Mission*, WMANT 50, Neukirchen-Vluyn: Neukirchener Verlag.

Orlinsky, H. M. (1967), *The So-Called 'Suffering Servant of the Lord' and 'Suffering Servant' in Second Isaiah*, VTSup 14, Leiden: Brill.

Osborne, G. R. (2002), *Revelation*, BECNT, Grand Rapids: Baker.

Oswalt, J. N. (1980), '*kābaš*', in *TWOT* 430.

—— (1986), *The Book of Isaiah: Chapters 1–39*, NICOT, Grand Rapids: Eerdmans.

—— (1997), '*nûaḥ* I', in *NIDOTTE* 3: 57.

—— (1997), 'Righteousness in Isaiah: A Study of the Function of Chapters 56–66 in the Present Structure of the Book', in C. C. Broyles and C. A. Evans (eds.), *Writing and Reading the Scroll of Isaiah: Studies of an Interpretive Tradition*, Leiden: Brill, 177–191.

—— (1998), *The Book of Isaiah: Chapters 40–66*, NICOT, Grand Rapids: Eerdmans.

—— (2009), *The Bible Among the Myths: Unique Revelation or Just Ancient Literature?*, Grand Rapids: Zondervan.

Ounsworth, R. J. (2012), *Joshua Typology in the New Testament*, WUNT 2.328, Tübingen, Germany: Mohr Siebeck.

Pao, D. W. (2002), *Acts and the Isaianic New Exodus*, Biblical Studies Library, Grand Rapids: Baker.

—— (2012), *Colossians & Philemon*, ZECNT 12, Grand Rapids: Zondervan.

Pao, D. W., and E. J. Schnabel (2007), 'Luke', in G. K. Beale and D. A. Carson (eds.), *Commentary on the New Testament Use of the Old Testament*, Grand Rapids: Baker, 251–414.

Parry, D. W. (1994), 'Garden of Eden: Prototype Sanctuary', in D. W. Parry (ed.), *Temples of the Ancient World: Ritual and Symbolism*, Salt Lake City, Utah: Deseret, 126–151.

Perrin, N. (1970), 'The Use of (Παρα)Δίδοναι in Connection with the Passion of Jesus in the New Testament', in E. Lohse, C. Burchard and B. Schaller (eds.), *Der Ruf Jesu und die Antwort der Gemeinde: Exegetische Untersuchungen Joachim Jeremias zum 70. Geburtstag Gewidmet von seinen Schülern*, Göttingen: Vandenhoeck & Ruprecht, 204–212.

Peterson, D. G. (2017), *Romans*, BTCP, Nashville: B&H.

Robertson, O. P. (2015), *The Flow of the Psalms: Discovering Their Structure and Theology*, Phillipsburg: P&R.
Ross, A. P. (2002), *Holiness to the Lord: A Guide to the Exposition of the Book of Leviticus*, Grand Rapids: Baker.
—— (2011), *Commentary on the Psalms*, Grand Rapids: Kregel.
Rowley, H. H. (1952), *The Servant of the Lord, and Other Essays on the Old Testament*, London: Lutterworth.
Sass, G. (1941), 'Zur Bedeutung von Δοῦλος Bei Paulus', *ZNW* 40: 24–32.
Schmid, H. H. (1968), *Gerechtigkeit als Weltordnung: Hintergrund und Geschichte der Alttestamentlichen Gerechtigkeitsbegriffes*, BHT 40, Tübingen: Mohr Siebeck.
Schoville, K. (1997), 'šāmar', in *NIDOTTE* 4: 182.
Schreiner, T. R. (2003), *1, 2 Peter, Jude*, NAC 37, Nashville: Broadman & Holman.
—— (2018), *Romans*, 2nd edn, BECNT, Grand Rapids: Baker.
Schultz, R. (1997), 'Servant, Slave,' in *NIDOTTE* 4:1184–1196.
Scott, J. M. (1993), *Adoption as Sons of God: An Exegetical Investigation into the Background of Huiothesia in the Pauline Corpus*, WUNT 2.48, Tübingen: Mohr.
Scroggs, R. (1966), *The Last Adam: A Study in Pauline Anthropology*, Philadelphia: Fortress.
Scullion, J. J. (1971), 'Sedeq–Sedeqah in Isaiah cc 40–66 with Special Reference to the Continuity in Meaning Between Second and Third Isaiah', *UF* 3: 335–348.
Seifrid, M. (2007), 'Romans', in G. K. Beale and D. A. Carson (eds.), *Commentary on the New Testament Use of the Old Testament*, Grand Rapids: Baker, 607–694.
Shelton, J.-A. (1998), *As the Romans Did: A Sourcebook in Roman Social History*, 2nd edn, New York: Oxford University Press.
Silva, M. S. (1994), *Biblical Words and Their Meanings: An Introduction to Lexical Semantics*, rev. edn, Grand Rapids: Zondervan.
—— (2014a), '*leitourgos*', in *NIDNTTE* 3: 104.
—— (2014b), '*oikonomia*', in *NIDNTTE* 2: 465–469.
—— (2014c), 'Introduction', in *NIDNTTE* 1: 5–14.
Smith, J. K. A. (2014), *How (Not) to Be Secular: Reading Charles Taylor*, Grand Rapids: Eerdmans.
Sonne, I. (1959), 'Isaiah 53:10–12', *JBL* 78: 335–342.

Spieckerman, H. (2004), 'The Conception and Prehistory of the Idea of Vicarious Suffering in the Old Testament', in B. Janowski and P. Stuhlmacher (eds..), *The Suffering Servant: Isaiah 53 in Jewish and Christian Sources*, Grand Rapids: Eerdmans, 1–15.

Strathmann, H. (1976), '*latreuō, latreia*', in *TDNT* 4: 60.

Stuhlmacher, P. (1968), *Das Paulinische Evangelium*, Göttingen: Vandenhoeck & Ruprecht.

—— (2004), 'Isaiah 53 in the Gospels and Acts', in B. Janowski and P. Stuhlmacher (eds.), *The Suffering Servant: Isaiah 53 in Jewish and Christian Sources*, Grand Rapids: Eerdmans, 147–162.

—— (2018), *Biblical Theology of the New Testament*, Grand Rapids: Eerdmans.

Taylor, C. (1989), *Sources of the Self: The Making of the Modern Identity*, Cambridge, Mass.: Harvard University Press.

—— (2007), *A Secular Age*, Cambridge, Mass.: Belknap Press of Harvard University Press.

Towner, P. H. (2006), *The Letters to Timothy and Titus*, NICNT, Grand Rapids: Eerdmans.

Tsumura, D. T. (1989), *The Earth and the Waters in Genesis 1 and 2: A Linguistic Investigation*, JSOTSup 83, Sheffield: Sheffield Academic Press.

Wagner, J. R. (1998), 'The Heralds of Isaiah and the Mission of Paul', in W. H. Bellinger and W. R. Farmer (eds.), *Jesus and the Suffering Servant: Isaiah 53 and Christian Origins*, Harrisburg, Pa.: Trinity, 193–222.

—— (2003), *Heralds of the Good News: Isaiah and Paul in Concert in the Letter to the Romans*, Leiden: Brill.

Waltke, B. K., and C. J. Fredricks (2001), *Genesis: A Commentary*, Grand Rapids: Zondervan.

Waltke, B. K., and M. P. O'Connor (1990), *An Introduction to Biblical Hebrew Syntax*, Winona Lake: Eisenbrauns.

Walton, J. H. (2006), *Ancient Near Eastern Thought and the Old Testament: Introducing the Conceptual World of the Hebrew Bible*, Grand Rapids: Baker.

—— (2011), *Genesis 1 as Ancient Cosmology*, Winona Lake: Eisenbrauns.

Watts, R. E. (1998), 'Jesus' Death, Isaiah 53, and Mark 10:45: A Crux Revisited', in W. H. Bellinger and W. R. Farmer (eds.), *Jesus and the Suffering Servant: Isaiah 53 and Christian Origins*, Harrisburg, Pa.: Trinity, 125–151.

—— (2000), *Isaiah's New Exodus in Mark*, Biblical Studies Library, Grand Rapids: Baker.

Wenham, G. J. (1979), *The Book of Leviticus*, NICOT, Grand Rapids: Eerdmans.

—— (1994), 'Sanctuary Symbolism in the Garden of Eden Story', in R. S. Hess and D. T. Tsumura (eds.), *I Studied Inscriptions from Before the Flood: Ancient Near Eastern, Literary, and Linguistic Approaches to Genesis 1–11*, SBTS, Winona Lake: Eisenbrauns, 399–404.

White, J. (2016), 'Paul Completes the Servant's Sufferings (Colossians 1:24)', *JSPL* 6: 181–198.

Wilk, F. (1998), *Die Bedeutung des Jesajabuches für Paulus*, FRLANT 179, Göttingen: Vandenhoeck & Ruprecht.

Wilkins, M. J. (2012), 'Isaiah 53 and the Message of Salvation in the Gospels', in D. L. Bock and M. Glaser (eds.), *The Gospel According to Isaiah 53: Encountering the Suffering Servant in Jewish and Christian Theology*, Grand Rapids: Kregel, 109–132.

Williamson, P. R. (2000), *Abraham, Israel, and the Nations: The Patriarchal Promise and Its Covenantal Development in Genesis*, JSOTSup 315, Sheffield: Sheffield Academic Press.

Wilson, T. A. (2004), 'Wilderness Apostasy and Paul's Portrayal of the Crisis in Galatians', *NTS* 50: 550–571.

Winter, I. J. (1997), 'Art in Empire: The Royal Image and the Visual Demonstration of Assyrian Ideology', in S. Parpola and R. M. Whiting (eds.), *Assyria 1995 : Proceedings of the 10th Anniversary Symposium of the Neo-Assyrian Text Corpus Project, Helsinki, September 7–11, 1995*, Helsinki: Neo-Assyrian Text Corpus Project, 359–382.

Witherington, B. (1998), *The Acts of the Apostles: A Socio-Rhetorical Commentary*, Grand Rapids: Eerdmans.

Wright, N. T. (1992), *The Climax of the Covenant: Christ and the Law in Pauline Theology*, Minneapolis: Fortress.

—— (1999), 'New Exodus, New Inheritance: The Narrative Substructure of Romans 3–8', in S. Soderlund and N. T. Wright (eds.), *Romans and the People of God: Essays in Honor of Gordon D. Fee on the Occasion of His 65th Birthday*, Grand Rapids: Eerdmans, 26–35.

—— (2013), *Paul and the Faithfulness of God*, Christian Origins and the Question of God, vol. 4, Minneapolis: Fortress.

Index of authors

Index of Scripture references

Exodus

1 Kings (*cont.*)

2 Kings

1 Chronicles

2 Chronicles

Nehemiah

Job

Psalms

Proverbs

Isaiah

Index of ancient sources

Titles in this series:

1 *Possessed by God*, David Peterson
2 *God's Unfaithful Wife*, Raymond C. Ortlund Jr
3 *Jesus and the Logic of History*, Paul W. Barnett
4 *Hear, My Son*, Daniel J. Estes
5 *Original Sin*, Henri Blocher
6 *Now Choose Life*, J. Gary Millar
7 *Neither Poverty Nor Riches*, Craig L. Blomberg
8 *Slave of Christ*, Murray J. Harris
9 *Christ, Our Righteousness*, Mark A. Seifrid
10 *Five Festal Garments*, Barry G. Webb
12 *Now My Eyes Have Seen You*, Robert S. Fyall
13 *Thanksgiving*, David W. Pao
14 *From Every People and Nation*, J. Daniel Hays
15 *Dominion and Dynasty*, Stephen G. Dempster
16 *Hearing God's Words*, Peter Adam
17 *The Temple and the Church's Mission*, G. K. Beale
18 *The Cross from a Distance*, Peter G. Bolt
19 *Contagious Holiness*, Craig L. Blomberg
20 *Shepherds After My Own Heart*, Timothy S. Laniak
21 *A Clear and Present Word*, Mark D. Thompson
22 *Adopted into God's Family*, Trevor J. Burke
23 *Sealed with an Oath*, Paul R. Williamson
24 *Father, Son and Spirit*, Andreas J. Köstenberger and Scott R. Swain
25 *God the Peacemaker*, Graham A. Cole
26 *A Gracious and Compassionate God*, Daniel C. Timmer
27 *The Acts of the Risen Lord Jesus*, Alan J. Thompson
28 *The God Who Makes Himself Known*, W. Ross Blackburn
29 *A Mouth Full of Fire*, Andrew G. Shead
30 *The God Who Became Human*, Graham A. Cole
31 *Paul and the Law*, Brian S. Rosner
32 *With the Clouds of Heaven*, James M. Hamilton Jr
33 *Covenant and Commandment*, Bradley G. Green

34 *Bound for the Promised Land*, Oren R. Martin
35 *'Return to Me'*, Mark J. Boda
36 *Identity and Idolatry*, Richard Lints
37 *Who Shall Ascend the Mountain of the Lord?*, L. Michael Morales
38 *Calling on the Name of the Lord*, J. Gary Millar
40 *The Book of Isaiah and God's Kingdom*, Andrew T. Abernethy
41 *Unceasing Kindness*, Peter H. W. Lau and Gregory Goswell
42 *Preaching in the New Testament*, Jonathan I. Griffiths
43 *God's Mediators*, Andrew S. Malone
44 *Death and the Afterlife*, Paul R. Williamson
45 *Righteous by Promise*, Karl Deenick
46 *Finding Favour in the Sight of God*, Richard P. Belcher Jr
47 *Exalted Above the Heavens*, Peter C. Orr
48 *All Things New*, Brian J. Tabb
49 *The Feasts of Repentance*, Michael J. Ovey
50 *Including the Stranger*, David G. Firth
51 *Canon, Covenant and Christology*, Matthew Barrett
52 *Biblical Theology According to the Apostles*, Chris Bruno, Jared Compton and Kevin McFadden
53 *Salvation to the Ends of the Earth*, Andreas J. Köstenberger with T. Desmond Alexander
54 *The Servant of the Lord and His Servant People*, Matthew S. Harmon

An index of Scripture references for all the volumes may be found at http://www.thegospelcoalition.org/resources/nsbt.